FINANCIAL PREP 101:
Simple Tips for the Next Generation

Second Edition

JANIS R DICKEY, PH.D.

ISBN Number: 978-0-9828141-0-9

Original Cover & Book Design By: Lisa Corcoran

Second Edition Editor: Angela Blomberg

Print On Demand By: IngramSpark, INC., U.S.A. La Vergne, TN 37086 USA

Disclaimers:

Internet sources cited herein have been checked prior to publishing this handbook. However, the author has no control over these internet sources and makes no representation or warranty that the content published from those sources will remain unchanged. Accuracy of completeness of the data from these internet sources is expressly disclaimed for liability/errors and omissions.

Investments are long-term, designed to help meet investment and retirement needs and goals. Account balances will fluctuate and are subject to market risk, including the possible loss of principal. Investors may receive less than their original amount they invest. Some investments have contingent deferred sales loads and tax penalties for withdrawals. Some insurance investment products and riders may be at risk, the contracts are subject to the ability and strength of the insurance company you invested with; i.e. contract guarantees are the responsibility of the insurance company issuing the contract and are based on the insurance company's 'claims-paying' ability.

None of the information presented in this handbook is intended to provide investment, tax, accounting, or legal advice. Any investment, tax or legal statements included in this handbook are not to be used for the purpose of avoiding the U.S. federal, state or local tax penalties.

Please consult your outside professional advisors for specific investment, tax, accounting, or legal opinion regarding statements made in this handbook.

The information presented in this handbook, to include text, graphics, links or other items as offered "as is." Some of the information contained in this handbook was gathered from publicly available sources that are considered to be reliable. The absolute accuracy of the data cannot be confirmed. Accuracy of completeness of the data is expressly disclaimed for liability/errors and omissions for the information.

No guarantee of any kind, expressed or implied, including, but not limited to, the warranty of non-infringement of third-party rights, title, merchantability, etc. is promised by the author.

These materials are offered for education purposes only.

The information presented in this handbook does not represent an endorsement of any entity, nor is there an endorsement of any source suggested by author.

Check web-site sources carefully to determine if they are promoted from a 'product-featured AD,' investigate the article to ensure that there is no bias.

This document was not intended or written to be used, and cannot be used, to: (1) avoid tax penalties, or (2) endorse, advertise, or propose any tax plan or legal arrangement.

Most/some charts are for illustration purposes only.

Dedication

I have been blessed with such love and support from my wonderful husband John and my sons Matthew and Michael, and brother, extended family, and caring friends.

My sincere thanks to the Jump$tart Coalition® for loaning me their Financial Literacy Standards. The work they do is so valuable. The organization strives to improve/advance Financial Literacy in the United States which provides an important benefit for all of us.

So please…

Join me on my journey as I share my story, and the story of others, with you. My wish is that you find yourself eager to explore how you can master the art of becoming financially solvent and improve your quality of life for yourself and your family.

Preface

'Hindsight' is not always 20/20'

Has our human race captured 'lightning in a bottle?' Just think what mankind has accomplished in the last century! As we reflect, we realize that we are a part of many great technological, humanitarian and economic achievements –all aimed at improving humanity's reality and quality of life. However, as we stand back to examine the economic landscape, we must consider if we are really making meaningful progress towards advancing our fiscal circumstances? At first blush, it appears our economic domain may be lagging other areas and negatively affecting our well-being. Consider, as you read through this handbook, how we might reverse this trend.

This handbook is offered in an independent effort to incite us to improve our financial knowledge. My quest is to present what I believe to be factual, and I am NOT promoting any company or specific strategy. This handbook is simply an introduction to some of the complex financial subjects that you face today and those issues you may face tomorrow. Information presented is intended to offer a menu of financial information, to ultimately assist you in becoming better prepared to create your own comprehensive personal money management plan. Education is proactive. Utilize this information to gain a greater understanding of the financial world, to help you become a better money steward, and to assist you in becoming more fiscally accountable. Simply put, the objective for writing this text is to help you become Smart with your money.

LET'S MAKE A 'WAY' WHERE THERE SEEMS THAT THERE IS NO 'WAY.' LET'S GET MOVING FORWARD TOWARDS A BRAVE NEW WORLD OF FINANCIAL FREEDOM.

Table of Contents

Introduction

As stewards of our own financial responsibilities, TAKE CHARGE. In this context, the decisions you make about how you will manage your *personal finances* will have a far-reaching impact on your quality of life, for you, your family, and your community.

Background

It appears that too many of us feel we have not been given the proper tools to help us achieve financial excellence. Are we adequately educated in the area of money management? Consider these statistics:

- Forbes.com (Dani Pascarella) presented 4/2018, *"4 Stats that Reveal How Badly America Is Failing At Financial Literacy,"* stating:

    1. "44% of Americans don't have enough cash to cover a $400 emergency.

    2. 43% of student loan borrowers are not making payments.

    3. 38% of U.S. households have credit card debt.

    4. 33% of American adults have $0 saved for retirement."

"Overall, people want to make good financial decisions that set them up for success both today and in the future, but most never had the opportunity to learn how to do it. Case in point: two-thirds of American adults can't pass a basic financial literacy test." (1)

Additionally, it is possible that some of our school systems are lagging in providing the financial education some of us need, i.e.:

The Consumer Education Services Inc® reports that a 2011 Charles Schwab® survey indicated that of, "teens between ages 16 and 18… 42% wanted their parents to talk more about finances and money. [And only] A mere 32% stated they knew how credit card interest and fees work." Additionally,

- "More than half of states don't require high school students to take an economic class.

- Only 17 states require high school students to take a course in personal finance."(1)

Bloomberg® reported that according to an Experian® study (9/2019), "Three out of four recent high school graduates said they wish a class on personal finance had been a mandatory part of their education." (1)

☒ The FINRA® Investor Education Foundation's 2018 Financial Capability in the US study reported: (2)

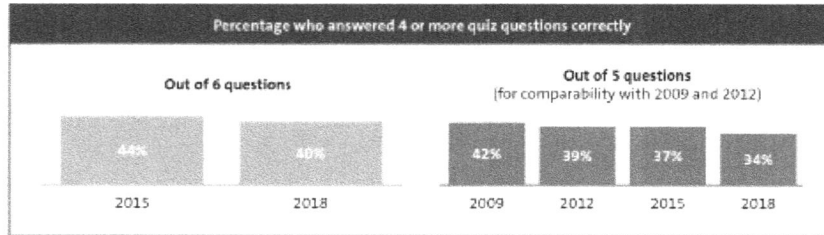

Percentage who answered 4 or more quiz questions correctly

Out of 6 questions		Out of 5 questions (for comparability with 2009 and 2012)			
44%	40%	42%	39%	37%	34%
2015	2018	2009	2012	2015	2018

☒ In 2008 President George Bush signed an Executive Order 13455, creating the 16-member President's Advisory Council on Financial Literacy "The Council assert sthat any individual completing a comprehensive financial literacy program should have an understanding of the following skills and concepts:

- the capital market system and financial institutions;

- the participant's household cash flow situation, and how to develop and maintain positive cash flow;

- how to develop a spending plan that is consistent with their resources and priorities;

- the reasons for having an emergency fund and how to establish an emergency fund;

- the fundamentals of credit granting, including how to evaluate, select, and manage credit, and how to maintain a good credit rating;

- the process of deciding when to rent and when to buy a home, and the process of home ownership;

- the process of identifying various financial risks, including development of a risk management strategy to decide which risks they should take on and which should be transferred to an insurance provider;

- how to identify and protect themselves from identity theft and various financial frauds, and what to know and do if they think they have been victimized;

- basic investment products, the relationship between risk and return, and the what, when and why of choosing the best investments at the right time in their life;

- how to evaluate and take advantage of employee benefits and tax-advantaged savings accounts.

- the various components of retirement planning, and how to develop an appropriate plan for a secure retirement; and

- how to develop a plan to assure financial security in the case of unexpected loss of income (disability or death) for those who depend on their earning power, and to assure the smooth transfer of assets to appropriate heirs." (Department of the Treasury, 8) transfer of assets to appropriate heirs." (Department of the Treasury, 8)

☒ 2010 Perspectives: *'American Association of State Colleges and Universities,'* published a paper by Thomas L. Harnish, *"Boosting Financial Literacy in America: A Role for State Colleges and Universities – Fall 2010."* The chart below indicates 2009 numbers from this report and the 2018 Finra® report (2). *(https://www.aascu org/policy/publications/perspectives/financialliteracy.pdf)*

United Sates Consumer Trends 2009/2018	
2009	2018
15% of Americans do not have a checking account	6% of Americans do not have a checking account
50% of Americans disclosed they have trouble meeting monthly expenses	50% of Americans disclosed they have trouble meeting monthly expenses
Some 42% admitted they had trouble calculating what they needed to set aside for retirement	Some 54% admitted they had trouble calculating what they needed to set aside for retirement

To help us improve these statistics, individuals sometimes request guidance from trusted advisors, i.e. financial advisors, tax advisors, lawyers, and others, to help them sort out their financial lives. For example, among other things we use our advisors to:

- ☒ consult with other financial experts on our behalf;

- ☒ research and recommend appropriate investment products to us;

- ☒ describe the pros and cons of different investment products in terms that we can understand;

- ☒ advise us regarding tax implications of our financial actions;

- ☒ guide us in financial planning for the future;

- ☒ assist us in our budgeting process and savings strategies;

- ☒ help us establish a spending/disbursement plan in retirement to protect us from outliving our money;

- ☒ advise us regarding wealth transfer strategies;

- ☒ assist us in planning for the protection of our assets; and

- ☒ prepare us for the potential unforeseen events in life by reviewing insurance solutions with us.

In short, informed individuals sometimes request guidance from trusted advisors in the areas of savings and budgeting, credit and lending, general money management strategies, investments, retirement strategies, and wealth transfer.

Check with a couple of individuals you know, determine who they would list as their 'trusted advisors,' note them here.

_____

_____

_____

Being successful in managing your money takes initiative and discipline. Reading this handbook is only a place to start. Read the terms and ideas presented here and embrace the concepts to customize and develop your own financial plan. Only YOU can manage your financial life responsibly.

This handbook was truly inspired by my family and friends; however, further recognition is given to the *Jump$tart Coalition®*. The wonderful people at *Jump$tart Coalition®* 'loaned' me their *Jump$tart Coalition® National Standards in K-12 Personal Finance Education* to use as the foundation for this writing. Their organization strives to help youth in many ways, here is their mission statement:

"Jump$tart Coalition® is a national coalition of organizations dedicated to improving the financial literacy of pre-kindergarten through college-age youth by providing advocacy, research, standards and educational resources. Jump$tart Coalition® strives to prepare youth for life-long successful financial decision-making."

> *"The quality of a person's life is in direct proportion to their commitment to excellence, regardless of their chosen field of endeavor."*
>
> Vincent Lombardi

To be committed to moving towards excellence is a start. Education is a path. Dedication and discipline are avenues to solutions.

CHAPTER 1

An Introduction To Budgeting And Saving

Learning Objectives

After reading Chapter 1, you should be able to:

a. Identify the six financial literacy competency areas outlined by Jump$tart Coalition® National Standards.

b. Articulate and demonstrate your understanding of the advantages of constructing a budget.

    • Explain a strategy for creating a budget.

    • Create both a short-term and long-term budget.

c. Describe the differences between a savings and a checking account; and the relevance for each.

d. Identify the differences between a credit and debit card, provide examples for how you will use each type of card.

e. Understand the different taxes imposed on your income; discuss how those taxes impact your 'net' income.

f. Recognize the differences in various payment methods, i.e.: checks. credit/debit cards, etc.

Chapter 1

An Introduction To Budgeting & Saving

Financial Literacy Defined
How Money And I Were Introduced
Why I focus on financial stewardship

My family and money:

On my Mom's side, my grandfather (Granddad) only had a 3rd grade education, but he became wildly successful in his own right. Granddad had a trade, he was a meat butcher. Granddad started out working in the mines when he was very young. Yet, shortly after he married my grandmother, he went to work as a butcher in my grandmother's (Nana) father's grocery store. Eventually Granddad bought the grocery store where he was the butcher, then he bought the strip mall where the grocery store was located, then he purchased nearby apartments…. etc. Granddad and Nana must have had a heck of a savings discipline! When my Granddad passed away in 1981, he left my grandmother with sufficient funds so that she could live comfortably for almost 20 years… and there was also an inheritance left for their three children.

My father worked as a Real Estate Broker selling inexpensive starter homes while my mom stayed home and took care of the family. Neither of my parents went to college, and as far as I knew college wasn't in the cards for me either. We had everything we needed…just not everything we wanted. My parents made many sacrifices for us and they learned how to stretch every dollar.

My grandfather and father took different paths in life, but each man was successful in providing for their family. Each man demonstrated an ability to manage his money and served as a role model for their family to watch and follow. My family also provided me with a great foundation to formulate my own saving and budgeting philosophy. Without scrimping and saving, neither my grandparents, nor my parents, would have been as financially successful as they were. Not everyone has a sound saving and budgeting process modeled for them, but everyone is capable of searching out resources to help them put together a personal saving and budgeting plan.

Navigating How to Budget and Save

Here's how I developed my saving and budgeting plan... Dad gave me the world when he introduced me to the wonderful world of finances. He taught me about how to manage money, and just as important, he confirmed, through his actions, the value of managing money in a prudent manner. To begin with, my Dad demonstrated the importance of saving every month, how to 'live within a budget,' and how to make 'wise' money decisions. He and I developed a budget together, and then Dad helped me monitor my spending against that budget; he explained the difference between simple and compound interest; he took me comparison shopping for my first car; and he also walked me through the process for buying my first real estate property. My Dad exposed me to a myriad of valuable financial skill sets I would need in life.

My Dad's hands-on approach included lots of questions! He quizzed me on my pre-preparation for every financial decision. He checked to make sure I had done my homework: He checked to determine:

☒   How much money had I saved for the purchase?

☒   Where had I comparison shopped?

☒   Did I have a general understanding of what the procedure or steps might be for negotiating a purchase?

☒   Had I reviewed the forms, signatures, notary items and so forth that I would be asked to sign?

☒   Did I know what the on-going, after-purchase expenses for each item were likely to be?

And so forth.

Believe me, this process was not fun. At the time, I thought that the procedure was a lot of unnecessary work. I pretty much thought that my Dad was crazy. I thought he was being unfair and that I should be able to just go and 'buy it.' I thought a lot of things, but what I realize now is how invaluable those early lessons were.

My childhood and my experiences are most likely nothing like yours. You will decide how you will proceed with your fiscal life; you will determine your money priorities. What else is different? We are more-than likely light years apart when it comes to your personal relationship with money. I am hoping that some of the experiences that I relay here may cause you to give a little more thought to how you will interact with your money.

Ask Yourself This:
How Important is The All-Mighty Dollar?

> *"Show me the money!"* *A famous line from the movie Jerry Maguire (1996) is almost a family staple for that generation, and a 'catchy sound-bite' for employees in the workplace.*
>
> (Loftus, 2013, "Don't Just Show Me the Money," Show me the Total Rewards.)

Several: Adrian Furnham (1984), Spann (2018) have studied the relationship between people's attitudes, belief systems, money usage and money management. Today our society has a very different relationship with money than my parents, and their parents before them, had. The importance of acquiring material possessions has risen to a whole new level. The possession of money and material goods seems now to be analogous with status. I believe that we are entrenched in a 'media frenzy' focused on the promotion of indulgent behavior directed towards the acquisition of products and material wealth. Today it seems like our society has become obsessed with MONEY. (16)

The construct of debt has also been transformed through the years and the stigma of being in debt appears to be waning. Our personal debt is growing, and the acceptance for this philosophy is modeled by our government's growing deficit. Is being in debt (over and above your car and mortgage payment) now the acceptable norm? Especially today, with the condition of our World credit and financial circumstances (US Debt is about $ 28 trillion, 08/03/2021 www.npr.org), I believe we need to reassess our attitudes towards debt and credit consumption.

Education And Knowledge Imparts Power

> *"To succeed, you will soon learn, as I did, the importance of a solid foundation in the basics of education—literacy, both verbal and numerical, and communication skills."*
>
> Alan Greenspan

Learning and possessing important facts about a topic provides you the opportunity to analyze information and make informed decisions. Lack of information can invoke stress. Financial stress can cause a loss of productivity or personal satisfaction. Bailey, Woodiel, Turner & Young (1998) report that, *'Satisfaction with life has been found to be a counter-balance against stress in both the personal and the work aspects of life.'* (3) And the same seems to be still true today. CNBC/Money reported, *"30% of Americans are 'Constantly' stressed out about money."* Varo, 3/2018. (4) Developing a financial strategy during your employed years can potentially increase work satisfaction and productivity. Increase in productivity can help you in a very dynamic way; with the right skill set in place, you may be able to better achieve a higher level of personal satisfaction, both today, and for your future. (3) Education and critical thinking skills are crucial to your success in life. It's no different with managing your finances. Without financial education, you may experience a higher level of stress.

Financial Literacy Perspectives

> *"No matter who you are, making informed decisions about what to do with your money will help build a more stable financial future for you and your family."*
>
> Alan Greenspan – Federal Reserve System (2002)

It is no secret that Financial Literacy among our youth is lacking and that in the recent past our educators have been attempting to introduce personal finance courses into our educational system. So… Let's start with a review of some Financial Literacy commentary: An article written by Jonathan Fox, Suzanne Bartholomae, and Jinkook Lee, *'Building the case for financial education'* (5), suggests that, 'The need for financial education among Americans is often demonstrated with alarming rates of bankruptcy, high consumer debt levels, low savings rates, and other negative outcomes that may be the result of poor family financial management and low financial literacy levels.' (5) Indeed, financial education is critical for promoting strong individuals and and communities.

Here are the statistics, they form a **baseline** for subsequent research…

- ☒ According to EverFi, Inc® (the education technology company that teaches, assesses, and certifies students in critical skills including financial literacy), "Nearly half of U.S. high school students do not know how to establish good credit…" (9) And the *2019 Money Matters on Campus Report/ EverFi®* College student report indicated, [Only] "53% [of college students] were prepared to manage money."

  - ○ "When asked about specific financial behaviors they have engaged in recently, only 59% claimed that they had checked their account balances, and even fewer had created (40%) or used (38%) a budget to manage their personal finances." (file:///C:/Users/Dell/Documents/ MoneyMatters-2019.pdf); and

  - ○ " …only 16% of the entire sample reported using a money management app or program to support their efforts and only 15% used a spreadsheet to generate a budget."

- ☒ The Guardian®, US Edition (https://www.theguardian.com/money/2017/nov/11/schools-ignore-personal-finance-lessons-fail-generation-debt?CMP=share_btn_link) reported this in a 2017 article, *" Schools ignore personal finance lessons and fail Generation Debt – 2017 study, "* that,

  - ○ "Most students find the terminology of finance very confusing. They don't, for example, understand the difference between a credit card and a debit card …

  - ○ …feedback from ex-pupils now at university suggested that a huge number wish they had left school with more financial awareness."

- ☒ "LAS VEGAS, Sept. 26, 2019 /PRNewswire/ -- Recent data indicate that people across the U.S. believe that financial literacy should be taught in schools. In a survey conducted between August 13th and August 15th, 2019, the National Financial Educators Council® asked 1,211 people, "Do you think high school students should take personal finance courses in high school?" More than 81% responded that students should take financial literacy coursework." (https://www.prnewswire. com/news-releases/survey-results-over-81-of-americans-agree-schools-should-teach-high-school-students-financial-literacy-coursework-300925844.html)

I encourage you to utilize the many 'financial' web resources and other educational sources to broaden your understanding of financial terms and processes. Here are a few:

- ☒ *"Money Math®: Lessons for Life,"* is an educational tutorial published by The Curators of the University of Missouri to help promote financial literacy. (10)

- ☒ When I searched for *'financial literacy'* on the **National Institute of Adult Continuing Education's®** (NIACE) website (9/2019), 442 results were offered. NIACE is an independent, non-government organization and charity devoted to the promotion and development of financial learning for adults. (11)

- ☒ The National Endowment for Financial Education® (NEFE) is a foundation that partners with others for the "financial well-being of the public." Visit the *https://www.nefe.org* website to discover another resource for financial literacy, specifically they offer a *'High School Financial Planning Program (HSFPP)'* that is very popular. (12)

- ☒ *https://www.mymoney.gov* is the U.S. government's website that is committed to financial education for all Americans.

- ☒ Neighbor Works America's® website, *https://www.nw.org*, also presents *"Financial Security/ Health"* programs to assist families and individuals in developing "sound money and management skills."

- ☒ The *"Money Smart®"* program was developed by The Federal Deposit Insurance Corporation (FDIC). The purpose of this program is to acknowledge, *"...the importance of financial education, particularly for people with little or no banking experience. That's why we created Money Smart, a training program to help adults outside the financial mainstream enhance their money skills and create positive banking relationships." (https://money.com/money/collection/money-101/)* (14)

- ☒ *https://www.Money.com* has a, *"MONEY 101® educational program–A step by step guide to gaining control of your financial life."* It is a series for educating individuals on a variety of financial literacy areas. The program is delivered in a simple and easy to understand format. (13)

Research and find 4 internet sites that provide financial terms, data, education, etc. Write those sites here for future reference.

_____

_____

_____

_____

Becoming financially literate is imperative. Jump$tart Coalition® defines Financial Literacy as,

> *"...the ability to use knowledge and skills to manage one's financial resources effectively for [a] lifetime [of] financial security. [Furthermore,] Financial literacy is not an absolute state; it is a continuum of abilities that is subject to variables such as age, family, culture, and residence. Financial literacy refers to an evolving state of competency that enables each individual to respond effectively to ever-changing personal and economic circumstances." (6)*

To help us define this 'continuum of abilities,' Jump$tart Coalition® outlines six financial literacy competency areas for us to consider. These standards provide a good barometer for you to use in evaluating whether or not you are 'Financially Literate.' As we move through this handbook, we will review information in an effort to help you to satisfy each standard, and at the end of each section we will review these standards to determine your progress towards improving your competency against each.

JumpStart Coalition® National Standards in K-12 Personal Finance Education:

Financial Responsibility and Decision Making

"Overall Competence: Apply reliable information and systematic decision making to personal financial decisions.

1. **Spending and Saving:** Apply strategies to monitor income and expenses, plan for spending and save for future goals.

2. **Credit and Debt:** Develop strategies to control and manage credit and debt.

3. **Employment and Income:** Use a career plan to develop personal income potential.

4. **Investing:** Implement a diversified investment strategy that is compatible with personal financial goals.

5. **Risk Management and Insurance:** Apply appropriate and cost-effective risk management strategies.

6. **Financial Decision Making:** Apply reliable information and systematic decision making to personal financial decisions." (6)

Let's start with first things first, a **BUDGET.**

Budgeting

> *"Never spend your money before you have it."*
>
> Thomas Jefferson

Just saying the word 'budget' out loud can elicit a 'deer in the headlights' look from some individuals.

I believe many people probably manage their finances without a budget. Let's face it, identifying and setting financial goals is a tough place to start. But, without a compass you don't know where you are, or where you're going. You need a plan of action. How many templates are there for putting a budget together? Hundreds? Thousands? If you want a template, the internet has plenty to choose from!

> *"Nearly 40 percent of Americans would struggle to cover an unexpected $ 400 expense."*
>
> *'Report of Economic Well-Being of U.S. Households in 2018 – Federal Reserve' (www.federalreserve.gov 0519)*
>
> *https://www.cbsnews.com/news/nearly-40-of-americans-cant-cover-a-surprise-400-expense/*

Budgets are the yardsticks against which you can monitor your spending. Creating a budget is one of the first steps you take in managing your money. You may be surprised the number of people that admit that they haven't really ever developed a formal budget. They have a budget, but just "never have the time to write their budget down."

> *"Accessing the American Dream of Financial self-sufficiency is not based on obtaining a loan or buying a new car; it is the very basics of education – knowing the importance of savings, how to balance a checkbook, budgeting, or investing for retirement."*
>
> National Credit Union Administration® (15)

Whether you think you know what you spend each month, or if you have never given it much thought, to manage your money effectively you will need to write down your budget and review it periodically. Often, in the past, when someone has articulated what they think they spend each month, and we then created a budget, the reality of what they actually spent was typically vastly different from what they thought they spent. This exercise is a good reality check.

> *"Annual income twenty pounds, annual expenditure nineteen six, results happiness. Annual income twenty pounds, annual expenditure twenty-pound ought and six, result misery."*
>
> Charles Dickens credited to David Copperfield

Take a minute this weekend and ask a few people if they actually have a WRITTEN budget. Record your findings.

_____

_____

_____

I believe there are a couple of reasons for this budget disconnect:

1. It is, quite frankly, a pain to write down what you spend and then go back and add it up, month after month.

2. Devising a plan to TRACK – retaining receipts, etc. is just NOT FUN!

3. People just don't want to believe that they spend as much as they do.

4. People are averse to conflict and don't want to conduct 'budgeting' discussions.

5. Budgeting is typically an area where discipline to stay on track, and interest in the process, wanes over time.

6. A consensus on how much to spend is difficult to obtain.

Life

I was a single mother in 1997 and was finishing my schoolwork while working as an adjunct professor at a local University --not making a lot of money. I was raising two children, so I was also watching every penny I spent.

I purchased one of those small, fit-in-your pocket notebooks and literally wrote down every purchase. (I even wrote down when I bought coffee for a $1.00.)

At the end of the month I added up what had I spent and put the expenses in categories. I then analyzed how much I was actually spending, and I found that I was spending too much in a couple of categories (clothes is one area that was out-of-hand).When I saw where I was over-spending, I reduced expenditures in those areas. I repeated my review every month or so.

Without this exercise I wouldn't have known exactly where my money was going. It seems logical now, but the exercise wasn't a lot of fun then.

PS: You should have seen the look on my new financial advisor's face when I showed up in his office with my spread sheets!

"Financial lessons that parents, schools should teach kids: Money Matters®," provides the following comments – they apply to individuals of ALL AGES!:

1. Save first, pay yourself first.

2. Learn how to budget and distinguish needs vs. wants.

3. Learn how bank accounts work, as well as checks, debit cards and credit cards.

4. Understand debt. Learn about loans and credit cards, and understand compounding interest and how to manage repayment of loans or credit cards.

5. Learn the importance of paying bills on time and building a solid credit history. Understand how a credit score affects not just your ability to qualify for loans or credit cards.

6. Understand the importance of protecting your personal information. This is huge.

7. Know how to make doctor's appointments, fill a prescription and make appointments for oil changes and other car maintenance.

8. Read what you sign and don't sign anything you don't read or understand.

9. Know when to ask for help.

10. Learn about income taxes and how to file tax returns.

11. Keep your receipts, car maintenance records, leases, bank statements, etc."

(Posted Sep 15, 2019; https://www.cleveland.com/moneymatters/2019/09/11-lessons-that-parents-and-schools-should-teach-kids-money-matters.html. Excerpt)

> *"A budget is telling your money where to go instead of wondering where it went."*
>
> John Maxwell

Reasons To Budget

I found an article on https://www.thebalance.com/how-to-budget-and-save-money-in-5-easy-steps-4056838, *"Strategies for Budgeting and Saving Money."* (17) Check it out. Here are a couple of pros that I offer to you for designing and sticking to a budget:

- ☒ Having a road map of where you want to go, and a plan to get you there can be invaluable. Having a plan can provide you with a sense of power and ownership over your financial affairs.

- ☒ Creating a strategy can help you to focus on the goals; can help provide a reason for you to stay the course; and can reduce stress regarding financial decisions.

- ☒ Watching your spending closely can help reduce the amount of money that is spent on 'impulse purchase' items.

- ☒ A budget should detail spending categories, and therefore highlight where your money is spent. This exercise may uncover areas of extravagance and produce 'extra' cash for savings.

- ☒ A budget helps to monitor your financial direction to ensure that you are not living beyond your means (you're not able to pay off credit cards each month or are neglecting to save money).

- ☒ A budget may help you STAY OUT OF DEBT; or at least help you plan to incur debt responsibly.

What are four reasons for budgeting that you feel are important to you?

_____

_____

_____

_____

Building A Budget

> *"A budget tells us what we can't afford, but it doesn't keep us from buying it."*
>
> William Feather

The topic of Budgeting is an important one for individuals, companies and government agencies. I work best with a plan, and you probably do as well. While you may not need a budget at your current stage in life, knowing how to create a budget could prove to be invaluable to you as you begin to manage your money yourself. However, you may already have a job and be saving for a car? Looking ahead will be important. To help you plan for the future, I have put together a 5-step approach for you to review as you consider putting together a budget. Use my **ASARR** formula (**AS ARR**). You might be able to remember it by saying, "**AS** you **ARR**." Start with the exercise of figuring out where you are: **A**ssess, **S**et goals and prioritize, **A**nalyze, **R**educe/eliminate, **R**evise and review periodically.

ASARR

Assess

Set goals/prioritize

Analyze

Reduce/eliminate

Revise/review

> *"The American people deserve a budget that invests in the future, protects the most vulnerable among us and helps to create jobs and economic security."*
>
> Carl Levin

1).   **ASSESS -** Start with your income, record all of the sources of your income; then record expenses like your car payment, car insurance costs, cell phone bill, etc. Later, when you own your own home, your expenses may include expenses, like: electric, gas and water bills; your mortgage; car payments; insurance payments; home owners association dues, etc. Don't forget to put down your Health and Beauty Aids, items like shampoo, haircuts, paper goods, prescriptions, etc. List your fixed expenses first. When you purchase your items … be sure to KEEP ALL of the RECEIPTS. to KEEP ALL of the RECEIPTS.

After you have recorded all of the fixed expenses, make a list of variable expenses. Variable expenses are the expenses that change from month to month. One of the hardest items to monitor is what you spend on food. Other variable items might be: clothes, gifts, entertainment, eating out, dry cleaning, gas and periodic expenses for the car (oil changes), etc.

Life

When John and I were married I asked him to save EVERY receipt and use the credit card for every purchase over $5.00. At first, he thought I had lost my mind. But, when we review our budget every 6 months or so, he sees how valuable it is to have all of the charges recorded for easy addition.

2).   **SET GOALS and PRIORITIZE -** Remember to set aside money for savings: personal, vacation, college, retirement, planned purchases (like a car).

Refer to Exhibit A to determine if you have forgotten any items in the budget you created and add items to it if necessary.

- **Hint: Don't forget any charitable contributions or tithing/ donating that you do.**

3).   ANALYZE – 4). REDUCE – 5). REVIEW - These last steps require constant review, elimination, and revision of your budget and spending. Without these steps the budgeting process is virtually useless. Checking yourself is really important. Analyzing is an essential step in the process. When you analyze, you refocus—then you will tend to reduce. Be sure you don't forget this step.

Identify a time frame to revise and time to review your budget. In the beginning a monthly review is warranted, but later you may fall back to quarterly reviews. Waiting 10 to 12 months is typically too long, and corrections cannot be made in a timely manner.

Be diligent. Develop your budget and review it on a regular basis.

Remember **ASARR... Assess, Set goals/prioritize,
Analyze, Reduce/eliminate, and Revise/review.**

Review your Budget worksheet now. Start tracking what you spend... Complete the exercise for a minimum of two weeks and review where your money is going. Use the Budget Sheet as a Tracking Sheet for this exercise.

Sometimes individuals put together a budget that allows for extra spending money for the weekend. Free time does seem to cost more.

> **Use the following information to fill in a hypothetical budget. Talk to someone you know and use the following outline and record your observations for comparison.**

Married couple with two children:		
Taxes	$ 235 a month	
Home and car insurance	$ 178 month	
Utilities	$ 199 a month	
Car payment	$ 150 a month	
Health & Beauty aids/haircuts	$ 72 a month	
Gas for car	$ 75 a month	
Food	$ 495 a month	
Savings	$ 100 a month	
College Savings	$ 125 a month	
Entertainment	$ 75 a month	
Misc.	$ 50 a month	
Tithing	$ 150 a month	
Vacation fund	$ 200 a month	

This step will require you to develop a system for tracking your income and spending…
VERY IMPORTANT! DO NOT IGNORE how critical keeping track of your spending is/ and the spending categories.

Do What? Stop Spending??? Are You Kidding?

Once you determine that you are on track with your budgeting and spending, the next step is to save and economize. The following information and ideas for economizing may not be new to you. I am going to guess that you have heard many of them before. What might be new: Read them a couple of times and attempt to implement one or two of them. Try to choose one or two of the ideas to apply to your lifestyle and see if you can stick with it/them for a week, then a month, etc.

As a start, you can begin to reduce spending by adhering to these rules:

1. Buy one item, make a smart purchase, and keep your item a long time. Don't forget to comparison shop, check the quality of the item you purchase and KEEP the item until it WEARS OUT.

Life

I had a client who just bought a new USED car; she had driven her old car for about 16 years!

2. Stick to a pre-determined shopping list. Allow yourself only one or two small items off the list.

Life

My husband and I make it a game. If I go to the store John asks me what I bought 'extra,' and if he goes, I ask him the same question. We make it a competition to see who just sticks to the list.

3. Stay out of the stores. Stay off the internet purchase sites. Do not watch the home-shopping channels or shop on-line. Nothing new here... common sense. It's hard to spend money if you aren't somewhere to spend it. If you find you are overspending, modifying behavior is critical.

Life

My husband John and I used to stop for coffee frequently. It was a fun outing, and relatively inexpensive. One day we just decided that we would stop BUYING the coffee out, and we would just start MAKING coffee AT HOME.

Let's say we were buying 8 cups a coffee each week (4 times for each of us),

At $ 2.50 a cup. That is roughly $1040 a year for coffee that costs about 20 cents a cup to brew at home. $1040 a year, at 5% interest, is about $1092 a year more that we have to put towards savings. After 10 or more years (at simple interest), that's $10,920 we can be ahead!

4. Having a 'buying process' is also important. Predetermine your criteria for your purchases.

With 6 children, John and I developed our process early on in our marriage…we needed to be EXTRA careful with our money. So, here are some questions that John and I ask ourselves prior to a purchase:

Life

a) *If we are replacing an item (car, TV, couch, chair, etc.) … How long have we had the item we are replacing? For cars we try to keep them around 6-8 years, based on the mileage. Other household items? Some furniture I have literally owned for 25-30 years! (and it still looks new!) Appliances (toaster/coffee pot) are typically kept until they don't work anymore (we think we have had our blender for over 15 years and it still works just fine, but it definitely doesn't look new!).*

b) *Why are we considering a replacement? (the item no longer functions?) High mileage, dependability issues? Torn/damaged and cannot be repaired?*

c) *Is 'safety' and 'accessibility' a motive?*

d) *Do we 'need' an additional item? For instance, my parents obviously didn't feel they 'needed' furniture in the living room, but I would definitely have a problem with an empty room right off the foyer that I looked at every day. I might look for 'used furniture' to fill the room up as a low-cost option.*

After we decide that we are going to make a purchase:

We need to do a 'price comparison' and compare the facts.

- ☒ *Pricing the cost at the various carriers was imperative. (Use online comparison websites – I saved over $ 900 on our refrigerator!)*

- ☒ *Product warranties are also considered.*

- ☒ *Product consumer ratings are also important.*

The most important part of the process was – once the BENEFIT and cost were determined – COMMITING to keeping the item is imperative.

Using this type of logic-based 'buying process' helps us to evaluate the validity of each purchase and determine whether or not the item should be budgeted for.

Develop your own spending process, set your own criteria for you and your family to follow. If you haven't 'thought through' the buying process, purchases should not be made.

5. Spend more time on activities that don't cost money. (Can you spend time reading to school children, or donating your time to a worthy cause, doing an extra-credit assignment, or playing outside, how about READING A BOOK?)

Life

I had a client who enjoyed visiting the Kansas City gambling casino a few times a week. The gentleman was retired, with a lot of free time. He spent about $300-$500 each visit. I noticed that money was draining out of his account each month. I got to know him, and his family and I became quite fond of him.

During one visit he commented on his activities and gave me an opening to say something. I took the opportunity to ask him about other hobbies he might have. Could he 'read to children?' or 'volunteer at his church?' He didn't comment at the time, but I noticed that a month or so later he had brought home a new puppy. The new puppy took up a lot of his time…. His visits to the casinos were dramatically reduced. Coincidence?

6. Just reduce spending. Whatever strategy you employ to help you reduce your spending, set a goal for each month and review your spending against your objective on a timely basis. The ultimate goal is to reduce your spending and increase your saving habits. I suggest that you visit these websites:++

   • https://www.consumer-action.org/english/articles/66_ways_to_save_money_en, ("66 Ways to Save Money – Consumer Action.") (17)

   • https://www.fool.com/personal-finance/2018/09/18/20-ways-to-cut-spending.aspx, ("20 Ways to Cut Spending;" 9/18/2018.)

- https://www.thesimpledollar.com/trimming-the-fat-forty-ways-to-reduce-your-monthly-required-spending/, ("40 Ways to Save Money on Monthly Expenses"). (18)

- https://www.daveramsey.com/blog/the-cure-for-excessive-spending, ("How to Stop Spending Money"). (19)

There are also many, many books available to help you uncover additional ideas for saving money.

Choose one item from your budget that you have identified that you would like to reduce. Monitor/write down what you spend in that area for one month. CHALLENGE YOURSELF

> *"You cannot afford to wait for perfect conditions. Goal setting is often a matter of balancing timing against available resources. Opportunities are easily lost while waiting for perfect conditions."*
>
> Gary Ryan Blair

Budgeting – The Short And Long Of It

After you are satisfied with your short-term budget, a longer-term budget should be considered.

Life

I once was watching a program on TV where the couple wrote down their longer-term 'dream list' items on pieces of large poster board and hung their poster board in the basement. From time to time when they visited the basement, they were reminded of those items for which they were sacrificing. They indicated that this exercise made it easier to keep on their savings track

What item(s) are you saving for longer-term?

_____

_____

What's The Magic Number?
How Much Should I Be Saving?

Your savings allocation will be an important budget category. How much you should save each month is the question of the day. Of course, we know that the savings percentage number will be different for each person. "The appropriate amount to save will depend on your individual situation and what your lifestyle goal is." The facts presented by _statista®,_ (M. Szmigiera, Oct. 28, 2019), _"Monthly personal saving rate in the U.S. 2016-2019,"_ states:

> _"American's annual personal savings rate was 8.8% in 2018, compared to 10.4% in 1960, 9.4% in June of 2021."_
>
> https://www.statista.com/statistics/246268/personal-savings-rate-in-the-united-states-by-month/

Here are a couple of suggested savings rates.

☒ Walter Updegrave, *Money Magazine*® senior editor wrote an article in 2007, *"Retirement: How Much to Save - Ten percent is better than nothing, but it's really only the beginning, our expert explains."* In this article Mr. Updegrave suggests that just using the 10% 'rule-of- thumb' doesn't allow for a margin of error. He suggests that 15% might be more prudent. (20)

☒ In her article, *"How Much Should You Save Each Month?"* Ms. Ilyce R. Glink suggests that Americans save, "perhaps 5 percent of our income. Some people save more, most save a lot less." (21)

☒ Jarred Kriz, 08/23/2011, in a *Fisher Investments*®, *Market Minder* article reported, "Despite the stubbornly high unemployment rate and contrary to what many would think, personal savings and income are growing. Today's savings rate of over 5% is well above average, causing the consumer's aggregate balance sheet to improve every payday…" (22)

☒ In Chris Taylor's (NEW YORK | Fri Sep 21, 2012 9:08am EDT) article: *"Are we saving enough to retire? No (but we think we are),"* published on https://www.reuters.com/article/ us-column-save-retirement/are-we-saving-enough-to-retire-no-idUSBRE88K0NB20120921, Taylor reports, *"the goal [is] having at least eight times your annual salary socked away by the time you retire."*

  o "While Fidelity's savings yardsticks aim for at least eight times your annual salary, T. Rowe Price financial planner Stuart Ritter thinks you should crank that up to 12.5 times."

See the following Bankrate® informational chart to review how much we save on average…

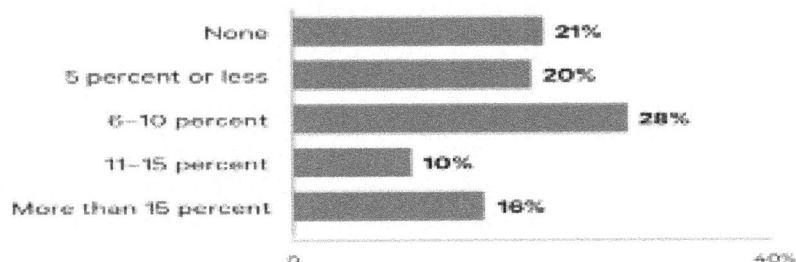

What percentage of annual income do you save?
How much Americans set aside for retirement, emergencies and other financial goals.

Category	Percentage
None	21%
5 percent or less	20%
6–10 percent	28%
11–15 percent	10%
More than 15 percent	18%

Note: Percentages may not total 100 due to rounding.
Other responses: Don't know/refused to answer: 6 percent.
Source: Bankrate's Financial Security Index, Feb. 26-March 3

Bankrate

Source: Bankrate's® Financial Security Index
https://www.bankrate.com/banking/savings/financial-security-march-2019/
https://www.cnbc.com/2018/03/15/bankrate-65-percent-of-americans-save-little-or-nothing.html

Check with someone to see what they budget for savings. Do you have a goal in mind?

_____

_____

Saving for everyday emergencies is imperative and saving for your retirement is also crucial. A rule of thumb for your emergency fund should be about 6-8 months of living expenses… 12 months is even better. To help you determine how much you should save for retirement income needs, you should utilize a retirement calculator. There are scores of retirement savings calculators offered via the internet. Find one and put in your specific numbers: your age, your salary, the growth rate you believe you will achieve according to your investment style, how long you think you will continue to work and save towards retirement, and your ultimate retirement income needs (i.e. your lifestyle income objectives), etc. Understanding that some items may impact your 'bottom-line' or tax status is also an area to explore with your tax advisor. Keeping accurate records of your expenditures will come in handy to help you in this area as well.

Life

I don't remember exactly that I ever put a percentage number on saving when I was younger. But recently, I would say the last 8-10 years or so, John and I tried to 'catch-up' by putting away about 20%.

Building a short-term budget can be easy. It's the getting started that is difficult. Take a couple of hours to gather some of your bills, checkbooks, paycheck stubs, last year's federal income tax return, account statements, and any other relevant financial information. Block out a two-hour time frame on your calendar and use a pre-formatted worksheet to get you started. I have provided a *Budget Worksheet - Exhibit A* for you to use, or you can go on-line and find another worksheet. You can also purchase one of a variety of 'budget builder' programs that are available.

Depending on your age, you may not have incurred some of the expenses discussed in this section. If that is the case, as you work through this handbook, ask an adult to share their financial experiences with you. Most individuals who are already of an adult age, will undoubtedly use some of the budgeting and savings principles cited here. As we have noted, one you have your budget in place, there are a few other housekeeping items you might consider: how to calculate a tip, understanding how to open a savings account, the differences between compound and simple interest; and understanding tax and other deductions that show on your pay stub. These are all important topics for keeping you on tract with developing your budget.

Also, in the MarketWatch® article, *"The astounding difference that can come from saving an extra 1% of your pay,"* (2/2015) it is important to note that small differences in savings over time, make LARGE differences overall. Calculate with your advisor what those 'extra savings' dollars may provide for you! *(https://www.marketwatch.com/story/how-a-1-savings-boost-could-sweeten-your-retirement-2015-02-20)*

Dave Ramsey.com (19) provides a Free Budgeting Tool, https://www.daveramsey.com/blog/the-cure-for-excessive-spending, available for download for free… one of many you can find on the internet.

Keeping Track of Your Money

A Savings Account

> "The habit of saving is itself an education. It fosters every virtue, teaches self-denial, cultivates the sense of order, trains to forethought, and so broadens the mind."
>
> Thornton T. Munger

Opening a savings account is typically your first exposure to becoming financially savvy. To help you get started, here are a couple of points to consider when you open a savings account:

- Is there a required minimum balance?

- What interest rate does the account pay you for letting them hold your money?

- Will you receive simple or compound interest?

- How is the interest calculated? i.e. annually, semi-annually, quarterly, daily?

- Is there a monthly fee for the account?

Typically, your money will be harder to access when you deposit it in your savings account. When you want to withdraw some money for a purchase, you will need to re-visit the bank to get your cash in-hand (or move the money online into your checking account and withdraw from an ATM). Because you don't have quite as easy an access avenue to your money, you may tend to rethink your spending decisions and leave the money in the savings account to grow. Try to avoid acquiring a debit card that is directly tied to your savings account.

A Checking Account

On-the-other-hand, a checking account **provides you with easy access to your money**. Writing a check is just like reaching into your pocket and taking out 'cash.' The checks are a replacement for your available 'cash.' But remember, when you reach into your pocket and there isn't any cash left, so it goes with your checking account. Keeping meticulous records… i.e. subtracting every check, every purchase, and every ATM withdrawal from your 'cash' balance is critical.

One of the financial skills you learn when you open a checking account is how important it is to keep your checking account 'balanced.' Your checkbook has two parts, the checks themselves, and a *ledger*. Balancing your checking account to insure you do not 'overdraw' what money you actually have in the account involves keeping track of the checks you write. You record the check amount, the check number, and to whom you wrote the check for every check you write in your ledger. You will then subtract the amount of the check from your previous balance total and note your new balance in the ledger. Do not ignore the 'ledger,' the small notebook-like accounting pad that comes with your checks. **Use the ledger every time to record what you have spent (and subtracted) from the previous balance.** Do not forget to subtract your ATM withdrawals or debit card purchases as well. Keeping up with this process keeps you aware of how much money you have left in your account. Just like reaching in your pocket to get out your cash, if you reach into your checking account and don't have 'cash,' (your balance will show you this 'cash' amount) you shouldn't make the purchase. **It is crucial to be sure you never write a check for more than you have in the account.** If you 'over-draw' the account, you are charged a processing fee and you 'bounce' the check. If you bounce a check: 1) you will need to re-write the check at a later date or make the payment in cash or use your debit/credit card; 2) it will cost you extra money in the form of a penalty. So be sure you balance your checking account frequently; know exactly how much money you have in your checking account at any given time. Check your on-line account frequently to compare the transactions and balance against your running ledger. Your on-line account will keep your transaction ledger as well and also balance your checking account for you. Compare the two tallies.

A Debit Card

Closely tied to a checking account is a 'debit card.' **A debit card is issued directly from your financial institution, like your bank, and permits you, the owner, to pay for purchases with a plastic card, 'same as cash.'** In a sense the debit card is a plastic check. The card provides you with instant access to your money. When the debit card is swiped, it automatically and electronically pulls money directly out of your checking or savings account.

The problem arises when you do not have enough money in your checking account to cover your purchase. Unlike a check, if your account doesn't have enough money in it to cover the cost of the purchase, the purchase may be 'declined.' If you don't have enough money in your account, one of two things can happen: 1) your purchase will not be approved and your transaction will be declined, or 2) if you have 'opted in' for 'overdraft protection' your purchase will he paid for – your purchase will not be declined.

In 2009 Congress passed some Debit and Credit Card reforms. One of the changes enacted by the reform is the ability to elect 'overdraft protection' for your debit card. To receive 'overdraft protection' you usually 'opt in' for this service. However, if you have 'opted in' for the 'overdraft protection,' and you need to use it, you typically will be charged a fee. The reform also prohibits banks from automatically adding 'overdraft protection' for your debit card. Therefore, you cannot automatically be charged the 'overdraft fees' that accompany this service without your consent. (Of course, new legislation can change this.)

> • Remember that debit card purchases also need to be subtracted on your check ledger from your previous checking account balance. Do not forget this important step. Keeping current with your balance will save you money in the end.

A Credit Card

When you read this article (https://www.360financialliteracy.org/Topics/Credit-and-Debt/Credit-Cards-and-Reports/Credit-Cards-The-Pros-and-Cons), "*Credit Cards: The Pros and Cons*," note:

☒ *"Credit cards often get a bad reputation, but the truth is they can be a key financial tool if used responsibly... [Review] some of the top advantages and disadvantages to consider before you add a shiny new card to your wallet."*

The credit card is very different from a debit card. When you use your credit card, money is not automatically taken from your account when it is swiped. **A credit card is NOT directly linked to your checking or savings account.** The credit card stands alone. When you swipe a credit card it records the purchase and sends it to your credit card company. **The credit card company pays the vendor where you have used the card to make your purchase.** So, in a sense you have 'borrowed' the money from the credit card company. At the end of the month the credit card company adds up the charges (the amount of money loaned to you that you charged on the credit card) and sends/emails you a bill to pay. If you have a balance from the last month, interest will be added as well. When you receive the bill notice, you write a check or move money from your checking account online and send it in to the credit card company to reduce your charge balance down to 'zero' again for the next month. Failure to pay off the charges (resulting in a NON 'zero' balance) each month results in a penalty, or interest charge added onto your account balance. The next month charges are then added to the previous month's balance and interest charge and the result is an even larger balance for the next month's bill. MONITOR CHARGES ON-LINE every few days.

Life

In church one Sunday morning our pastor posed this question:

If a student graduated college, got her first job in an office environment, and then decided that she needed some new clothes to wear to the office... went shopping and charged $2500 for those clothes on her credit card, and set up a payment schedule to pay the minimum $50.00 a month, "How long would it take to pay the original $2500 charge off at an interest rate of @ 23%?"

I turned and whispered to my husband, "She will never pay the charge bill off completely."

Actually, the pastor said it would take her over 83 years to pay off the credit card balance—I don't recall how much in interest she paid, but it was a lot!

When you apply for a credit card you sign a contract that indicates that you agree to specific terms. **Once you use the card, you are legally bound to the terms of the contract**; please understand that the credit card application is a legally binding contract. When you open a credit card account, be sure you read through the opening account information carefully. (I'll be the first one to admit that most of what you read is difficult to understand, the contract contains a lot of legal jargon, ask for clarification.) If there is something in the contract that you don't fully understand, don't be shy – ask for an explanation.

When you open the account, ask questions about the rate and fees. Some credit card companies charge an 'introductory interest rate,' this is the initial rate that lasts for a stated period. This introductory rate can be much lower than the rate you will be charged once the introductory period is over. Be sure you understand if your credit card will automatically change the rate at a pre-determined date, and if so, what the new (post-introductory) rate will be. Ask questions about extra charges that might be assessed, like: telephone payment fees, late fees, the annual membership fees, penalties for using your credit card overseas, rates that escalate the more items you purchase, etc. Extra fees just add to your monthly payment and, if your goal is to pay-off the credit card balance each month, you won't want any unbudgeted surprises.

The manner in which you pay your bills has an important effect on your credit score. And, we will later discuss how your credit score has a long-term effect on how much money you can borrow, and the interest rates you may get charged for loans, and IF you can borrow for larger purchases – such as a car or your mortgage. In the Financing Section, more information about credit cards, and compound and simple interest will be provided.

Please complete: True or False

1. Credit cards have a monthly bill for you to pay. _____

2. Debit cards are more like "cash" than credit cards. _____

3. Debit cards have a monthly bill for you to pay. _____

Plan For Taxes

> *"The hardest thing to understand in the world is the income tax."*
>
> Albert Einstein

The subject of taxes is definitely a complex one. I am not a tax advisor, but I am frequently asked questions about tax issues and I always defer to a TAX ADVISOR. Our tax legislation is forever changing, and it is very difficult to navigate the tax laws. If you are curious to learn more about tax legislation history, one resource is the June 2008 issue of Research Magazine®. The issue provides a brief review of tax legislation: '*18 Notable events in the history of American taxation.*' And Wikipedia also provide a "*History of Taxation in the United States,*" (https://en.wikipedia.org/wiki/History_of_taxation_in_the_United_States). Be sure you consult a tax advisor to help you decipher the many ins and outs of tax laws and requirements.

Why are we discussing taxes here? For one reason, you cannot develop a budget without considering the impact of taxes. Examine your pay stub. Not only do you need to check that the calculations of your income are correct, you also need to review what taxes and deductions have been withheld. For example, you will see four tax lines: one for your state income taxes, one for federal income taxes, and two for FICA taxes (one each for Social Security and Medicare).

FICA

The Federal Insurance Contribution Act (FICA) withholds money from your paycheck to support Social Security and Medicare/Medicaid programs. While you are not likely to use these programs any time soon, these programs should be available to support you when you are retired or if you become disabled. These programs disburse money to retirees after they turn a specific age. Individuals are eligible for social security payments when they reach the age of 62. Our Social Security program is funded by today's workers for a) current retirees, and b) disabled individuals and their dependents. FICA money also funds Medicare. Medicare is a health insurance benefit for the elderly and disabled; and Medicaid provides health and hospitalization benefits to individuals with low incomes. Individuals are currently eligible for these health benefits at age 65. Websites like: https://www.ssa.gov, https://www.aarpmedicareplans.com/medicare-education, and https://www.medicare.gov provide more detailed information; visit them when you have questions in the future.

One of the most popular questions I am asked concerns, "When should I begin to take my Social Security income?" We'll address this question and discuss more about the Social Security program in the Retirement Section.

Income Taxes

Income taxes are payments to the government, based on your income level. The state you live in may also receive money from most working citizens by deducting taxes from their income. However, each state has a different tax rate. Some states even waive the state income tax, so you will need to check to see what your state's income tax rate is.

In addition, most individuals who exceed the minimum income limits (the minimum limits also can change from year to year) will likely pay federal income taxes. The federal income tax is a 'progressive tax' structure. That means that in theory the more money you make, the more money you pay in taxes. When you consult a Tax Schedule (Exhibit B provides several websites that offer tax schedules that you can review) you will notice that you pay a lower percentage of taxes on the first XX dollars, and a slightly higher tax rate on the next tier of XX dollars, and so forth. Through the years our government revises the tax brackets frequently; in fact, according to the IRS website, the tax brackets changed again for 2018. (https://www.irs.gov/pub/irs-pdf/p5307.pdf) Be sure you understand your tax deductions so you can accurately compute your income for your budget.

Look at your pay stub (or someone else's) – note: FICA (Social Security, Medicare), State, Federal Tax Amounts here.

_____

_____

There are two additional tax subjects that we will examine in the Investment Section:

1. The tax-deferral of some types of retirement savings, and

2. How the long- and short-term gains realized from investment sales are taxed.

Tips on Tips

I am including information about how to calculate a tip here, in the tax section, because both subjects concern calculating percentages. Calculating a tip is a life skill. I am certain that you will want to know how to calculate a tip for services you receive from hairdressers/barbers, waiters and waitresses, etc. Some people have trouble with this activity.

Here it is, plain and simple. If you review your sales ticket or dinner check you will see that taxes are added. Look at your bill closely and you will note that your items are subtotaled, then a tax is shown, and then the total is recorded. There are a couple of schools of thought on how to calculate a tip. I generally think that most people look at the total bill, including the tax, and add somewhere between 15% and 20% for services rendered, if they are satisfied with the service they received. See the example below.

Tipping, how you calculate the tip, and what percentage you tip, is a personal preference. You decide.

Life

Example: 20% Tip	Example: 15% Tip
$30.00 food 2.40 tax	$30.00 food 2.40 tax
$32.40 subtotal	$32.40 subtotal
$6.48 20% tip	$4.86 15% tip
$38.88 total	$37.26 total

Calculate a 15% and a 20% tip on a $ 47.00 food ticket.

_____

_____

What To Save For, Maybe A Family?

Aside from buying a home, another primary expense might be raising a family. While not everyone is planning on having children, no conversation about saving money would be complete without a mention about how much children cost. With the responsibility of children comes the responsibility of providing for those children. And, providing for children takes money, time, effort and dedication. Of course, the decision to have children is not merely a dollars and sense decision, but financial preparation for having children is not only imperative, but just plain smart.

In her article, "*Baby bust: 5 charts show how expensive it is to have kids in the US today*," (3/2018) Heidi Steinour suggests that the cost to raise a child from birth to age 17 is:

- "As of 2015, American parents spend, on average, US $233,610 on child costs from birth until the age of 17, not including college. This number covers everything from housing and food to childcare and transportation costs." (24)

Another article, "*Average cost to raise a kid: $241,080*," (8/2015, Melanie Hicken) states,

- "From day care to the monthly grocery bill, the cost of raising a child is climbing at a rate that many families can't keep up with." (25)

Note that the costs provided DID NOT include the cost of college.

College?

If you plan to attend a secondary school, or save money to help fund college for you, or a family member, please read about a couple of different college planning savings options below:

☒ Research the various types of College Savings Accounts as rules, limits, distribution amounts change periodically. The following outlines 3 College Savings Account options for you to review.

    i.   **The 529 College Savings Plan** is most likely the most popular savings vehicle for college expenses today. There are several aspects of the 529 plan that are very attractive:

         a.   The 'owner/participant' (typically a parent) opens an account for a named beneficiary.

         b.   The contribution gifting limits are very generous; however, the limits can change each year.

         c.   The beneficiary of a 529 account can be changed during the lifetime of the account.

         d.   You do not pay federal taxes on the earnings if the earnings of the account (assuming the account value grows over time) are utilized for qualified higher-education expenses.

         e.   The owner, not the beneficiary, retains control of the account.

         f.   Some states may allow you to deduct some amount of your contribution from your state taxes.

         g.   Age or income limits do not apply for your contributions. (29)

College Savings accounts are sometimes used because they offer the benefits listed here… As you can see, these 'College Savings Account' features are different from a typical Savings Account. Just like other investment products, 529 College Savings plans are not all created equal. Several states sponsor 529 College Savings plans, and each will offer specific investment choices. Before you choose which 529 plan to invest in, be sure you: evaluate the 529 plan investment options against your objectives, research fees, investment choices, historical performance, etc. Inquire about state tax deduction options as well.

ii. **A Coverdell Education Savings Account** is a college savings account that permits withdrawals to be applied to Kindergarten through High School (laws may change periodically), as well as college expenses, when used for educational expenses only. These withdrawals are federally tax-free. The account has a custodian, typically a bank or a financial institution, so control over the account and changes of beneficiaries can be different than with other college savings plans. The contribution limits for a Coverdell account are considerably lower than those for a 529 plan, and income limits do apply.

iii. **UTMA or UGMA (Uniform Trust/Gift to Minor Account)** are custodian accounts that can also be utilized for college savings. These types of accounts have a less favorable tax treatment than the other two account types described here. The UTMA/UGMA accounts do not permit a beneficiary change during the life of the account. However, there are fewer restrictions for the use of the money than with the other two account types. The money in these accounts must be used to benefit a Minor, and the Minor gains control of the assets at the age of majority (someone under the age of 18 or 21 is a Minor, depending on each state's definition of 'Age of Majority') because the account is actually owned by the Minor (the account is opened using the Minor's social security number).

☒ Consider the account fees of any account and make note of any withdrawal charges.

☒ Be sure to determine which type of expenses are eligible for payments (tax-free withdrawals) from the College Savings Account you choose.

☒ Consult a financial and tax advisor to obtain specific information and to discuss which type of college savings account may be appropriate for you. (29)

Free Money?

There are a host of opportunities for college funding, here are a list of organizations that offer scholarships or grants for students who want to attend college:

- https://www.scholarships.com/

- https://www.collegescholarships.org/grants

- https://www.comparetopschools.com

- https://www.financialaidfinder.com/financial-aid/financial-aid-programs/coverdell-educational-savings-account/coverdell-529-college-plan-comparison/

While there seem to be scholarships available, you will need to do your homework to find them. Check first with your high school and college counselors to inquire about where to go to find the scholarships and how to apply for them; read the requirements CAREFULLY.

Conclusion:

The most important activity you can do to prepare yourself for financial independence is to PLAN, PLAN, and PLAN. Creating a budget, both for short-term and longer-term purchases will prove to be immensely helpful if you monitor your spending against your budget. Understanding where your money goes will enable you to responsibly manage your money. Your budgeting and saving activities will prove to be invaluable to you if you focus on being disciplined in both areas.

> *"Practice does not make perfect. Only perfect practice makes perfect."*
>
> Vince Lombardi

Exhibit A General Budget Worksheet

Item	Budgeted Spending	Suggested	Actual
Charitable Gifts		10-12%	
Saving		5-10%	
Housing		25-35%	
Utilities		5-10%	
Food		5-15%	
Transportation		10-19%	
Clothing		2-7%	
Medical/Health		5-10%	
Personal		5-10%	
Recreation		5-10%	
Debt		5-10%	
Other		5-10%	

Exhibit A-Items For Your Budget

Exhibit A Items For Your Budget	Month1	Month 2	Month 3	Month 4
PERSONAL INCOME				
Other Income				
TOTAL INCOME				
PERSONAL EXPENSES				
Mortgage/Rent				
Property Taxes				
Telephone				
Utilities				
Car Gas				
Car Payment				
Food				
Clothing				
Cable/Internet				
Car/Home Maintenance/Repairs				
Health & Beauty Aids				
Misc.				
Doctor visits/medicine/college savings				
Insurance - home				
Insurance - car				
Insurance - life				
Insurance- long term care				
Insurance benefits (health/medical)				
Retirement savings				
Personal savings				
Charitable contributions				
Vacations				
Taxes				
Gifts				
Tax preparation				
Legal expenses				
TOTAL EXPENSES				

What We Forget To Budget For

Everyone has different priorities. Some of the following willl not be appropriate for your budget, and you most certainly have other items that aren't listed here.

Here is a preliminary list of "hidden What We Forget To Budget For

a.   Gifts For Family and Friends

b.   Wardrobe For Specific Events (Work, Party, Vacation

c.   Shoes

d.   Suits

e.   Accessories

f.   Dry Cleaning/Laundry

g.   Contacts/Glasses

h.   Doctor/Dentist Visits

i.   Hosting Parties, Bringing Food And Beverage to Social Gatherings

j.   Car/Home Repairs

k.   Oil Changes

l.   Routine Home Air Conditioner/Furnace Check-Ups

m.   Landscaping Expenses

n.   Stamps/Stationery Items

o.   Cleaning Products

p.   Babysitters

q.   Small Appliances

r.   What You Really Spend On Entertainment

s.   Legal Expenses

t.   Tax Preparation Expenses

u.   Medicine/Vitamins

Exhibit B- Tax Schedules

Remember: Tax schedules can and DO charge, check a website for the up to date-version. Here are a few to start you off.

- https://www.credit.com/taxes/how-many-tax-brackets-are-there/

- https://www.bankrate.com/finance/taxes/tax-brackets.aspx

- https://taxfoundation.org

- https://www.irs.gov/site-index-search?search=federal+tax+brackets&field_pup_historical_1=1&field_pup_historical=1

There are ample other resources available on the internet.

Sources:

(1)   https://www.bloomberg.com/news/articles/2019-09-21/young-people-are-starving-for-classes-on-finance-tips-on-taxes, *"Young People Are Starving for Classes on Finance,"* Virginia Van Natta (9/2019); *"4 Stats That Reveal How Badly America Is Failing At Financial Literacy,"* 4/3/2018, Dani Pascarella; https://www.forbes.com/sites/danipascarella/2018/04/03/4-stats-that-reveal-how-badly-america-is-failing-at-financial-literacy/. *"Kids Need Financial Education"* (3/2019), https://www.cesisolutions.org/2019/03/should-financial-education-be-taught-in-schools/, https://www.bea.gov/data/income-saving/personal-saving-rate; https://blog.aicpa.org/2019/04/cpas-are-playing-a-leading-role-in-financial-literacy.html#sthash.GFztGFZI.dpbs, *"CPAs play a leading role in financial literacy."*

(2)   FINRA® Investor Education Foundation's *"2018 Financial Capability in the United States,"* https://www.usfinancialcapability.org/downloads/NFCS_2018_Report_Natl_Findings.pdf., ©2019 FINRA. All rights reserved. FINRA is a registered trademark of the Financial Industry Regulatory Authority, Inc. Reprinted with permission from FINRA; .https://www.investmentnews.com/article/20190302/FEATURE/190229936/financial-literacy-an-epic-fail-in-america, *"Financial literacy: An epic fail in America,"* Greg Iacurci, 3/2019.

(3)   William C Bailey, D. Kay Woodiel, M. Jean Turner, and Jenifer Young, B.S., *"The Relationship of Financial Stress to Overall Stress and Satisfaction,"* 1998, Vol. 2, No. 2, https://citeseerx.ist.psu.edu/viewdoc/download?doi=10.1.1.536.7683&rep=rep1&type=pdf.

(4)   CNBC/Money, 3/2018, *"30% of Americans are 'constantly' stressed out about money- but you don't have to be,"* Shawn M. Carter. https://www.cnbc.com/2018/03/19/30-percent-of-americans-are-stressed-out-about-money-constantly.html.

(5)   (2005) Jonathan Fox, Suzanne Bartholomae, and Jinkook Lee, *"Building the case for financial education,"* The American Council on Consumer Interests®, Volume 39, Number 1, March 2005, 195-214(20), https://onlinelibrary.wiley.com/doi/abs/10.1111/j.1745-6606.2005.00009.x.

(6)   https://www.jumpstartcoalition.org, *"The Financial Literacy of Young American Adults"* (2008), https://www.stockmarketgame.org/assets/pdf/2008%20JumpStart%20Financial%20Literacy%20Survey.pdf, https://www.jumpstart.org/what-we-do/support-financial-education/standards/.

(7)   https://youth.gov/youth-topics/financial-capability-literacy/facts, *"Facts About Youth Financial Knowledge & Capability,"* Organization for Economic Co-operation and Development®, 2014.

(8)   Varcoe, Karen P.; Martin, Allen; Devitto, Zana & Go, Charles (2005), Association for Financial Counseling and Planning Education®, *"Using A Financial Education Curriculum for Teens,"* 63-71.

(9)   *"Survey Reveals that US High School Students Lack Adequate Financial Knowledge,"* 4/13/13, https://everfi.com/press-releases/survey-reveals-that-us-high-school-students-lack-adequate-financial-knowledge/.

(10)   https://www.treasurydirect.gov/indiv/tools/tools_moneymath.htm, Curators of the University of Missouri; *"Money Math, Lessons for Life®,"* Mary C. Suiter & Sarapage McCorkie, Center for Entrepreneurship & Economic Education®, University of Missouri-St. Louis (2001); https://www.moneyinstructor.com.

(11)   https://www.local.gov.uk/our-support/research/partner-organisations/national-institute-adult-continuing-education-niace, (NIACE); https://www.fdic.gov/consumers/consumer/moneysmart/.

(12)   https://www.fdic.gov/consumers/consumer/moneysmart/adult.html, *"Money Smart Adult Financial Education Curriculum®;"* https://www.nefe.org/education/school-based/hsfpp.aspx, "HSFPP."

(13)   ('Personal Finance' drop-down – 'Money 101,' Lessons), *"Top things to know; Money 101 Lessons 1- 23;"* https://money.com/money/collection/money-101/.

(14)   https://www.fdic.gov/consumers/consumer/moneysmart/index.html, FDIC's *"MoneySmart®."*

(15)   http://www.plattscsdfcu.org/Includes/Services/financial_resources.htm; Financial Resources.

(16)   1/2018, Scott Spann, https://www.forbes.com/sites/financialfinesse/2018/01/14/are-your-money-beliefs-holding-you-back/?sh=549cc4cf79bd, *"Are your money beliefs holding you back?"* https://www.semanticscholar.org/paper/MANY-SIDES-OF-THE-COIN-THE-PSYCHOLOGY-OF-MONEY-Furnham/e90cb4c26b8e57d01b83114c12bd2b57a3df043c, *"Many Sides of the Coin-The Psychology of Money Usage,"* Adrian Furnham, (1984).

(17)   *"Budgeting and Saving Money;"* https://www.thebalance.com/how-to-budget-and-save-money-in-5-easy-steps-4056838, https://www.consumer-action.org/english/articles/66_ways_to_save_money_en, *"66 Ways to Save Money – Consumer Action."*

(18)   https://www.thesimpledollar.com/trimming-the-fat-forty-ways-to-reduce-your-monthly-required-spending/;TheSimple Dollar.com; Trent Hamm 6/22/19; *"40 Ways to Save Money on Monthly Expenses".*

(19)   https://www.daveramsey.com/blog/the-cure-for-excessive-spending, Dave Ramsey blog; *"How to Stop Spending Money".*

(20)   Updegrave, Walter (1/8/2007), *"Money Magazine®,"* *"Ten percent is better than nothing, but it's really only the beginning, our expert explains,"* https://money.cnn.com/2007/01/08/pf/expert/expert.moneymag/index.htm.

(21)   https://www.ThinkGlink.com, Added September 9, 2009 by Ilyce R. Glink, *"How Much Should I Save Each Month and For Retirement,"* https://www.thinkglink.com/2009/09/09/how-much-should-i-save-each-month-and-for-retirement/.

(22)   https://www.fisherinvestments.com/en-us/marketminder/a-discussion-on-consumer-credit-trends; Jarred Kriz, 08/23/2011, *Fisher Investments®, Market Minder, 1/2011. By the Number$,* Sunlife Financial©.

(23)   https://wealthpilgrim.com/share-financial-data-family/, *"How To Share Your Financial Data With Family,"* Neal Frankle, CFP, WEALTH PILGRIM, 2019.

(24)   https://theconversation.com/baby-bust-5-charts-show-how-expensive-it-is-to-have-kids-in-the-us-today-91532, *"Baby bust: 5 charts show how expensive it is to have kids in the US today,"* Heidi Steinour, 3/2018.

(25)   https://money.cnn.com/2013/08/14/pf/cost-children/, *"Average cost to raise a kid: $241,080,"* 8/2013, M, Hicken. (25a) *'The cost of raising a child in America has soared – it's a price tag fit for a prince,"* Heidi Steinour, 4/2018 . https://www.marketwatch.com/story/these-5-charts-show-how-expensive-it-is-to-raise-children-today-2018-03-29.

(26)   https://research.collegeboard.org/pdf/trends-college-pricing-2007-full-report.pdf; *"College Board's Trends in College Pricing 2007,"* 2012-full-report-121203.pdf; https://research.collegeboard.org/trends/college-pricing, CollegeBoard®, *"Trends in College Pricing 2018."*

(27)   https://research.collegeboard.org/pdf/trends-college-pricing-2019-full-report.pdf, *"Trends in College Pricing 2019,"* CollegeBoard®.

(28)   Christine Benz (3/8/2005, 9/30/2008, 10/27/2010), *"The Late-Start Guide to College Savings:"* https://www.
         morningstar.com/articles/357111/the-late-start-guide-to-college-savings; *"Late start" college savings options,"*
         Richard Barrington, 3/2018; https://www.moneyrates.com/savings/late-start-college-savings-options.html.

(29)   https://www.fremontbank.com/wealth-management/invest/college-savings-plans, Fremont Bank, *"College Savings
         Plans;"* https://www.financialaidfinder.com/financial-aid/financial-aid-programs/coverdell-educational-savings-account/
         coverdell-529-college-plan-comparison/, *"Financial Aid Finder - Coverdell ESA and 529 College Plan
         Comparison."*

Chapter 1

Check For Understanding

For a chapter review, read and complete the following follow-up activities.

☒ Prepare a list of areas that encompass your definition of Financial Literacy.

☒ Record some resources for developing a budget.

☒ Make a list of subject areas for your short and long-term budget goals. Offer at least 15 categories.

☒ Translate the 5 Steps of Developing a Budget into your own words – rename the steps to make them appropriate for you and your lifestyle.

☒ Consider why individuals may procrastinate in creating a budget and sticking with it.

☒ Describe in your own words why you think a budget is hard to create and monitor.

☒ Demonstrate your 'system' for keeping track of your income and spending.

☒ Find and employ a budget you have found through research. Record the website/source here.

☒ Illustrate how you might be able to realistically reduce monthly spending.

☒ Compare the differences between a debit card and credit card.

☒ Contrast a checking account with a savings account, how are they alike or different?

☒ Examine your recent pay stub, how did taxes impact your 'net' verses 'gross' income?

About Experience Talks...

Individuals save and budget in so many different ways... everyone has their own approach. What follows are some vignettes that offer a brief insight into how some people who I have encountered over the years have shaped their own approach to accumulating wealth. These examples are presented so you can begin to formulate your philosophy towards budgeting and saving, copy what you think might work for you. But, create your own budgeting strategy according to your own style.

Nearly everyone has a car story... Here is my personal Budget/ 'saving for a car story'....

I was changing jobs and I needed a larger car. I had been saving for several years for my next car. I began by researching how much my current car was worth for the trade-in.

So, on a hot June afternoon (@ 90+ degrees) a friend and I set out to visit three dealerships in Kansas City. We were shopping for a used model but discovered that a special sale was going on for the new models.

The NEW model was actually being offered at a better price than the used model.

I knew the trade-in value of my car, and I had allotted $ X amount for my budget. I had saved for the car for over 5 years.

We arrived at the third dealership at about 3 pm in the afternoon, test- drove a car, and I began negotiations. For approximately five and a half hours I kept repeating that I only could write a check for $ X amount. ($X amount is the amount I had saved.) At 9:05 p.m. my friend and I left the dealership after I had written a check for $300 over my budget for my new car.

I guess I just plain wore them out!

Experience Talks...

Jane worked at a Fortune 500 company for 31 years and saved like crazy

Jane lived modestly; paying off a mortgage for a house that was bought in the 1970s that cost less than $30,000. Jane paid off her automobile and kept it for years; and she spent very little on material objects and personal entertainment.

Jane was referred to me by a friend when she retired. Up until that point, Jane had not invested outside of her 401k at work, although she did have a savings account where she kept some cash in a money market. When I sat down with Jane. I was amazed to learn that she had saved over $1,000,000. Very methodically, over the course of the 31 years, Jane had diverted a large portion of her salary into her retirement account and had watched it grow. She must have realized a healthy rate of return to achieve that level of wealth accumulation.

And Jane was not the only person I know who saved like this. Betty was another client that put somewhere between 35-50% of her salary into investment and retirement accounts for over 20 years. When I met Betty, she was in her mid-forties and had over $1,000,000 put away as well.

You should understand if you met either of these women you would not be able to guess that they had as much money as they did. Even Betty's sister had no idea how much money Betty had saved.

Moral of the story: If saving money is a priority, and you are disciplined, you can accumulate money.

Experience Talks...

Saving Becomes A Habit

Damon went to work after school when he was only 14 years old. Damon developed a plan to buy a car… he saved money every week out of his paycheck. At the age of 17 he had saved enough money to put about $ 3,000 down on a brand-new car.

A year later he got a different job as a sales representative for a consumer product company. His new job came with a company car. Damon waited six months, just to be sure that he liked the new job… and he sold his new car. Fortunately, Damon not only got his $ 3,000 back that he had put down on the car, but he netted about $ 3850.

Damon had also been able to save some money during the six months he worked at his new job; he had saved close to a total of $ 5,000. Damon put $ 4,000 down on a small condo which was selling for $27,000. He bought the condo during the early 1970s. (Probably can't find too many $ 27,000 condos today!)

Two years after he purchased the first condo, Damon sold the condo for @ $ 46,000 and bought a different home.

Moral of the story: Start small but start somewhere.

Experience Talks...

Pay Yourself First

Jacqueline married Steve when she was 27 and Steve was 34 years old. Steve was a marketing executive, and Jacqueline was a sales representative. Both came to the marriage owning a condominium. After just a few months of marriage, it became apparent to Jacqueline that she and Steve were not adhering to a comprehensive budget and could be doing a much better job of saving money. Jacqueline approached Steve and asked him if they could set up a budget they could both agree upon and she would manage the household finances. Steve readily agreed.

Jacqueline was convinced that she and Steve could live on Steve's income and save hers. First, Jacqueline analyzed where they were spending their money. Her first task was to reduce their food expenses. Jacqueline started this process by keeping a running 'food list' handy in the kitchen. By grocery shopping once a week and sticking to the list, Steve and Jacqueline reduced their 'last-minute-dinner-dash' behaviors.

Secondly, by setting up their fixed bills on a monthly auto-pay program, Jacqueline was able to determine what their fixed expenses were. This allowed both Steve and Jacqueline to better understand what they had left-over for discretionary spending. Jacqueline had reviewed where they were spending their money, so the next task was to determine if their discretionary spending could be reduced or re-routed. One simple tactic that Jacqueline used was to 'save first.'

By putting money into 'savings categories,' Jacqueline was in a sense paying her and Steve first. For example: both Steve and Jacqueline began to fund their 401ks at work, they contributed to a vacation 'savings bucket,' and because Steve and Jacqueline only had one car, (the vehicle was paid-for) Jacqueline set up a separate savings account to begin to accumulate money for a second car purchase in the future.

Once they began funding these savings buckets (different categories or vehicles for savings), it was easier to be disciplined in their savings. Jacqueline also reported that because they were essentially saving her salary, they did not feel guilty about spending any left-over money from Steve's income.

Moral of the story: Can being organized help you find extra/free money?

Experience Talks...

You Can't Live On ALL Credit

Jeff worked for a large corporation. He was an executive and was paid a high salary. Because of his income, Jeff was able to purchase an expensive home. Jeff didn't seem to worry too much about finances. His home, cars, and credit cards were 'mortgaged,' he owed quite a bit on his material assets, but he managed to pay the 'minimums' on the balances and keep afloat. Jeff wasn't concerned about saving.

Jeff was married with a teenage son. When asked about his college savings plan for his son, Jeff remarked that he would just use his annual bonuses to fund college expenses. It appeared that he would just handle the cost of his son's education 'when the time came.'

Since so many companies reduced their workforce and salaries and bonuses in 2008, and Jeff's employer probably followed suit.... I always wondered if Jeff's plan has taken a dramatic turn???

Moral of the story: The prudent planner constructs Plan A, and has (at least) a back-up *Plan B.*

Experience Talks...

My Money, Your Money, Somebody Else's Money... It's Still Money

G retchen and Mike had three children. Two of the children were twins, and their eldest daughter was just two years older than the twins.

Both Gretchen and Mike were wonderful financial role models.

Gretchen told me that she and Mike devised a plan to help instill money management strategies for their children when the children were in middle school. What Gretchen and Mike did was give each child an 'allowance.' This allowance was to be spent by each child as the child deemed appropriate. The money was to be used primarily for clothing and discretionary spending items.

Gretchen reported that after she and Mike had started this plan, shopping trips took on a different tone. When one of the children asked to buy items, Gretchen would ask, "Are you going to spend your own allowance money on the item?" Over time, it became apparent that the children were less willing to buy items with their own allowance money, the kids seemed to be more discerning about what they purchased and made fewer purchase requests.

Overall, Gretchen and Mike thought that the plan worked. Not only were the children more 'in tune' with what items cost, but they also began to practice restraint. As time went on, budgeting techniques were actually employed voluntarily by the children.

Moral of the story: Does other people's money spend differently than your own?

Experience Talks...

Loans Are Supposed to Be Paid Off... REALLY

Christian graduated Graduate school at age 26 with @ $94,000 in school loans.

While school loans used to carry a low interest rate, about 3-4%, Christian's loans averaged @ 6.75%.

After graduation, Christian's first order of business was to get a job. While he worked two part-time jobs, Christian diligently searched for a full-time job in his field of training. After about 8 months, he landed a position that paid him close to $ 60,000 a year. He waited three months and then moved out of his parents' house to begin living independently.

I checked back with Christian about 6 months later and found that he: a) did not have any credit card debt, b) was driving a 2004 car that he had bought used and paid cash for, c) was sharing an apartment with a roommate, and his living expenses were 'reasonable,' d) kept himself on a tight discretionary spending budget, taking his lunch to work and cooking at home almost every night... spending very little on entertainment (he reported that his dating life was suffering), and e) he had not only begun to pay back his student loans, he was adding an additional $ 500- $600 a month toward his loan principal. Christian calculated that he was able to accelerate his re-payment schedule over the next 5 years; he might be able to pay the loan off in about 8 years. If he can pay his loan off early, his interest payments can be dramatically decreased. Discipline will be critical if his plan is to succeed.

Moral of the story: Reduce debt to save real money (interest payments) over time.

PS: Christian's loan did get paid off in 7 years!

Experience Talks...

Autopay Is Not a German Highway

John has a flat dollar amount, $150, automatically transferred into his savings account from his paycheck each pay period. John uses this special account as an emergency account to pay for unexpected expenses.

Moral of the story: Autopay yourself and your bills to ensure you take care of the important tasks first. What you don't see you won't miss.

CHAPTER 2

An Introduction To Borrowing/Finance Options

LEARNING OBJECTIVES:

After reading Chapter 2, you should be able to:

a. Exhibit an understanding of what 'credit' is, and how and when you will use credit.

b. Describe the differences between simple and compound interest; and the relevance for each.

c. Demonstrate an understanding of various ways 'finance' charges can be calculated; and identify various finance terms.

d. Understand what 'credit scores' are; and what factors affect your credit score.

e. Identify behaviors to help establish 'good' credit.

f. Learn the fundamental facts about mortgages; convey where you will find assistance when the time arrives for you to apply for a mortgage.

  • Outline and give details of some of the different mortgage rate options.

  • Be aware of some of the mortgage terms.

  • Understand and be able to describe the difference between specific use loans and mortgages.

g. Comprehend and be able to describe what 'bankruptcy' is.

Experience Talks...

Take Borrowing Seriously

My parents bought their first home in the 1950s. They had been married for less than 10 years and had saved diligently. According to my Mom, going into debt to that extent was a frightening experience. When Mom and Dad bought their first home in southern California, during the1950s home prices for a 3 bedroom/two-bathroom home were running about $ 20,000! When the cost for new cars were $1,500- $2,000, a $20,000 debt was daunting. My parents, like their parents, did not use credit frivolously… borrowing was a serious endeavor.

My parents did not use credit cards. They paid cash or used checks for purchases for almost everything. They balanced their checkbooks with EVERY entry, and my Dad knew to the penny what the balance was. My father calculated meticulously how much money my Mom could spend each week, he knew exactly what his fixed expenses were, and how to be, and remain, solvent. This behavior helped me learn important finance principles. So, when I was 18 years old, working and living away from home, bringing home about $83 a week, paying rent and all living expenses, I also stayed away from using credit cards.

Debit cards may not have been available at the time. I was diligent at balancing my checkbook and went without rather than go into debt. My roommate at the time worked at a dental office as a dental assistant. My roommate paid her half of the apartment expenses, and we both pitched in for food. At the time, neither of us over-extended ourselves… meaning we didn't spend more than we afford, or more than our jobs paid us. I believe that in the 1970s the thought of going into 'debt' for purchases other than your car or home was frowned upon. The 'loose' credit environment had not evolved as yet.

Navigating Credit and Financing

Even though there may not be the same stigma attached to using 'credit and financing' today, going into debt can severely impede your savings plan and your standard of living.

Understanding how to navigate the complex world of 'credit and financing' is invaluable to assisting you in properly managing your finances. The next section will introduce you to some of the credit and financing terms that will be important for you to learn as you face credit and financing options in your future.

Chapter 2

An Introduction To Borrowing/Finance Options

Borrowing Money

> *"Remember that credit is money."*
>
> Benjamin Franklin

How to Borrow

Today, Americans live in a very consumer-oriented, 'get-it-now' society. As previously discussed, my mother and father saved and sacrificed. Accordingly, I was brought up that if you can't buy it without using credit, with the exception of a home mortgage or car loan, then you go without. Period. That goes for the credit card too. Therefore, if you use a credit card, pay it off each month. What about the idea that you DO NOT go out to eat or buy new clothes, or get whatever might be on your 'want list,' until the money is saved and it is sitting in your checking account ready to pay for the items? What about the concept that you contribute to your savings account each month, BEFORE you buy that new item? And savings accounts, along with retirement accounts, are not used for any 'want list' items. The answer? You guessed it…. "No compromising."

I realize that this line of thinking is antiquated in today's easy-credit-crazy environment. I also admit that this philosophy is easier said than done. Discipline is difficult. To accomplish these objectives, you will probably need to modify your behavior. You will not be alone. And, contrary to popular belief there are individuals who do live by these standards.

Life

Because of what I did for a living, I come into contact with people from all walks of life. Their fiscal management styles are different; their approach to saving is different, and of course, their approach to spending is also varied. But be assured, there are many, many individuals living on a fixed income amount that would seem impossible to survive on to others.

Some people in the financial arena have been concerned about the status of the 'American debt' for quite some time, and it didn't surprise them to learn that we were in trouble with our financing. This statement may summarize it all. 'Credit consumption' has caused severe problems in the financial system. So, the question of the day is, "How are you preparing to safe-guard you and your family against finding yourself in an over-extended credit position?" The logical answer is: use debt wisely.

Make a list here of the loans you current have.

_____

_____

Understanding the complicated world of credit can help you make wise borrowing decisions. The choices you make regarding the use of credit can have a dramatic and far-reaching impact on your borrowing power and your credit score (either positively or negatively). Carefully read through this section to determine how you might protect and elevate your credit status to improve your future.

> *"It is well that the people of the nation do not understand our banking and monetary system, for if they did, I believe there would be a revolution before tomorrow morning."*
>
> Henry Ford

Even if Henry Ford made this statement in a 'tongue-and-cheek' manner, as responsible citizens we certainly do not want to be a 'people of the nation that [do] not understand our banking and monetary system.' You want to be knowledgeable about the banking system and how you borrow money. Therefore, in order to further your financial competency, you will need to become familiar with some financing terms. The following section provides a review of some financing concepts.

> *"Rather go to bed without dinner than to rise in debt."*
>
> Benjamin Franklin

Collateral Can Be Very Important

> *"A bank is a place that will lend you money if you can prove that you don't need it."*
>
> Bob Hope

Mr. Hope's words can be somewhat confusing, nevertheless often very true. For some loans, you will need to substantiate the fact that you have the assets, or collateral, to repay the money you borrow. Collateral are the assets, or your items of value, that you can convert to cash in order to repay the loan if you run out of other available funds. You 'pledge' your collateral to the lender with the agreement that the lender may take your collateral if you do not repay the loan according to the agreed-upon terms of your loan contract. The value of your collateral can help to determine how much money you can borrow. There is a relationship between the amount of money you can borrow and the amount of assets, or collateral you pledge for the loan. This ratio is referred to as, the loan-to-asset ratio. Your cash, or capital, is also factored into the loan ratio equation and helps to determine the loan-to-asset ratio for your loan. The more collateral you own, typically the more money you can borrow…. Because, in theory, you can convert the collateral you own to cash to help repay the loan.

Life

When I purchased my first home, in @1975, I was required to have a specified amount of collateral, and cash ($5,500), to borrow @ $24,000 to purchase a three-bedroom condominium, not too far from the beach in California. I bought the condo for @ $27,000.

At that time, in order to obtain my loan, I needed a minimum of 20%, or $5,400 to put down. Collateral that I had at the time included cash in the bank. I also had NO other debt, I did not owe anything on a car, nor did I have any outstanding credit card debt. I had enough cash in the bank, was employed and had a strong bill payment history. This allowed me to secure the loan.

In other words, I also had to an income that could support my re-payment of the loan. Not just a job, but a track-record of income, and a track record of paying my bills.

What you should also know is that the loan-to-asset ratio requirements can dramatically differ between financial institutions. The ratios are a moving target, meaning that different lenders, in different geographical locations, can use very different ratio formulas.

During the past several years some of the parameters have shifted regarding the ***loan-to-asset ratio*** and they have become less stringent. However, given our current economic environment, the pendulum could be swinging back the other way… ratios are becoming more rigorous. This means that getting approved for a loan may require you to produce more collateral, creating a lower loan-to-asset calculation.

Life

For example:

In the past if you wanted to purchase a $ 100,000 home you may have been able to do so with only $10,000 down. And if now, a $20,000 down-payment is required, this is a lower ratio. Carefully compare ratio requirements when you apply for a loan.

Note: Your loan-to-asset ratio should not be confused with your ***debt-to-income ratio.*** Your debt-to-income ratio is **calculated by dividing your outstanding loan amount by your income total.** This ratio gives you an idea of how much of your income is being spent on servicing your debt. The lower your debt-to- income ratio, the more financially solvent you are.

What has also shifted is that Americans have now begun to re-focus on our 'capacity' for repaying a debt. The capacity is the income stream or available capital that the borrower possesses; it is a hypothetical mathematical calculation that projects whether or not you can pay back a loan. If you do not have the capacity for paying back a loan, in theory, the lender will deny your loan request. If you obtain a loan and cannot repay it, you 'default' on the loan. If you default on the loan, the bank, or lending institution takes your collateral in lieu of the loan payment. Again, requirements will differ from financial institution to another. Carefully compare requirements when you apply for a loan.

Buying On Time

> *"In God we trust; all others must pay cash."*
>
> Unknown Source

Acquiring items and paying for them over time is not a new idea. You probably already have a credit card, or have taken out a loan for your car. I believe that credit may have originally been created so that the purchaser, you, could spread out payments over time for large, expensive purchases (like a home or car). I don't think credit cards were originally meant to be used to purchase a cell phone. Case in point, credit may have been designed for these purposes:

- Back in the early days, landowners offered farmers the opportunity to farm their land for a period of X years, and in return the landowner gave the land to the farmer at the end of pre-determined time period;

- Storekeepers offered the opportunity to local farmers and townspeople to 'buy' goods in advance of harvesting time, and pay for the goods after their crops were in; and

- Early indentured servants sometimes worked on a landowner's property for X amount of years in exchange for their freedom.

The occasion of how and when individuals use credit has shifted. When we look at how credit is offered today, it appears that we use credit in a very caviler manner. Quite simply, I think we take credit for granted. Doing so has contributed to the unfortunate financial situation that we are in today.

Are You Credit Card Savvy?

> *"Credit card debt now averages $8,500 per U.S. household."*
>
> (30) (October/2019)

While the average credit card debt was reported to be about $ 8,300 in 2008 (30), Tim Chen suggests that there is an additional consideration:

- "The average US household credit card balance now stands at $16,140, counting only those households carrying debt," wrote NerdWallet CEO Tim Chen in a recent commentary." (31)

In the Sunday section of the *Kansas City Star*®, September 28, 2008, an article on credit cards appeared, written by Patrick May. The headline read, *'50 YEARS OF PLASTIC MONEY.'* The article chronicled the history of credit cards, stating that nearly 50 years ago, "Bank of America® mass-mailed every home in Fresno, CA, a small piece of plastic called the Bank Americard®." (32) Accordingly, this reportedly launched the era of the *credit card.* The credit card has dramatically altered our world of credit. May's article suggests that the long-term effects could not have been predicted, and I totally agree!

What was the credit card originally intended to be used for? I want to believe that our credit cards were designed to be utilized in a case of an emergency. Or maybe the cards were intended to allow the credit card owner to carry less cash, providing a 'safer' means of currency. A credit card is a powerful resource that can quickly become your enemy if you're not careful. I have met with people who are reluctant to tell me how high their credit card outstanding balances have grown. I have counseled many individuals that found themselves with a credit card balance that was 'overwhelming.' Their balances were so high they would need years of saving to pay down the balances completely. What I mean is, they could not make the minimum payment on the amount they owed (principal and monthly interest charge) each month. In this case, additional charges were then added to their balance each month, causing them to go deeper and deeper in debt. Here are a couple of avenues you can pursue if you find that you are not able to pay off your credit card balance each month.

☒   If you get into trouble and overuse your credit card:

- Make it a priority to pay off the cards as fast as you can. Cut back on other spending categories until you can get back to a '$ 0' balance.

- Consult a professional if you need to.

- Develop a plan to pay off those high interest outstanding credit card balances first. Believe it or not, calling your credit card companies and asking them to get involved may also prove to be worthwhile.

    ○ Sometimes you can secure a 'rescheduling' of payments, can extend your loan, refinance, or consolidate.

- The National Foundation for Credit Counseling® (NFCC) is a ready resource for you to work with (33).

- There are several websites that offer tips for evaluating credit features and debt reduction options advice. Check which options may be available to you.

Interest Rates: Not All Interest Rates Are Created Equal

Knowing the interest rate you will pay on the money you borrow (same for a credit card) is typically the first question on which we all focus. However, the subject of interest rates is broader than you might realize. First of all, the reason that you pay an interest rate on the money you borrow is simple: **You are reimbursing the lender for money you borrow today that is worth less tomorrow. Because the money is worth less tomorrow, you are compensating the lender with a higher re-payment amount.**

If you have a loan or a credit card, what is your current interest rate?

_____

_____

Monetary Policy Affects The Interest Rate

Monetary policy is complicated for most of us, me included. **The monetary policies are directed through the efforts of one government agency, the Federal Reserve (the Fed).** The Federal Reserve Act was passed in 1913. "The U.S. Federal Reserve was designed to present the country with a more secure, more elastic, and more stable economic and financial structure… the Federal Reserve is in charge of the nation's monetary policy and oversees the regulation and management of banking institutions." (34) These policies can influence interest rates though the process of setting the '**discount rate**.' (In simple terms, the discount rate is the interest rate that banks pay on short-term money loans they receive from the Fed.) How the rates are set impacts how you and I can borrow money, and at what rate. (33) The Federal Reserve's monetary policy impacts how money flows down through our banking and financial systems. In theory, their policy dictates the actions that the Fed's regulatory body takes. Specifically, the Fed's charge is to: regulate Federal banks; facilitate inter-bank money transfers; promote stability of interest rates; stimulate full employment; and to control inflation. (35)

Understand that the actions of the Federal Reserve impact interest rates, the economy, and the job market. What interest rate you pay at a particular time is determined by a number of factors:

a.   Do the markets offer a lot of 'loan-able' money right now; or is money 'tight?'

b.   What is the status of inflation? It is high or low?

c.   What is a connection between the risk of the loan and the interest charged?

d.   What is the duration or length of a loan?

e.   Is the taxable interest higher than tax-free interest?

f.   Can the lending institution 'use' your money?

Simple Or Complex?

When discussing interest, the difference between 'simple' interest and 'compound' interest is important:

> - **Simple interest:** interest that is paid exclusively on the principal or borrowed amount – nothing else.
>
> - **Compound interest:** interest that is paid both on the principal and accrued interest (interest amount that has already been added) amount.
>
>   (https://www.investopedia.com/terms/c/compoundinterest.asp)

Life

Here are the calculations for a 5 Year Loan calculated at
10% COMPOUND interest:

YEAR	LOAN AT START	INTEREST CALCULATION	LOAN AT YEAR END
1	$1,000.00	($1,000.00 X 10%)=$100.00	$1,100.00
2	$1,100.00	($1,100.00 X 10%)=$110.00	$1,210.00
3	$1,210.00	($1,210.00 X 10%)=$121.00	$1,331.00
4	$1,331.00	($1,331.00 X 10%)=$133.10	$1,464.10
5	$1,464.10	($1,464..00 X 10%)=$146.41	$1,610.51
	$1,610.51	INTEREST PAID $610.51	

Here is a simple formula for calculating the compound interest:

- Calculate the interest (what the original loan amount is $1000.00) x (the interest rate of 10%).

- Total the amount of interest plus principal at the end of each year times 10%. Add $1000.00 together with the $610 interest: you've paid $1,610.51 over the 5 year period. This equals 'pay-off.'

Here are the calculations for a 5 Year Loan calculated at 10% SIMPLE interest:

YEAR	LOAN AT START	INTEREST CALCULATION	LOAN AT YEAR END
1	$1,000.00	($1,000.00 X 10%)=$100.00	$1,100.00
2	$1,000.00	($1,000.00 X 10%)=$100.00	$1,100.00
3	$1,000.00	($1,000.00 X 10%)=$100.00	$1,100.00
4	$1,000.00	($1,000.00 X 10%)=$100.00	$1,100.00
5	$1,000.00	($1,000.00 X 10%)=$100.00	$1,100.00
	$1,000.00	INTEREST PAID $500.00	

Here is a simple formula for calculating the compound interest:

- Interest = $1000.00 x 10% x 5 years = $500.00

- To calculate loan payoff, add $1000.00 together with the $500 interest: you've paid $1,500 over the 5 year period.

Finance Charges And Credit Card Contract Terms

There are many fees associated with loans. One such fee is the finance charge. The finance charge is the interest rate you will be charged on your outstanding loan balance; meaning if you do not pay off your credit card balance each month; you will be charged a finance charge of some type. The finance charge can be calculated a variety of ways. Check your credit card contract to determine which of the finance calculation methods your credit card company is using. For example, an article, *"Ways Finance Charges Are Calculated,"* (36) provides this daily balance calculation method explanation:

> *"The daily balance method of calculating your finance charge [interest fee charged on revolving credit accounts] uses the actual balance on each day of your billing cycle [the period of time between billings]. Then divided the total by the number of days in the cycle. Your rate is then applied --- 1/365th of your APR [annual percentage rate is the interest rate charged on the amount borrowed]. This is your daily rate [1/365th of your annual percentage rate]. Finance charges are calculated by summing each day's balance multiplied by the daily rate."*

This quote demonstrates an important point: If you don't understand the credit card language, you might find yourself in a position you hadn't prepared for. Understanding the terms of the credit contract is extremely important. If I asked you what interest rate your credit card is charging you, would you be able to answer the question? As mentioned in the previous section, credit card contracts are complicated. Always do your research and understand what the basic terms of the contract are. There are a few different methods for calculating the finance charges on your monthly balance. It is important to understand how you are being charged for the use of the money (the balance) you have 'on-loan.' (This assumes that you do not pay the entire balance off at the end of each month.) Familiarize yourself with each type of method and then investigate which type of calculation is utilized for the credit card you use. Finance charges are applied to the 'balances' outstanding on your card. Here are a couple of ways your finance charges might be calculated, as well as a few additional credit card and finance terms for you to research: (36)

Finance Terms

Adjusted Balance: The adjusted balance method can be the least expensive method for calculating finance changes. This method starts with the balance you owed at the beginning of the billing cycle; and then any payments you made are then subtracted; new purchases are not included in the balance.

   a.   **Adjusted Balance:** payments are subtracted daily from your outstanding balance (nets a lower balance).

Average Daily Balance: This is the most common manner to calculate finance charges. The average daily balance method calculates the average of your balance during the billing cycle. Each day's balance is added together and divided by the number of days in the billing cycle, and the interest charge is applied to this balance number.

   b.   **Average Daily Balance:** all daily balances added together and divided by the number of days, then the average daily balance is multiplied by the card's monthly periodic rate.

Daily Balance: The daily balance calculation method uses the ending day's balance; then multiplies each by the daily rate; and adds each number together.

Ending Balance: This method seems simple. The ending balance method takes your beginning balance; subtracts the payments you made; and adds the charges and you made during the billing cycle. The number of days in the billing cycle doesn't affect the amount of the finance charge.

   c.   **Ending Balance:** your balance at the end of the month.

Previous Balance: This method of calculation does not consider any of the payments or charges in the immediate billing cycle. The balance at the beginning of the billing cycle (which is also the ending balance of the last billing cycle) is utilized for the calculation. The number of days in the billing cycle doesn't affect the amount of the finance charge. (36)

   d.   **Previous Balance:** beginning monthly balance, net of any additional charges during the current month.

More Finance Terms

- **The annual percentage rate (APR)** is the annual rate of interest that includes the fees and costs you pay for the loan. Lenders are required by law to disclose the APR. To calculate the rate, the compound interest rate is averaged over the term of the loan.

- **Card-holder contract/agreement** – The contract you sign to obtain your credit card. The contract is required by Federal Reserve regulations to have the following information: Annual Percentage Rate, the monthly minimum payment formula, annual fee if applicable, and the cardholder's rights in billing disputes. With prior written notice, changes in the cardholder agreement may be made at any time by the issuer.

- **Cash-advance fee** – If you utilize your credit card to get a cash advance, you will be charged a fee by the financial institution. This fee can be assessed as a flat, per-transaction fee; or as a percentage of the amount of the cash advance.

- **Finance charges** are fees assessed for using a credit card, i.e. interest costs and other fees.

- **Grace period** is the interest-free time between the transaction date and the billing date before interest is assessed on any balance in the account.

- **Interest rate floor** – The minimum interest rate that can be assessed, after any initial introductory rate period has passed.

- **Introductory rate** is the initial interest rate presented to attract customers to change credit card companies or lenders.

- **Minimum payment** is the amount you can pay to keep the account from going into default.

- An **Over-the-limit fee** is charged for exceeding the credit limit on your card.

- **Variable interest rate** moves up or down periodically based on changes in other interest rates. (36-38)

A Little Grace?

Everyone appreciates a little grace now and then. In finance terms, the **grace period** is the time interval allotted for you to pay for new charges before a finance fee is added. To elaborate: the grace period is the point in time after your purchase date when you will pay your total balance to prevent a finance charge to be assessed; the period of time during the billing cycle when no interest is charged on certain transactions or balances.

Do not get caught waiting on grace. The grace period is *definitely not an extended time period to allow for you to send in your payment for last month's bill.* Pay close attention to credit card due dates; late payments will affect your credit scores.

The world of credit card financing is a difficult one to unwind. Be sure you use your card responsibly… rates can change if you are not diligent about paying your balances down to zero each month. I am not passing judgment on the credit-card industry here, whether you agree with the standards or not… It is your responsibility, as a consumer to understand the contracts that you enter into, and the consequences of your actions. If you do not fulfill your contractual obligations, you may suffer penalties.

Interview someone who has a 'late-pay' or 'delinquent-pay' experience. Relate what they reported are the consequences of their actions:

_____

_____

_____

Here is my story: One of my clients had open-heart surgery. She was the one in her family who paid the bills. She asked her husband to send in their credit card bill payment, and he did so. However, the payment arrived just a few days late to the credit card company. My client reported that their interest rate was then changed from 9.9% to @ 29%!

Credit Scores Mean What?

> *"The most important thing for a young man is to establish credit - a reputation and character."*
>
> John D. Rockefeller

A lot of people ask me about their credit scores. Credit scores are vitally important to you. Building, maintaining, and protecting your credit score should be a primary goal for you. Credit scores are compiled by various sources and the ranges of scores vary. For example: a FICO® credit score is a number from 350-850, and a VantageScore® scores credit between 501-990. (41) The lower the number, the higher the 'credit risk.' The higher the number, the less risk of default. The independent credit rating bureaus, like Equifax®, Experian®, and TransUnion® Corporation, credit karma®, keep a record of your credit history and provide your credit reports to you upon request. Some of the areas the reports consider in calculating your score are your debt-to-income ratios, public records, and payment history. According to Fair Isaac and Consumer Federation of America® (42), there are varying opinions of the average percentage of the components that make up your credit score, here is one example and the information illustrated in the chart below is gathered from several sources:

- 10% - Types of Credit in Use

- 35% - Payment History

- 10% - Requests for New Credit

- 15% - Length of Credit History

- 30% - Current Total Debt

A free credit report can be accessed from a variety of website resources: https://www.nationaldebtlaw.com/how-does-fico-credit-score-work/, https://www.annualcreditreport.com, https://www.creditcards.com/credit-card-news/help/5-parts-components-fico-credit-score-6000.php, https://medium.com/@MLeachRealEstate/components-of-a-credit-score-cb7beae2efe1.

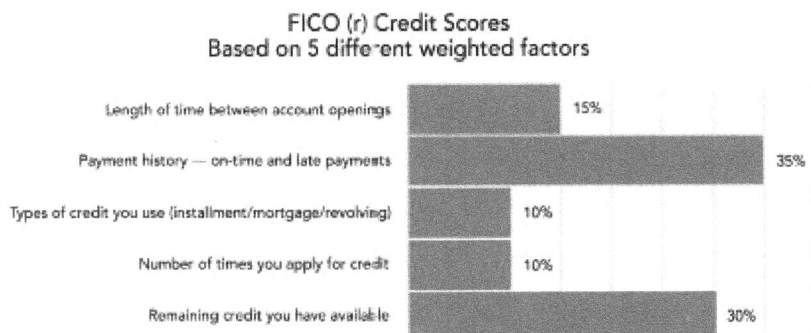

FICO (r) Credit Scores
Based on 5 different weighted factors

Length of time between account openings	15%
Payment history — on-time and late payments	35%
Types of credit you use (installment/mortgage/revolving)	10%
Number of times you apply for credit	10%
Remaining credit you have available	30%

Life

Here's what happened to me not too many years ago!

I applied for something, and was told the company would conduct a credit check... okay – no problem, right? Well, I went on to double-check that everything was 'okay,' and found that two of the three credit reporting agencies had just added a $36 failed collection notation. WHERE DID THAT COME FROM?

So, I did what anyone would do, I started frantically calling one of the credit bureaus to get an answer. After a series of automated answer machine queues and speaking with several individuals who attempted to transfer me – and ended up disconnecting me – (about 2 hours) I finally got someone who would check on the entry for me.

"I am sorry Mam; it appears we made a 'mistake.' The item is not tied to your social security number, we will remove that notice and send letters to all three credit bureaus."

Okay, but that took a minimum of about 30 days, and probably still has hurt my credit score. However, if I hadn't of checked... it might have remained on my social security number forever.

Be sure you review your credit history frequently. You can use Equifax®, Experian®, and TransUnion® one time a year at no cost. Alternate using these three sources, use them about every 4 months to avoid charges and to keep on top of your credit score. Evidently credit Karma® is available for more frequent use. DO NOT keep pulling your credit as this activity may harm your credit score (note: 'Requests for New Credit'). Check the reports for accuracy. As reported on https://www.debt.org/credit/report/, (Max Fay, 7/2018), "A recent government survey says that 20% of consumers found at least one error on their credit report."

> **Remember that incorrect reporting can cause your credit score to be lower. Visit a credit education website, note three things you learned here.**
>
> _____
>
> _____

☒ At a minimum, be sure to check your credit score every year.

Different banks and lending institutions have various criteria for granting a loan to you. Having a good credit score is imperative. Why? The better interest rates are provided to the individuals with higher credit scores. As we have learned earlier, your credit score is an indication of risk. In other words, having a poor credit score can cost you money… or may cause you to be turned down for a loan all-together.

How Does Someone Establish Good Credit?

Here are a couple of ideas for building/establishing good credit (42):

FIRST, with the exception of your mortgage, car purchase, an emergency, or a very large purchase which you have already budgeted: Use a credit card to make purchases when you have the money in your checking account to pay the balance off at the end of each and every month. In other words, pay your credit cards balances down to $0 each month. No exceptions. Spend responsibly, go without if need be.

SECOND, pay all of your bills on time. All types of payments are recorded, even those for your car payment, car insurance, gas, electric, water, etc. Your payment history for all of these expenses can affect your credit. 'Late-pays' on ANY bill can be damaging to your credit.

Paying your bills on time is very, very, important. Even if it is the gas or electric bill, you need to pay them on time. Today, with the automatic bill payment options available there is virtually no excuse for tardiness. John and I have all of our 'fixed' bills paid automatically, and consequently only write one or two checks a month for items that are atypical expenses for the month. Along with knowing that I will not be late, it takes some of the stress out of my life as well. (However, no one is perfect… but making a concentrated effort to pay on-time is critical to helping you establish good credit.)

Remember – if you have set up automatic 'fixed' bill payments to take money out of your account each month, you need to deduct those bill amounts first from your account balance, or you can over-draw your account and then your bills will not be paid. You need to be diligent about balancing your checkbook, considering all means of withdrawals. (Don't forget ATM withdrawals as well.)

THIRD, avoid using your credit card for a 'cash advance.' Some credit card companies charge a higher fee or interest rate for a cash advance and you could find yourself paying much more for the 'loan' of that money than you would ever guess. Typically, a cash advance does not carry a 'grace period.' So that means that as soon as you receive the money, the interest begins to accrue. (43)

Be sure that the 'cash advance' is not offered at a much higher interest rate, and that the contract does not read, "Allocates your payments to balances with lower APRs before balances with higher APRs." This means that the payments you make each month go to the lower APR charges first… leaving you to pay the higher 'cash advance' APR interest rate. Be very careful, guard against this scenario. (44)

Life

I had a client who was a business owner and traveled quite a bit. He made a very good salary by anyone's standards and had a nice savings account and retirement account. This gentleman told me that he had applied for a mortgage and had been turned down. He came to me to see if I could help him.

In researching the situation, I found that he had 'late-paid' his mortgage a few months prior. When I asked him about the late-pay he said he had been out of the country on business. In a nutshell, the mortgage company didn't care what the excuse was, they only considered the facts. He ended up going to a different lending institution that more-than-likely charged him a higher interest rate.

Here are a few additional tips to help you with your credit:

○ "Comparison shop to help you secure the 'best' credit terms.

○ Carefully read the terms of the credit agreement to ensure that you understand the terms before you apply for, and accept, a loan or credit card contract.

○ Create a monthly budget for the credit charges and adhere to it.

○ View your loan and credit card purchases as 'cash' and spend your money as carefully with credit as you do with cash.

○ Budget for monthly credit payments and do not 'borrow' on credit unless you're certain you can meet those monthly obligations.

○ Pay your bills promptly and in full to keep finance charges low.

○ Use a debit card for day-to-day expenses so you do not have a monthly credit balance for them… however, if you do use your credit card for day-to-day-expenses, pay the credit card balance in full each month.

○ Guard your credit cards against loss or theft. But, if your cards are stolen, be sure you have recorded your credit card information (including phone number of issuer) and have put that information in a safe place.

○ Save the copies of your sales slips and compare the charges against the when bill when it arrives. If there's a mistake, call your issuer right away." (42, 44)

⊠ i.e.: One-time John and I looked at our receipt from a fast-food restaurant we had been to for lunch and noticed that we had been charged $ 62.00 instead of $ 6.20! (We only had tacos.)

There is an excellent information brochure titled, *"7 Credit Card Tips Everyone Should Know"* at https://www.nerdwallet.com/article/credit-cards/credit-card-tips-everyone-should-know/. (44)

I suggest you review that information, and list out the pertinent points here:

_____

_____

Repairing Your Credit

There are also opportunities offered to help you repair your credit if you find yourself in a less-than-desirable-credit position. Check these website or contact your local credit counselors for assistance –

https://www.nfcc.org/ (National Foundation for Credit Counseling®); https://www.consumer.ftc.gov/articles/0153-choosing-credit-counselor (Federal Trade Commission Consumer Information®, CFBP - Consumer Financial Protection Bureau, FTC -Federal Trade Commission, FCRA - Fair Credit Reporting Act);): https://rescoreyourlife.com/.

Janna Fox, CEO of ReScore reports;

"79% of all credit reports contain errors according to a study conducted by the Federal Trade Commission (FTC)." (consumerfinance.gov; https://www.creditlawcenter.com/credit-repair/79-of-all-credit-reports-contain-errors-credit-law-center/; consumer.ftc.gov)

"Paying a collection that appears on your credit report could harm your credit scores." https://www.experian.com/blogs/ask-experian/can-paying-off-collections-raise-your-credit-score/ (44); myFico.com)

" Paying 30 days or more past due could drop your score as much as 100 points." (https://www.nerdwallet.com/article/finance/late-bill-payment-reported; Experian.com)

The more credit responsible you are, the higher your credit score will be, and the easier it will be for you when you move towards buying your first car or really big purchase- your home. When the time comes and you are ready to access credit, you will want to be able to borrow at a 'prime' credit rate (prime credit is sometimes available if you have previously demonstrated that you are 'credit responsible'). The prime interest rate is the rate that commercial banks offer their best customers (their most 'creditworthy' clients). What you want is to be able to borrow money as close to the prime rate as you can. However, if you have no credit history, or have not demonstrated fiscal responsibility on prior debts, it may be necessary for you to borrow money at a higher 'sub-prime' rate. The sub-prime rate typically means the lender will loan you money at a higher interest rate, costing you more money out of your pocket. So, help guard against making credit mistakes early on that may affect your credit score at a later date. Minimize the use of credit, and when you do access credit, repay the money you borrow in a timely and fiscally responsible manner. Determine your strategy for minimizing your use of credit, do what works for you.

What are you doing right to help your credit score? Do you need to make any necessary changes in behavior?

_____

_____

Ready To Buy Your Own Home? You Might Need Lots Of Money

Generally, the biggest purchase that you will ever make is your home. And, unless you have a lot of excess cash, you will need to attain a mortgage to afford buying your home. Mortgages can be obtained from several types of lenders, such as: commercial banks, credit unions, mortgage companies, and thrift institutions. The navigation of the mortgage process can be daunting but equipping yourself with the facts can help to eliminate some of the stress.

> *"Financial education fosters financial stability for individuals, families, and entire communities. The more people know about credit and banking services, the more likely they are to increase savings, buy homes, and improve their financial health and well-being. The Money Smart® curriculum helps individuals build financial knowledge, develop financial confidence, and use banking services effectively." (48)*

One comment about Foreclosure…Finding yourself in a position that dictates that you cannot make the payments on a mortgage sometimes can lead to Foreclosure: "Foreclosure is the legal process by which a lender attempts to recover the amount owed on a defaulted loan by taking ownership of and selling the mortgaged property." (Investopedia.com) Homeowners do not want to enter into a foreclosure situation.

The problem of home foreclosure itself is not new, evidenced by the fact that in 2002 the FDIC and the Neighborhood Reinvestment Corporation® developed a pilot program to, "train adult educators and teach money management skills to thousands of people, primarily low-income consumers, minorities or women who are potential home buyers or existing homeowners having problems making ends meet." (47) This is also a part of the *"Money Smart®"* program. *The Money Smart®* program states clearly that,

"Financial education fosters financial stability for individuals, families, and entire communities. The more people know about credit and banking services, the more likely they are to increase savings, buy homes, and improve their financial health and well-being...." (48)

What Exactly Is A Mortgage?

When you have established a good credit score, have saved for a down-payment, and you are ready to purchase a home… you will apply for a mortgage. The following section will discuss some of the terms you will encounter when you apply for a mortgage to make a home purchase.

Life

Purchasing a home for the first time (even the second or third time) is a very scary endeavor. To-date I have participated in the purchase or sale of 18 homes or condos. So, I have helped negotiate 18+ times. Fortunately for me, I had real help from my real estate broker father for home number ONE. I was also fortunate that, when I made that first purchase in 1975 the variety of the varied mortgage products that exist today weren't offered.

The definition of a mortgage, taken from *http//www.investorwords.com* is:

> *"A loan to finance the purchase of real estate, usually with specifiedpayment periods and interest rates. The borrower (mortgagor) gives the lender (mortgagee) a lien on the property as collateral for the loan." (49)*

> **The Dictionary– defines a mortgage as***: "A legal agreement by which a bank lends money at interest in exchange for taking title of the debtor's property, with the condition that the conveyance of title becomes void upon payment of the debt." (50)*

The 'mortgage' document and the Good Faith Estimate, which accompanies the mortgage document, registers the customer's name and address, as well as the lender's name and address; and the fees that the lender/investor/broker are charging for the loan transaction. The mortgage is a contract that pledges a specific, named, property as security for the loan transaction. **The Good Faith Estimate** itemizes all closing fees, including pre-paid and escrow items, as well as lender charges; and the Good Faith Estimate must be made available to the borrower within three days after submission of a loan application.

The Truth in Lending is a federal law obligating a lender to give full written disclosure of all fees, terms, and conditions associated with the loan during both the initial period and the subsequent adjustable period when the loan rate changes to another rate. The Truth in Lending is also referred to as the **Consumer Credit Protection Act** (Regulation Z), which demands that lenders disclose to borrowers the cost of financing during the life of the loan; and disclosure of the APR and the prepayment penalties, if any apply. Simply stated: A mortgage document and the Good Faith Estimate identify the 'terms' under which the lender will give the loan to the borrower; these are, "document[s] signed by the borrower when a home loan is made that gives the lender a right to take possession of the property if the borrower fails to pay off the loan." (51) The primary functions of the contracts, beyond property descriptions, etc., are to state:

1)   how much money you are borrowing from the lending institution? How much money are you committing to repay?

2)   the interest rate you will be charged on the money you borrow... At what interest rate will you borrow the money?

3)   the length of the contract... What is the length of the term of your loan? and

4)   the fees involved in the transaction... What fees are assessed for other items associated with the mortgage?

Many lending institutions offer 'comparison charts' for different mortgage solutions. One such website is https://www.fanniemae.com/portal/index.html. Another great resource is the https://www.federalreserve.gov website. Review the Federal Reserve Board, "*Looking for the Best Mortgage,*" article for information, (https://www.federalreserve.gov/boarddocs/press/general/1999/19990210/default.htm) general tips and guidelines on how to shop, compare, and negotiate for a mortgage, as well as other sites to familiarize yourself with mortgage terms (51) prior to initiating a mortgage.

Types Of Mortgage Loans

Conventional loans are loans that are **NOT insured or guaranteed by a government agency**. On-the-other-hand, **non-conventional loans** are guaranteed by a government agency. FHA or VA loans are examples of non-conventional loans. Most loans issued are conventional loans, they are loans that most of us will get from financial institutions. Just as types of loans are different, so are the mortgage-payment options you may encounter. Here are a couple of the mainstream mortgage-payment options for your review, accompanied by a brief explanation of each:

A. A *fixed rate* mortgage is the type of mortgage that homeowners have historically used. The fixed rate mortgage locks in a specific interest rate for the length of the mortgage and the loan payment amount does not change. There is an Amortization Schedule that is disclosed during the loan process. The Amortization Schedule illustrates how much interest you will pay over the life of your loan if you do not change the terms or pay the loan off early.

B. *Adjustable Rate Mortgage* (ARM)

   o **ARMs have two rate periods:**

   - The first period is the time frame when the initial interest rate is fixed and locked-in. The length of this period is also pre-determined when the contract is signed.

   - After the first fixed-rate period has passed, then the next term is the **'adjustable'** rate period. The adjustable period could change every month, every quarter, every year, or on a multiple year schedule (like every 3 years or every 5 years), depending on which schedule you pre-select.

   o The **interest rate for an ARM is comprised of two parts:** the **index**, and the **margin**.

   - The **index** is typically the prevailing rate that lenders utilize as a benchmark rate for lending money in the market;

     ➢ The index upon which the mortgage is based can vary. Research which index your mortgage is tied to very carefully; understand how the index has historically fluctuated. **Examples of indexes that mortgages are tied to: Treasury, Libor, Prime Rate.**

   - The **margin** is the amount that the lender charges over-and-above the interest rate to hold and manage the loan.

     o Some lenders determine your margin based on the strength of your credit score.

○ **ARMS may have an 'interest-rate cap.'**

a. A lifetime cap identifies how high the interest rate may climb during the life of your loan. The lifetime cap must, by law, be disclosed to you when you negotiate your loan.

b. A periodic adjustment cap identifies how much the interest rate can move up or down during your adjustment period date. For example: If you have a 3-month adjusting loan, and it can move a maximum 2% up or down... every three months you may see a 2% or less change in rate.

- **Beware of any 'discounts' offered that may reduce the mortgage rate for an initial period, only to adjust upward after that initial period; which in turn increases the amount of your future payments.**

- **There are a couple of other ARM types. One is an Interest Only option. With this option your payment does not reduce the amount of principal you owe each month, you are only paying the interest rate charged on the money you borrowed.**

Life

One of my clients was researching his 5-year ARM because the fixed rate period is up soon. When he re-read his contract, he discovered that his loan was indexed to the Treasury. Lo and behold, the Treasury yield was at an all-time low... his mortgage rate will more than likely adjust DOWN!

Check with a couple of individuals you know, determine who they would list as their 'trusted advisors,' note them here.

_____

_____

Obtaining a mortgage is complex. Before you sign the mortgage document, realize that you are signing a contract, a written promise for performance. The following identifies a few of the other terms you should be familiar with when entering into a mortgage contract and closing the sale of your home.

Find someone who has a mortgage and record the following:

1. Is it a fixed or adjustable mortgage?   _____

2. What is the length of the mortgage?   _____

3. How many years are remaining on the term of the mortgage?   _____

4. What was the initial interest rate?   _____

5. What is the current or adjustable interest rate?   _____

Closing

The culminating event for purchasing or selling a home is called a 'closing.' The closing is the event where you sign your mortgage contract and all of the other documents associated with the purchase or sale of your home. The closing process can be a stressful event. Understanding what your responsibilities will be, what you are required to do prior to the closing, the documents you will need to bring to the closing, and what documents you will be signing at closing, is of vital importance to you.

There are many costs involved with purchasing or selling a home. You may be asked to bring money… not only for your mortgage, but to pay for other expenses associated with the sale or purchase as well. Some of those costs are listed here:

   a.   commission costs paid to the real estate brokers;

   b.   home inspection costs;

   c.   title searches;

   d.   up-front taxes and insurance costs;

   e.   'pre-pays' for homeowner association dues;

   f.   appraisal costs, g) extra insurance charges, etc

The following chart offers you an opportunity to check how much you know about some of the terms the near future, you can use the chart for later reference. See Exhibit D for a HUD Statement Example.

Put a checkmark by the terms you know.

Annual Percentage Rate (APR) identifies the rate, which includes: the interest rate, points, broker fees, and other credit charges.

____ **Application fees or Origination costs** can be assessed at the time you apply for the loan to cover administration costs for initiating the mortgage.

____ The **Escrow Account** is an account that holds the buyer's 'earnest money' that accompanies an offer to buy a home. The account is managed by an independent third party. At closing this earnest money is credited back to the buyer against his or her expenses.

____ **Appraisal fees** are paid by you for the services of a third-party appraisal company. The appraiser provides information to the lender that is analyzed to verify that the property you are purchasing is 'valued,' or is worth the amount of money the lender is loaning you.

____ **Prepayment penalties** are fees that can be assessed if your mortgage contract does not allow you to pay your loan off early. Appreciate that people do pay off their existing mortgage early… they refinance to a lower rate, or they need to move, or circumstances change, and they want to terminate their contract early. Be ready and watch for this clause in your contract.

____ **Conversion fees** are charged if your contract allows you to convert your loan from one mort- gage type to another. An example would be if you want to convert your ARM to a fixed-rate mortgage.

____ **Points** is a fee paid by the borrower to lower your mortgage interest rate. For example, if your mortgage was $50,000 you might pay a 1% point to reduce the mortgage rate. A breakeven can be calculated to determine the length of time you need to stay in the home to warrant you paying the extra $500 at closing.

____ The **Down-Payment** is the money you invest in the home at closing. The down-payment essentially equals your initial 'equity' in the home - until your home appreciates. (The home value grows.) The down-payment is generally referred to as a percentage of the mortgage.

____ **Lenders** customarily require a percent of your money to be invested in the property before they would loan you any money. I call it having 'skin in the game.' The thinking was that if you stand to lose some of your own money, then you will be more serious about paying the loan back to the lender.

____ **Private Mortgage Insurance (PMI)** is insurance that the borrower normally pays for over-and-above the cost of the mortgage if the borrower does NOT put at least 20% down. It is added to the monthly payments for the loan.

____ The **Closing** is referred to as the formal meeting when you and your lender assemble to sign the paperwork and you officially take possession of the home or sell the property.

____ **Transaction, settlement, or closing cost**s are a variety of fees associated with the transfer of the home from the seller to the buyer.

____ The **HUD Statement** is a Good Faith Estimate that identifies the costs and fee details involved in the purchase of the home. This statement is generally available a day or so before the closing so that the borrower and the seller have time to review the fee details and under- stands exactly how much money he or she should bring to closing. (51, 52)

A comprehensive *Mortgage Shopping Worksheet* is provided on the https://federalreserve.gov website. The worksheet provides an excellent vehicle for you to use to compare various loan criterions for several lenders at once. When you are contemplating obtaining a mortgage, ask your lender and/or broker to assist you in analyzing the data you compile. (https://www.fedsearch.org/board_public/search?text=mortgage+shopping+worksheet&Search=)

Adding a *Line of Credit* is sometimes offered when you obtain a mortgage. A Line of Credit allows the borrower to have access to additional money, over and above the mortgage amount, at a later date without having to re-qualify for a new loan. The Line of Credit typically can be accessed at any time after it is in place; money can then be borrowed and repaid. I have in the past sometimes added a line of credit at the time the mortgage was obtained because there was no cost to do so. Typically, the line of credit interest rate is higher than the mortgage rate, so ask questions. I believe that a line-of-credit is for emergencies only. So far, to the best of my knowledge, I haven't used even a $1 of my credit line over the years.

To be sure all individuals are regarded equally, the **Consumer Credit Protection Act**, the **Equal Credit Opportunity Act**, and the **Fair Housing Act** are in effect. These laws protect against discrimination towards a buyer based on any criteria. Also, as described above, the **Truth In Lending Act** requires that costs and conditions for borrowing money must be fully disclosed to the consumer/buyer. **The Fair Credit Reporting Act** ensures a consumer's privacy and protects the consumer from misstatement of their credit information. And in the event that a misstatement of credit information does occur, the **Fair Credit Billing Act** provides the consumer with a process to quickly correct any errors. (52)

Life

You never know when you may need to access your line of credit. I met with a new client a few years ago and we discovered that his credit card bills had gotten out of hand. He researched his various credit card interest rates and found them to vary from @ 9.89% to @ 19.9%. His line-of- credit interest rate that was tied to his mortgage was @ 5.6%.

He utilized his line of credit to pay off his credit card debt and consolidate his debts onto one monthly payment. The line-of-credit was the least expensive interest rate he had available. Then he could more efficiently 'pay-down' his debt and it was easier to manage. Of course, NO MORE using the credit cards until he was solvent.

Research websites to find a Mortgage Worksheet for keeping track of the questions you want to ask during the mortgage process. Report them here.

_____

_____

When you are ready to apply for a mortgage, be sure you check with several lenders and ask vigilant questions. If you have never purchased a home before, search out an experienced person to provide you with information, counsel, and support. Remember, rules and regulations change, so do your homework. Use the internet, research and read books, and ask your trusted advisors. The more you know, the better prepared you will be, and the confident you are likely to be throughout the process. More confidence generally leads to less stress!

Ready To Sell Or Buy That Home?

> _"The first step to preparing a home for sale is to let go of your emotional attachment to it."_
>
> Elizabeth Weintraub

I've often thought about the process of buying and selling a home. The process is very distinctive. In the process of offering your home for sale, you allow individuals to come into your intimate domain and, in a sense, critique your 'style.' The choices you make for your home: paint colors, wallpapers, furniture, room arrangement, etc. must translate favorably to a buyer. And, as a buyer, you have the privilege of being able to view a variety of homes and spaces to help you determine what type of layout, location, size, and style of home will fit your needs. And on top of that, the 'price' is sometimes… most of the time… negotiable. It is truly a unique proposition.

Because a home purchase is so important, probably the biggest financial investment one makes during their lifetime, individuals tend to take their time when they buy a home. And they should. On-the-other-hand, if you are selling your house, you may sell your home quickly or it may take quite some time for the 'right' buyer to find your home. However, whether you are the buyer, or the seller, the process can be very stressful. So, in an effort to keep your stress levels to a manageable level, Exhibit C presents a couple of ideas to help you prepare for the buy/sell process in your future.

Your Mortgage In Reverse

No discussion about loans and mortgages would be complete without a comment here about Reverse Mortgages. I am asked about reverse mortgages from time to time. The reverse mortgage should be used in very specific cases. If the individual(s) do not have enough income to live on, and they don't want to deplete their other assets, they can consider a reverse mortgage if they own at least 40% of their home. In this case, the reverse mortgage may offer an income stream, or a cash lump sum. An oversimplified description of a reverse mortgage is this:

- This type of mortgage is a "non-recourse" loan.

- A reverse mortgage allows the homeowner to take out the equity, or the money you have paid into your home over the years. This money will be paid by the financial institution that offers you the reverse mortgage and will be paid to you as a lump sum of cash, or in monthly payments, or through a line of credit.

- As long as you continue to live in the home; you never have to pay back the cash you were given by the financial institution. (53)

- The money you receive is tax-free.

- To be eligible for a reverse mortgage you must be 60 years of age or older (in most states) with a recommended 40% equity in your home.

- One owner must remain in the home. If all of the owners move out of the home, you, or your estate, has one year to repay the loan. If a profit is realized, the profit passes to your heirs. (53)

There are several primers available on the subject of reverse mortgages. For example, reversemortgage.org is an excellent resource. (This source is presented by the National Reverse Mortgage Lenders Association®.)

Need Anything Else? Another Loan?
For Something Special?

Besides credit cards and mortgages, 'specific use' loans are another source of accessing credit. A specific use loan is just that, a loan that covers a specific purchase (or use). For example, many people do not pay cash for their car, they take out a loan and pay finance payments over time. Financing a car also allows the first-time buyer to build a credit history. However, being able to buy a larger purchase with cash may provide you with additional bargaining power. Consider this story:

Life

Nearly everyone has an, 'I should have read the fine-print' story…

One of our boys had just bought his first home with his wife and they went to a large furniture store to shop for a couch and TV.

Finding the ones that they wanted was easy, so was getting a great deal! They were told that they could get a '0 (zero) interest' loan for 3 years <u>but needed to make the (smaller - @ $ 85) (monthly payments – ONLY!</u>

Since the purchase was a couple of thousand dollars, they were elated! So, they picked up their furniture and were on their happy way.

Everything went as planned for the first year or so… they made their monthly payments ON TIME and really didn't give the sales contract much thought.

However, for whatever reason they missed (at least) one payment and, to their surprise received a monthly statement that had a hefty interest rate payment added to their balance. Not just a 'one-time late payment' charge, but interest calculated back to the FIRST MONTH of their purchase.

Of course: 1) they called us to complain/ask questions; and 2) they had to PAY ALL the interest back.

Lesson learned… read, listen, ask questions about ALL contracts you sign. Understand the 'fine-print.

Before you embark on the purchase of a new car, consider whether you should buy a new car, or will a used car work for you just as well? Of course, there are pros and cons for both sides. You may have very specific reasons for purchasing that NEW car. However, if you can find a reliable used car you will not only save the initial out-of-pocket cost, but insurance costs should also be lower. I have read that new cars can lose about one-third of their value in just the first year alone. One source reports that, "New-car depreciation begins as soon as you drive off the lot. Your car's value decreases around 20% to 30% by the end of the first year." (54) Also consider that saving enough money to purchase a new car outright, without financing, is more difficult and can take a lot longer.

Check on-line to find a car Buying Guide, here are a couple of websites for you to start with: *https://www.boston.com/cars/car-guides/2018/01/24/15-used-cars-for-under-1500, or https://www.Cars.com.*

What else might you find yourself purchasing with credit? Furniture is another purchase that people tend to finance. Some of the larger furniture stores offer "NO Interest until X date," and you may want to consider this option. However, those offers only work if you actually pay the stated amount each month. If you fail to meet the payment requirement, interest can be recalculated back to your date of purchase. One payment miscalculation, or missed payment, might trigger unwanted consequences.

Do you already have a special use loan? If yes, for what?

_____

_____

Life

Here is a comparison for a $2,500 loan from two lenders: Lender A and B. Two sources were used: the Granite State Management & Resources (A nonprofit student loan servicer), *"The Cost of Borrowing,"* (55); and Bankrate® @ bankrate.com. Review this information to discover some loan features you might inquire about when you are considering lenders:

School Loan Comparison	
Lender A Interest Rate: 5%	Lender B Interest Rate: 6.5%
Fee: $50 (2% of loan amount)	Fee: $75 (3% of loan amount)
Loan Term: 60 months Grace Period: 10-year repayment Term: Following graduation	Loan Term: 60 months Grace Period: 10-year repayment Term: Following graduation
Monthly Payment: $47	Monthly Payment: $49
Finance Charge: @ $331 (total)	Finance Charge: @$435 (total)
Total of Payments: $2,831 Plus Loan Fee of $50	Total of Payments: $2,935 Plus Loan Fee of $75

Be careful NOT to engage in any 'Best Loan Companies for Bad Credit' schemes (mostly internet loan offers that do not require you to have good credit) -- as interest rates offered may be a cousin to the dreaded 'pay-day' loans. Avoid any use of 'pay-day/cash advance loans' which are typically very short term and carry very high interest rates. See the article: *"What Is A Payday Loan, and Why Is It A Really Bad Idea to Get One?"* (1/7/2020, Kevin Mercadante, https://www.moneyunder30.com/payday-loan). Keep your credit score in check and avoid those exorbitant interest rate pitfalls.

A Note Regarding The Dreaded Bankruptcy

A quote from and CNBC article (5/2019), presents that, *"Millions of Americans are only $400 away from financial hardship. Here's why ..."* The article supplies supporting documentation for creating and sticking to a budget; and guarding against over-extending your credit obligations. When Americans were asked how they would handle some 'unplanned' expenses, or a financial emergency, here is how they responded:

☒ "If faced with an unexpected expense of $ 400: 61% of adults could cover it with cash, savings, or a credit card paid off at the next statement. But 27% would have to borrow or sell something to pay for the expense; 12% would not be able to cover the expense." (55, 56)

When someone cannot pay their bills they sometimes consider filing 'bankruptcy.' Because of the consequences of filing for bankruptcy, this course of events should be considered as a last resort. "**Bankruptcy** is a legal status designating you as unable to pay off your outstanding debts.' (56) It provides you with protection under a federal bankruptcy code that may save some of your assets, keep your creditors at bay, and provide you with the help of a professional… "Protection from creditors is one important benefit of bankruptcy filing." (57) There are a couple of different types of bankruptcy, be sure you investigate your options fully before you file. You may encounter severe repercussions for filing bankruptcy. There are many websites that you can visit to become familiar with the consequences of filing bankruptcy; be sure to visit a few. (57) Before you contemplate filing bankruptcy, you will be required to visit with a creditor counselor, and it is advisable for you to also consult with an attorney as well to determine what consequences you may face if you file. The credit counselor will also help you file if you decide to proceed.

USCourts.gov (3/2017) reported:

"In the 12-year span from October 1, 2005 to September 30, 2017, about 12.8 million consumer bankruptcy petitions were filed in the federal courts."

https://www.uscourts.gov/news/2018/03/07/just-facts-consumer-bankruptcy-filings-2006-2017

Ms. Warren, a Harvard Law School professor who, among many projects, has researched why our middle-class American families are filing for bankruptcy in epidemic numbers. She suggested (2007) that, *"Families are not going broke over lattes. Families are going broke over mortgages."* (58)

Ms. Warren reported that our families are building their budgets around two incomes, and in doing so, they place themselves in a precarious financial position; they are exposing their budget to unstable economic conditions. Ms. Warren cites 'layoffs' as one important area of financial exposure. For example, when both the Mom's and Dad's incomes are required to cover monthly fixed costs, and a financial bump in the road occurs – Mom or Dad is laid off or becomes ill or unable to work – then financial disaster can strike. Financial disaster strikes when: a) one of the family paychecks disappears, or b) the family resorts to overuse of the family credit card, or c) the family borrows against the equity in their home by re-financing the mortgage, or d) borrows from 'payday' lenders, etc., to stay afloat. (58, 42) Even though the article is a little dated, I believe the concept still holds true today.

"One of the number one reasons for bankruptcy is [being] overextended on credit."

https://www.investopedia.com/financial-edge/0310/top-5-reasons-people-go-bankrupt.aspx

Others report the following causes for bankruptcy:

- Such as: "five main life events and changes that can make you much more likely to file bankruptcy.

    o Medical Expenses

    o Job Loss

    o Uncontrolled Spending

    o Divorce

    o Unexpected Disaster" (59)

- ClearBankruptcy, LLC®, reported in their article, *"10 Leading Causes of Bankruptcy,"* the following reasons for bankruptcy, and the percentage contributed by each reason.*

    o Medical Expenses (42%)

    o Job Loss (22%)

    o Uncontrolled Spending (15%)

    o Divorce (8%)

    o Unexpected Disaster (7%)

    o Avoiding Foreclosure (1.5%)

    o Poor Financial Planning (1.5%)

    o Preventing Loss of Utilities (1%)

    o Student Loans (1%)

    o Preventing Repossession (1%) (59)

* Percentages represent reasons an individual files bankruptcy. Sources were combined to average top reasons Americans file.

"More Americans are spending over half their income on housing," as reported By Jacob Passy, Marketwatch, February 4, 2020. (https://nypost.com/2020/02/04/more-americans-are-spending-over-half-their-income-on-housing/) Review this statistic compared to the Joint Center for Housing Studies® at Harvard University, who reported that in 2008, *"35% of all-American households spend at least 30% of their pre-tax income on housing."* (60) Housing costs, coupled with credit card and financing balances, are eating up the American paycheck.

Here's a more recent graph from the Bureau of Labor Statistics (9/10/2019), noted in an article written by Ester Bloom, which illustrates information (https://www.cnbc.com/2017/09/27/how-your-spending-compares-to-the-average-american-and-us-government.html)... *"See how your spending compares with that of the average American..."* regarding where individuals are spending their money. (2020 numbers are similiar.)

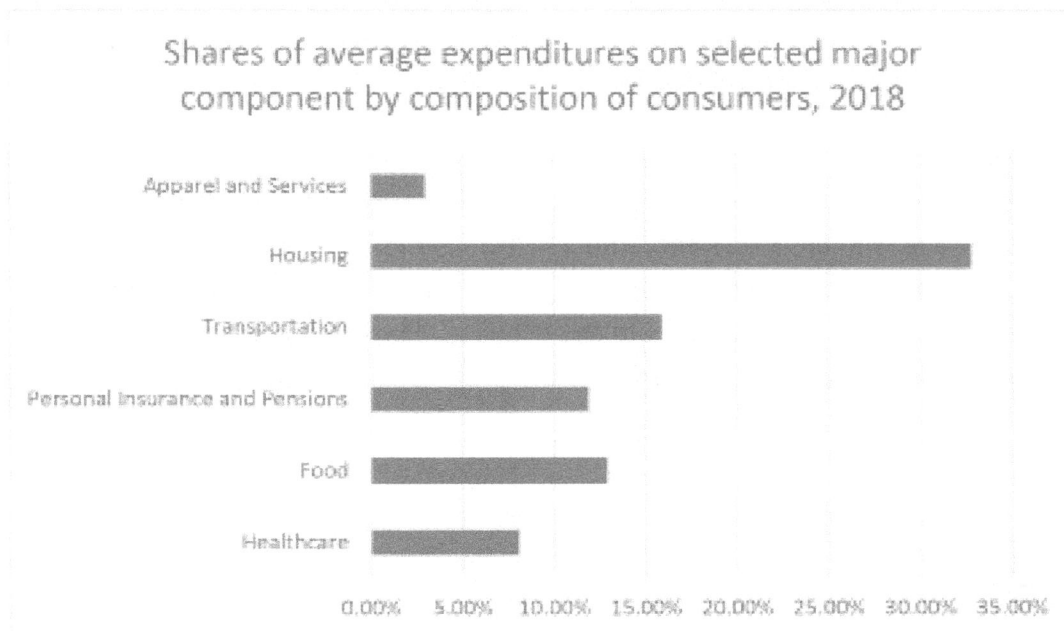

Shares of average expenditures on selected major component by composition of consumers, 2018

https://www.bls.gov/news.release/pdf/cesan.pdf

Healthcare	8.10%
Food	12.90%
Personal Insurance and Pensions	11.90%
Transportation	15.90%
Housing	32.80%
Apparel and Services	3.00%

Conclusion:

When developing your budget, be very realistic. Do not budget fixed expenses upon improbable, or variable, income numbers. If you can, budget for a single income. For example: In our family fixed expenses, and normal 'variable' expenses are planned to be paid by John's income. Savings, entertainment, vacations, 'extras,' new appliance/home furnishings, etc. come from my salary, or from savings. So, if one of us doesn't work, the fixed expenses (like the mortgage, utilities/phone, food, insurance, taxes, Health & Beauty aids, etc.) still get paid.

Staying out of debt might be a goal for all of us. However, if we find ourselves in a pickle, get help. There are many websites that offer tools and solutions to help you compare features of loans and interest rates. Many sites offer suggestions for reducing your debt. See these websites for more information:

- https://www.consolidatedcredit.org

- https://www.MoneyManagement.org

We have reviewed a few of the basics that you need to know about financing. I haven't covered every nuance of financing, that would be an insurmountable task. Remember, when you start to use credit you should find someone who has experience and ask them for guidance. Carefully monitor your use of credit. I strongly urge you to consult a trusted mentor when you begin your research for a loan or a finance purchase. Don't allow yourself to be rushed into any decision. There is no substitute for research, be sure you do your homework and ask lots of questions.

"A person who can't pay gets another person who can't pay to guarantee that he can pay. Like a person with two wooden legs getting another person with two wooden legs to guarantee that he has got two natural legs. It don't make either of them able to do a walking-match."

Charles Dickens

Exhibit C

Buying Or Selling A Home

Typically, your real estate company will have a website that provides you with information about making your experience of either buying or selling a home more enjoyable. Information is power. Do your due diligence and conduct some research before you jump right into the home buy/sell process. You should be able to find a variety of real estate websites which offer a wealth of information on buying and selling homes. For example,

☒ https://www.Realtor.com and https://www.fanniemae.com/portal/index.html are two great websites to visit when you are looking either to buy or sell a home.

☒ Look for this article on https://realestate.usnews.com/real-estate/slideshows/secrets-to-selling-your-home-faster: the *"15 Secrets to Selling Your Home Faster,"* (2/25/2021). (146)

☒ Other resources: *"10 Steps to Buying a Home," "Do These 11 Things Before Putting Your Home on the Market,"* (147) and *"Are You Ready? 10 Steps of Home Ownership,"* (148) also provide valuable information for buying/selling real estate.

☒ See the article, *"How to Prepare your House for Sale,"* by Elizabeth Weintraub, https://www.thebalance.com. Here are a few of the highlights of her article: (149)

1. Take your emotion out of the selling process – make the sale a business proposition. *"Disassociate Yourself With Your Home."*

2. Remove your very personal items – *"De-Personalize."*

3. Make your space look as big as possible by removing items you can live without for a short while – put them in storage. *"De-Clutter."* Remove your excess items in all of your rooms and storage areas– "Rent a Storage Unit" and put your 'over-load' items in storage.

4. Have someone help you stage your rooms, and – *"Rearrange Bedroom Closets and Kitchen Cabinets"* to make your space neat and orderly.

5. Walk around your home and be sure everything is in good working order; does any room need a new coat of paint; *"Make Minor Repairs"* where necessary. Don't lose a sale because of burnt-out light bulbs or fingerprints on the walls!

6. Clean like you never have before! – *"Make the House Sparkle!"*

7. Ask a friend, or your real estate agent to be brutally honest with you, what do they see that could be improved? – *"Scrutinize."*

8. Don't forget the landscaping and outdoor appeal – *"Check Curb Appeal."*

9. Make sure visitors can clearly read your house number. (149)

Here are a few other ideas to consider before you either buy or sell a home:

1. **Consider using a Real Estate Agent.** Of course, I am biased in this matter. I have tried a couple of times to sell my home by owner, without any luck. I feel that an agent has the expertise to market your home. The agent will charge you a commission for their services. Among other duties, the agent assists you with the contracts, inspections, appraisals, and a host of other details of the transactions.

Be sure you compare services, and the cost of the services, of at least three agents. Ask friends for referrals.

When selling your home, the agent typically will:

☒ List your home on the MLS (Multiple Listing Service) to provide you with the greatest exposure for your home.

☒ Help you determine the appropriate asking price for your home. The agent will provide you with *'comparables.'* These 'comps' are homes that are listed in your price range, and homes in and around your neighborhood that have recently sold. These homes would be considered as competition for your home (same general size, features, etc.) Left alone, it is sometimes difficult for the seller to be objective about the value of their own home.

☒ Market and advertise your home. Do you want the agent to hold Open Houses, or place newspaper ads, design brochures, or create internet listings? If so, you should inquire as to the scheduling to these during your agent interview.

When buying a home, the agent may also prove helpful.

☒ If you are buying a home, you can utilize the services of a real estate agent as well. Be sure you understand how the agent will represent you. Some agents require you to sign a 'Buyer's Agent' contract, and other agents may not. A Buyer's Agent contract will bind you to the use of a specific agent (with whom you have the contract) for the purchase of your home.

☒ Working with an agent will generally provide you similar services (only in reverse) as if you were selling a home with the assistance of the agent. Again, compare agent services and ask friends for referrals.

Review the negotiation process with your agent.

☒ Be sure you inquire about the negotiation process with your agent: the offer and counter-offer procedure. Discuss the 'everyone wins' goal with your agent as well. Being overly aggressive in price, on either side of the transaction can hamper your success for completing the transaction.

☒ Understand how the 'multi-offer' circumstances might be handled if one should arise. For example, will the agent be willing to counter with multiple variations? Will the agent want to offer a 'closed, one-time, best offer?' Approaches can be different, and some agents are more comfortable with one approach than another.

Review each line of the offer contract with your real estate agent. It is imperative that you understand the obligations to which you are committing. Failure to ask questions may put you at a disadvantage later.

2. **Research your financing options**. One of the most critical issues for you, as the seller is to understand the options available regarding your buyer's financing. Today, many buyers will obtain a **'pre-approval'** letter to present with the buying offer or contract. This 'pre-approval' letter from the buyer's bank will assure you that the buyer has done their homework and **already has financing in place**—with this letter you should be more confident that your buyer will be able to attain a loan for a specific amount of money. Be sure you carefully review what type of loan the buyer has secured... <u>do not sign a contract that does not have these details filled in.</u> Ask for clarification about the type of loan your buyer is obtaining. This information should be part of the contract and understanding how the buyer is financing the offer is important for you and your agent to know. Why, you ask? If your buyer has not secured financing, they may be unable to do so later, or in a timely manner. This 'hitch' could prohibit the sale from closing... not what you want.

Conversely, as a buyer you have the same financing preparation to do. Work with a mortgage broker to gain assistance in the loan process.

3. **Learn about the sale/purchase contract and the HUD-1 Statement.** These are two of the most confusing items you will encounter during the purchase, or sale.

☒ The actual *sale/purchase contract* itself. Please consult both your agent and a trusted advisor to read through each line – ASK QUESTIONS. The contract itself is filled with legal information, most of which will be foreign to you. In a nutshell, the contract provides all of the terms of the purchase or sale of the property. Among other items, the contract identifies the property selling price, the loan amount, the type of loan being used for the purchase of the property, the date of the transfer of property, the date of the closing, the terms for agent commission, rights for both parties, a myriad of 'what-ifs', etc.

☒ The HUD-1 Statement. Go on-line and search the https://www.hud.gov/ website for HUD-1. There is a line-by-line explanation for this extremely complicated document. The HUD -1 form identifies who will pay what at the closing. The settlement agent, or the title company, will prepare the HUD-1 document for both buyers and sellers to review prior to closing. Ask your title agent to review every line with you before you come to closing so you understand all of the itemized charges listed on the form. It is your responsibility as either the buyer, or the seller to review the HUD-1 **before** the closing. As the seller you may receive money at closing; however, if you owe more in expenses than you are receiving from the sale, you may also need to bring money to the closing. The buyer will almost certainly need to bring money to the closing.

4.   **Get advice.** The best advice I can give you is to work with a trusted advisor during the home sale or purchase process. Find a friend or family member who has previously bought or sold their home and ask them to participate in your purchase or sale as your mentor. I believe that people enjoy sharing their experiences and are eager to help others.

What is the single best idea you learned from reading this section of the Handbook?

_____

_____

Life in Exhibit C

If you don't think that mistakes can happen during a transaction on a home, think again. I read every page of my contract (except for the stock legal parts that never get changed). In fact, when we go to a closing my husband has been known to say to the mortgage officer, "You might as well get comfortable, Janis is going to read the entire contract, word-for-word."

I have found several discrepancies in the documents, here are a couple of examples that I can remember:

1) *The type of loan that a buyer on my house was going to use was left blank. I did not sign the contract until the information was provided. Why did this matter to me? Well - What if the buyer was asking for an 'unusual' type of mortgage? If his request was out of the ordinary, and he was denied a mortgage, this might have been a valid reason to allow him to renege on the purchase of my home. This would cost me time and money.*

2) *The interest rate was incorrect. (Self-explanatory).*

3) *Math calculations have been found to be incorrect (yes, do your own math).*

4) *Escrow amounts also can be very confusing. Double check to ensure that you are not paying for something up-front (to be put in escrow) that you might not have to. For example, your home insurance might be counted twice (what you have in escrow with your current home and what you are going to put into escrow for your new home). Sometimes you can just have the insurance company apply one balance to the other. You need to ask.*

5) *Real Estate Agent's commission was calculated incorrectly.*

Moving Made Easier

After you have accepted an offer for the sale of your home, or if you just purchased a new home, start thinking about the process of moving. Planning and budgeting for your move can be stressful. However, if you prepare properly you may find you will save time and money, and the move itself may go smoother than you thought. I have moved more than the average bear. It might surprise you to learn that, "As of 2018, the median duration of homeownership in the U.S. is 13.3 years," (150)…and "the average homeowner sells his or her home every 5 to 7 years." (151) When I tell people how many times I moved, the reaction is typically, "Ugh! I hate to move!" I am well aware of the fact that moving isn't any fun.

If you are moving from one apartment to the next, or into your first or next home, the more organized you can be, the better. If you are buying a new home, once you are all set with your mortgage and inspections, and before you have closed on your home, start planning your move immediately. There are many, many good sites on the web; and there are a variety of books available to help you organize your move. I suggest you do some research and diligently put a punch-list together.

Here are two websites that outline some tips on how to make your move go smoother: https://www.moving.org/top-10-tips-great-move: and https://www.moving.com/tips/tips-for-smooth-move/. These two articles are specific resources for you: "*Tips for a Smooth Move*," 7/2019; and The American Moving and Storage Association® (AMSA) article "*10 Tips for moving*." Visit the websites to get full details. Here are a few of their suggestions, along with a few of my own comments.

Life in Exhibit C

When preparing for your next move, consider these ideas:

1. *Get three written in-home moving company estimates, and always check the carriers with the Better Business Bureau® to review the company's ratings and consumer complaints. <u>Ask for a copy of their insurance documents for your file (Liability/Workers Comp, truck insurance, etc.)</u>*

2. *Obtain and read the "pre-move" required documents from your carrier to understand your liability and insurance needs. If you do your own packing, you may not be covered for some types of damages. Check the 'insurance' numbers carefully, ask your Home Insurance Agent for his/her opinion.*

3. *Avoid carriers that require (large) pre-payments.*

4. *Ask lots and lots of questions. How many movers will you have? Is there a maximum 'over-charge versus the estimate?' Will your salesperson be there the day of the move? How experienced is the lead-driver? What size of truck will be used for your move?*

5. *Plan to move in an off-peak season when possible.*

6. *Do your part and be ready. Avoid packing when the movers are trying to load the truck.*

7. *Supervise your move: it is important to be present to watch what is going on.*

8. *Don't be shy, speak up if there is something you have a question about or don't like.*

9. *Don't let the movers transport your valuables, take them with you in your own vehicle; to include your fragile items and the personal items you will need for travel/the first week.*

10. *Clean as rooms get vacated, it makes the task easier later, and gives you something to do while you are watching.*

11. *Make all of your 'change of address' and utility change calls weeks ahead of your move time.*

12. *Throw out what you do not need—don't take it with you!*

DON'T SWEAT THE DETAILS;
IT ALWAYS TAKES LONGER THAN THE MOVER ESTIMATES.
PLAN FOR THIS AND TRY TO 'CHILL OUT.'

Above are some helpful tips from a 'moving pro.' However, the most important tip I can provide is to START EARLY. Weeks ahead of the move start planning, making the arrangements, boxing up your stuff and THROWING things away. The day dawns way too fast. Don't forget your pets.

Sources For Exhibit C:

(146) https://realestate.usnews.com/real-estate/slideshows/secrets-to-selling-your-home-faster, *"15 Secrets to Selling Your Home Faster,"* (2/25/2021) Teresa Mears and Devon Thorsby.

(147) https://www.moving.com/tips/how-to-get-your-house-ready-to-sell/, *"Do These 11 Things Before Putting Your Home on the Market,"* 7/2018, Marian white; https://www.daveramsey.com/blog/ready-to-sell-your-home, *"Am I Ready to Sell My House?;"* https://www.discover.com/home-loans/articles/10-steps-to-buying-a-home, *"10 Steps to buying a Home,"*

(148) https://www.forbes.com/sites/davidrae/2019/01/21/6-things-first-time-home-buyers-need-to-know/#753a55f9cb7d, *"6 Things First Time Home Buyers Need To Know,"* David Rae, 1/2019); https://www.heartlandrealtyservices.com/10-steps-to-home-ownership, *"10 Steps to Home Ownership ."*

(149) Elizabeth Weintraub (8/2019), *"How to Prepare Your House for Sale."* https://www.thebalance.com/how-to-prepare-your-house-for-sale-1799018.

(150) https://www.valuepenguin.com/how-long-homeowners-stay-in-their-homes, Madison Miller, 6/2018, *"How Long Do Homeowners Stay in Their Homes?"*

(151) Elizabeth Weintraub, 8/2019, https://www.thebalance.com/why-home-owners-sell-1799021, *"Why Do People Sell Their Homes? The Top Reasons Homeowners Make a Move."*

Exhibit D: Sample HUD-1 Statement

A. U.S. Department of Housing and Urban Development		B. Type of Loan		
		1. [ ] FHA 2. [ ] FMHA 3. [ ] Conv. Unins		
FINAL		4. [ ] VA 5. [ ] Conv. Ins.		
		6. File Number	7. Loan Number	
Settlement Statement		8. Mortgage Ins. Case No.		

C. Note: This form is furnished to give you a statement of actual settlement costs. Amounts paid to and by the settlement agent are shown. Items marked ("POC") were paid outside the closing; they are shown here for information purposes and are not included in the totals.

D. Name of Borrower:

E. Name of Seller:

F. Name of Lender:

G. Property Location:

H. Settlement Agent: TIN:
   Place of Settlement:

I. Settlement Date: Proration Date:

J. Summary of Borrower's Transaction			K. Summary of Seller's Transaction		
100.	Gross amount due from borrower:		400.	Gross amount due to seller:	
101.	Contract sales price	302,000.00	401.	Contract sales price	
102.	Personal property		402.	Personal property	
103.	Settlement charges to borrower (line 1400)	7,177.30	403.		
104.			404.		
105.			405.		
Adjustments for items paid by seller in advance:			Adjustments for items paid by seller in advance:		
106.	City/town taxes		406.	City/town taxes	
107.	County taxes		407.	County taxes	
108.	Assessments		408.	Assessments	
109.	HomesAsc 600.00yr 6/5/2009 to 1/1/2010	345.21	409.	HomesAsc 600.00yr 6/5/2009 to 1/1/2010	
110.			410.		
111.			411.		
112.			412.		
120.	Gross amount due from borrower:	309,522.51	420.	Gross amount due to seller:	
200.	Amounts paid by or in behalf of the borrower:		500.	Reduction in amount due to seller:	
201.	Deposit or earnest money	1,000.00	501.	Excess deposit (see instructions)	
202.	Principal amount of new loan(s)	152,600.00	502.	Settlement charges to seller (line 1400)	
203.	Existing loan(s) taken subject to		503.	Existing loan(s) taken subject to	
204.			504.	Payoff of first mortgage loan Citimortgage	
205.			505.	Payoff of second mortgage loan First Horizon	
206.	Closing Costs Paid by	1,012.50	506.		
207.			507.		
208.			508.		
209.			509.		
Adjustments for items unpaid by seller:			Adjustments for items unpaid by seller:		
210.	City/town taxes		510.	City/town taxes	
211.	County taxes 1/1/2009 to 6/5/2009	1,558.23	511.	County taxes 1/1/2009 to 6/5/2009	
212.	Assessments		512.	Assessments	
213.			513.		
214.			514.		
215.			515.		
216.			516.		
217.			517.		
218.			518.		
219.			519.		
220.	Total paid by/for borrower:	156,070.73	520.	Total reduction in amount due seller:	
300.	Cash at settlement from/to borrower:		600.	Cash at settlement to/from seller:	
301.	Gross amount due from borrower (line 120)	309,522.51	601.	Gross amount due to seller (line 420)	
302.	Less amount paid by/for borrower (line 220)	156,070.73	602.	Less total reduction in amount due seller (line 520)	
303.	CASH (X) FROM ( ) TO BORROWER	153,451.78	603.	CASH ( ) FROM (X) TO SELLER	

Exhibit D: Sample HUD-1 Statement

	L. Settlement Charges	6/4/09 5:42 PM		Paid From Borrower's Funds at Settlement	Paid From Seller's Funds at Settlement
700.	Total sales/broker commission				
	Division of commission (line 700) as follows:				
701.					
702.					
703.	Commission paid at settlement				
704.					
705.	Broker Administration Fee	to	Realty Executives of Kansas City		
706.	Broker Administration Fee				
800.	Items payable in connection with loan				
801.	Loan origination fee	to	(1%)	1,525.00	
802.	Loan discount				
803.	Appraisal fee	to		415.00	
804.	Credit report	to		27.65	
805.	Lender's inspection fee				
806.	Mortgage insurance application fee				
807.	Assumption fee				
808.	Underwriting Fee	to		250.00	
809.	Flood Certification Fee	to		19.60	
810.	Tax Service Fee	to		85.00	
811.	Document Preparation Fee	to		175.00	
812.					
813.					
814.	Yield Spread Premium				
900.	Items required by lender to be paid in advance				
901.	Interest from 6/5/2009 to 7/1/2009 at $18.53000/day for 26 days			481.78	
902.	Mortgage insurance premium for				
903.	Hazard insurance premium for 1 year to Insurance			1,632.06	
904.					
905.	VA Funding Fee				
1000.	Reserves deposited with lender				
1001.	Hazard insurance 3 mo @ $127.6708 per mo			383.01	
1002.	Mortgage insurance				
1003.	City property taxes				
1004.	County property taxes 5 mo @ $309.6000 per mo			1,548.00	
1005.	Annual assessments (maint.)				
1006.					
1007.					
1008.					
1009.	Aggregate Adjustment to			(619.19)	
1100.	Title charges				
1101.	Settlement or closing fee to			275.00	
1102.	Abstract or title search				
1103.	Title examination				
1104.	Title insurance binder				
1105.	Document preparation				
1106.	Notary fees				
1107.	Attorney's fees to				
	Includes above items no.:				
1108.	Title insurance to			700.00	
	Includes above items no.				
1109.	Lender's coverage $152,500.00 $250.00				
1110.	Owner's coverage $302,000.00 $503.00				
1111.	Wire Fee/E-Mail docs/Delivery Fee				
1112.	Overnight Payoff				
1113.	Closing Protection Fee(s)				
1114.	Title Service Charge(s)				
1115.					
1116.					
1117.					
1200.	Government recording and transfer charges				
1201.	Recording fees				
1202.	City/county tax/stamps				
1203.	State tax/stamps Mortgage $396.60			396.50	
1204.	Recording Services to RTA			108.00	
1205.	Tender of release fee to Lender				
1206.					
1300.	Additional settlement charges				
1301.	Survey				
1302.	Pest inspection				
1303.	Home Warranty to				
1304.	Initiation Fee to			250.00	
1305.	Homes Asc transfer fee to Neighborhood Group			75.00	
1400.	Total settlement charges (entered on lines 103, section J and 502, section K)			7,177.30	

Mortgage Shopping Worksheet

Mortgage Shopping Worksheet	Lender 1		Lender 2	
Name of Lender:				
Name of Contact and Phone Number:				
Purchase Price of Home:				
Mortgage Amount:				
Information on the Loan:	**A**	**B**	**C**	**D**
Type of loan: Fixed rate or adjustable rate				
If the loan is a fixed rate: Initial rate:				
If the loan is an adjustable rate mortgage: Initial rate:				
Rate and payment caps each year:				
Rate and payment caps over the life o f the loan				
The frequency of rate change:				
The index that the lender will use to determine change:				
The margin the lender will add to the index:				

NOTES:

Mortgage Shopping Worksheet

Mortgage Shopping Worksheet	Lender 1		Lender 2	
Name of Lender:				
	A	**B**	**C**	**D**
Loan application fee				
Credit report fee				
Attorney fees				
Appraisal fee				
Recording &/or preparation fees				
Underwriting or origination fee				
Broker fee				
Lender fee				
Other costs at closing				
Amount you will 'prepay' for: interest, taxes, insurance, payments to escrow, Private Mortgage Insurance, etc.				
Title search/Title insurance – for you				
Title search/Title insurance – for lender				
Home inspections/surveys State and local taxes, stamp taxes, transfer taxes				
Flood determination costs				
Total Fees and Closing Costs				

Sources:

(30)   https://www.thebalance.com/average-credit-card-debt-u-s-statistics-3305919, *"Average U.S. Credit Card Debt Statistics,"* Kimberly Amadeo, 8/2019.

(31)   https://nypost.com/2015/12/05/increased-credit-card-use-fuels-household-debt/, *"Increased credit card use fuels household debt,"* Gregory Bresiger, 12/2015; https://credit.org/cccs/, Consumer Credit Counseling Service®, (2008).

(32)   May, Patrick, *"Kansas City Star®"* (September 28, 2008*), *'50 YEARS OF PLASTIC MONEY.'*

(33)   https://www.nfcc.org.; https://www.investopedia.com/terms/d/discountrate.asp; 6/2019, *"Discount Rate."*

(34)   https://www.federalreserve.gov/aboutthefed/structure-federal-reserve-system.htm, *"Structure of the Federal Reserve System,"* (3/2017).

(35)   https://www.federalreserveeducation.org/about-the-fed/history, *"History of the Federal Reserve;" "What is the Fed: History,"* (2010) Federal Reserve Bank of San Francisco, https://www.frbsf.org/education/teacher-resources/what-is-the-fed/history/.

(36)   http://www2.ca.uky.edu/agcomm/pubs/fcs5/fcs5111/fcs5111.pdf, *"How Finance Charges Are Calculated on Credit Card Accounts,"* University of Kentucky, 1991; https://www.thebalance.com/ways-finance-charges-are-calculated-960256, LaToya Irby, *"Ways Finance Charges Are Calculated,"* (6/25/2021).

(37)   https://www.bankrate.com/finance/financial-literacy/15-must-know-credit-card-terms.aspx, (8/8/2002), *"15 must-know credit card terms."*

(38)   https://www.creditcards.com/credit-card-news/glossary/, *"Credit Card Terms;"* https://www.thebalance.com/credit-card-terms-everyone-should-know-4687035, *"Credit Card Terms Everyone Should Know."*

(39)   https://wallethub.com/answers/cc/high-school-student-credit-cards-2140670429/, *"Are there any high school student credit cards?"* John Harter, 10/2018, https://www.yacenter.org/index.cfm?fuseAction=financialLiteracyStatistics. financialLiteracyStatistics, Young Americans Center for Financial Education® – *"Financial Literacy, The State of Financial Literacy in America."*

(40)   Bianoc and Bosco (2002, p.45), *"Ethical Issues In Credit Card Solicitation of College Students- The Responsibilities of Credit Card Issuers, Higher Education, and Students," "Teaching Business Ethics Journal,"* (Vol. 6/No. 1 2/2002, pages 45-62); https://link.springer.com/article/10.1023/A:1014206607573.

(41)   https://www.vantagescore.com/about/vantagescore_model.

(42)   (2005) Fair Isaac and Consumer Federation of America (FICO®); https://www.experian.com/blogs/ask-experian/credit-education/improving-credit/building-credit/, *"How to Build Credit;"*, https://www.thebalance.com/pay-more-than-the-minimum-961133, *"The Benefits of Paying More Than the Minimum on Your Credit Cards,"* Latoya Irby, 5/31/2021; www.creditcard.org/toptencredittips.htm, *"Top 10 Tips for Good Credit,"* (11/2002) Office of Fair Trading; , *"10 Credit Tips From Someone With a Perfect Credit Score;"* https://www.fool.com/the-ascent/credit-cards/articles/10-credit-tips-from-someone-with-a-perfect-credit/. https://www.thesimpledollar.com/trimming-the-fat-forty-ways-to-reduce-your-monthly-required-spending/, *"40 Ways to Save Money on Monthly Expenses,"* Trent Hamm, (04/22/2021), *"100 Ways to Save Money Fast,"* Trent Hamm, https://www.thesimpledollar.com/save-money/litttle-steps-100-great-tips-for-saving-money-for-those-just-getting-started/; https://www.moneycrashers.com/tips-living-on-one-income-family/, *"9 Tips for Families Living on One Income,"* Casey Slide.

(43) https://www.bankrate.com/credit-cards/how-to-minimize-the-cost-of-a-cash-advance/, 8/9/2019, Tim Maxwell (6/17/2021), Fred Williams, *"How To Minimize the Cost of A Cash Advance,"* https://www.thebalance.com/credit-card-grace-period-explained-960699, 7/16/2019. Latoya Irby, *"Credit Card Grace Period Explained."*

(44) https://www.nerdwallet.com/blog/credit-cards/credit-card-tips-everyone-should-know/, *"7 Credit Card Tips Everyone Should Know,"* Lindsay Konsko, 11/2014, https://www.ncua.gov › Resources › Documents › Cr-Crd-TRICKS; https://www.federalreserve.gov; *"Minimize Credit Score Damage From Late Payments,"* Bev O'Shea, 6/2/2021, https://www.nerdwallet.com/article/finance/late-bill-payment-reported#:~:text=Paying%2030%20days%20or%20more,as%20much%20as%20100%20points.&text=If%20you%20have%20otherwise%20spotless,but%20will%20still%20do%20damage.

(45) https://www.realtytrac.com/news/tag/foreclosure-report, *"424,800 US Properties with Foreclosure Fillings In First Six Months of 2017, Down 20 Percent from Year Ago"*; *"U.S. Foreclosure Activity Increases 23 Percent In First Quarter,"* (2008), RealtyTrac® Staff; https://www.realtytrac.com.

(46) https://www.reuters.com/article/us-usa-housing-foreclosures/-u-s-2009-foreclosures-shatter-record-despite-aid-idUSTRE60D0LZ20100114, Lynn Adler (1/14/2010), *"US 2009 foreclosures shatter records despite aid;"* (4/11/17)*"Q1 2017 Foreclosure Activity Below Pre-Recession Levs Nationwide..."*

(47) Neighborhood Reinvestment Corporation® (4/2002), *'FDIC and Neighborhood Reinvestment Corporation® Announce Program to Promote Financial Education and Home Ownership'* (PR-42-2002), https://www.fdic.gov/news/press-releases/2002/pr4202.html.

(48) https://www.fdic.gov/consumers/consumer/moneysmart/adult.html, *"Money Smart Adult Financial Education Curriculum®."*

(49) https://www.investopedia.com/terms/m/mortgage.asp, *"What Is a Mortgage?,"* Julia Kagan, Feb 25, 2021; https://www.lexico.com/en/definition/mortgage.

(50) https://www.federalreserve.gov/pubs; Dictionary; https://www.google.com/search?q=definition+of+a+martgage&rlz=1C1CHBF_enUS833US833&oq=definition+of+a+martgage&aqs=chrome..69i57j0l5.6151j1j8&sourceid=chrome&ie=UTF-8.

(51) https://www.federalreserve.gov/pubs/refinancings/glossary.htm, (8/27/2008) Federal Reserve Board, *"A Consumer's Guide to Mortgage Refinancing,"* https://www.federalreserve.gov, *"Looking for the Best Mortgage",* https://www.fdic.gov/consumers; https://www.hud.gov/sites/documents/BOOKLET.PDF; https://www.realtor.com/home-finance/buyers-basics/home-buyers-basics.aspx, *"10 Steps to Buying a Home;"* https://www.discover.com/home-loans/articles/10-steps-to-buying-a-home; https://www.realestateabc.com/index2.php; https://money.cnn.com/pf/money-essentials-home-buying/index.html, *"Buying a Home in 10 Steps,"* 2/2018; *"Reverse Mortgages,"* https://www.consumer.ftc.gov/articles/0192-reverse-mortgages; https://www.reversemortgages.com/guides/reverse-mortgages-what-to-know.pdf.

(52) https://www.ftc.gov/bcp/edu/pubs/consumer/credit/cre16.shtm, *"Disputing Credit Card Charges;"* https://www.google.com/search?q=fair+credit+reporting+act&rlz=1C1CHBF_.

(53) https://portal.hud.gov/portal/page/portal/HUD, Reverse Mortgages; (2/20/2009) Hud publication, https://hsh.com; https://www.consumer.ftc.gov/search/site/reverse%20mortgages, *"Reverse Mortgages."*

(54) https://www.nerdwallet.com/blog/insurance/car-insurance-basics/car-depreciation/, *"Managing the Hidden Costs of Car Depreciation,"* (Nicole Arata, 7/2017).

(55)   https://gsmr.org/financial-tips/the-cost-of-borrowing, "*The Cost of Borrowing*," Granite State Management & Resources®, A nonprofit student loan servicer working on behalf of the U.S. Department of Education®. https://www. cnbc.com/2019/05/23/millions-of-americans-are-only-400-away-from-financial-hardship.html, "*Millions of Americans are only $ 400 away from financial hardship. Here's why*." Eric Rosenbaum, (5/2019.); https://www.nationaldebtrelief. com/bankruptcy-only-option/, "*How to Figure Out if Bankruptcy Is Your Only Option*," 10/2017, Daniel Bauer.

(56)   https://www.rocketlawyer.com/family-and-personal/personal-finance/debt-and-bankruptcy/legal-guide//bankruptcy-protection-from-creditors, "*Bankruptcy Protection From Creditors*," https://www.citicards.com/cards/wv/html/cm/ managing-your-finances/gaining-financial-control/; https://www.citibank.com.au/usecreditwisely.htm, "*Use Credit Wisely*," Citigroup®.

(57)   https://www.wisegeek.com/what-are-the-consequences-of-filing-for-bankruptcy.htm; https://www.legalzoom.com/ articles/bankruptcy-basics-when-should-you-throw-in-the-towel; https://www.lectlaw.com/files/bnk06.htm.

(58)   (2007) Beth Potier (on Elizabeth Warren); Harvard University Gazelle® Archives: "*Middle-class income doesn't buy middle-class lifestyle*," Harvard News Office, President and Fellows of Harvard College®; https://news.harvard.edu/ gazette/story/2003/10/middle-class-income-doesnt-buy-middle-class-lifestyle/ .

(59)   https://www.cnbc.com/2019/02/11/this-is-the-real-reason-most-americans-file-for-bankruptcy.html, "*This is the real reason most Americans file for bankruptcy*," Lori Konish, 2/2019; https://www.debt.org/bankruptcy/statistics/; https://www.huffpost.com/entry/top-10-reasons-people-go-_b_6887642?guccounter=1&guce_ referrer=aHR0cHM6Ly93d3cuZ29vZ2xlLmNvbS8&guce_referrer_ sig=AQAAAJbEMQAk9WoVjIlpa2XmWMue2raA0dIs0zOZGjMOJYVlRqYA1aEnJrZNAepUwt__Lo3tE_d1 XtgMXUis4docM1N9UR7jl4hBlsYPggMAw4Z6vugfyfA2JC-L8MG-tI-FDCpVDdo0DyYoS7M85AjeIbDt-0nCMDn1X0194piE9INs, "*Top 10 reasons People Go Bankrupt*," 3/2015, HUFF POST; https://jamesjuliano.com/10-leading-causes -of-bankruptcy, "*10 Leading Causes of Bankruptcy*," James Juliano, 2/2018.

(60)   9/29/08) Transamerica®: "*By the Number$*," Joint Center for Housing Studies® at Harvard University®.

Chapter 2 Check For Understanding

For a chapter review, read and complete the following follow-up activities.

- ☒ Estimate how much you will pay in interest if you are charged 5% simple interest (annualized) over a 3-year period for a $ 500 purchase.

- ☒ List how an Adjustable Mortgage Rate is different from a Fixed Mortgage Rate.

- ☒ Discuss how the Federal Reserve policies impact you.

- ☒ Name two sources for obtaining your credit report- credit score.

- ☒ Describe your plan for attaining a good credit score.

- ☒ Explain some of the potential consequences of having a lower credit score.

- ☒ Identify what you believe to be some of the reasons why individuals may not understand their credit card contracts/mortgage documents.

- ☒ Evaluate what you believe your responsibility is for using credit; and does your philosophy coincide with current society trends? Explain.

- ☒ Discuss a Home Equity Line of Credit, when might you use one?

- ☒ Describe Private Mortgage Insurance (PMI).

- ☒ Explain some of the fees that may be accessed during the process of buying or selling a home.

- ☒ Identify an item you may obtain a loan to purchase. Identify and research the terms for a hypothetical loan.

- ☒ Locate some of the agencies that are available to you for solving credit issues.

About Experience Talks...

I offer some examples of real-life experiences regarding financing and borrowing situations on the next few pages. The stories record experiences that have been shared with me through the years. Of course, the names have been changed to protect the identity of the individuals. As you read through the stories, attempt to understand what 'worked' and what 'didn't work' for each individual. The stories are offered in an effort to assist you in the formulation of your own perspective on **borrowing and financing.**

Experience Talks...

Don't Be Late... Its Costly

Darren is a man in his late 60s. He plans to work until he is 70 years old. Darren has two children who live in a house or condo that he helped them purchase.

Darren hopes that his children will one day be able to 'buy him out' and return the equity he invested in the homes.

Darren decided to relocate his business to Florida, so he needs to sell his house and purchase a new home in Florida. However, Darren has a problem. When he began looking for his new home, he first attempted to get his 'pre-approval mortgage letter' from his bank. When Darren started this process, he was unaware that one of his children had missed several mortgage payments along the way. Since his name was on the mortgage, this 'late-pay' history dramatically affected his credit score. In fact, it was doubtful that he was going to be able to secure another loan in Florida unless his credit score was repaired.

Through some very hard work, and over the course of several months, Darren and the mortgage broker were able to work through the red-tape and get some of the credit issues taken care of. The process involved documentation of recent good credit behavior, sending letters of explanation for items, and many telephone conversations with various retailers and credit managers. Eventually, Darren should be able to secure his 'pre-approval letter' for a new mortgage.

Moral of the story: Maintain total control of any debt you are responsible for.

Experience Talks...

Don't Let Debt Control Your Life

At the age of 27 Gary had never actually financed anything in his life. However, his girl-friend Alice has. Alice bought a house about 2 and a half years ago.

So when Gary and Alice decided to refinance their house earlier this year, Gary was surprised to learn how much of the monthly payment went to paying off the interest in the early years of the amortization mortgage schedule. Gary hadn't seen an amortization schedule before. An amortization schedule provides the borrower with a schedule to pay back the loan.

An amortization schedule was provided when Gary and Alice refinanced their home and acquired a new 30-year loan. The schedule illustrated the point that in the early days of owning a home, most of the money is paid towards the cost of the mortgage interest, and only a small portion of the monthly payment is applied towards paying down the actual principal (dollar loan amount). The following amortization schedule is for a 30-year loan, with a fixed interest rate of 6%. Notice how much of the payment in the early years goes straight to interest…. very little money of your monthly payment goes towards paying the principal back.

If you think of it this way… for a $ 100,000 home, if you add in the $ 115,838 in interest payments, you really pay $ 215,838 for the $ 100,000 home (at a 6% interest rate).

Loan Summary	Payment Summary	
Principal: $100,000	Number of Payments:	360
Interest Rate: 6%	Monthly Payment:	$599.55
Loan Term: 30 years	Total Principal Paid:	$100,000.00
Total Interest Paid:		$115,838.19

The moral of the story: The 'equity' you earn in the home is built very slowly, however accelerating your payments, or adding 'principal' money each month, can reduce the total interest you pay.

Yearly Amortization Schedule

Payments	Yearly Total	Principal Paid	Interest Paid	Balance
Year 1 (1-12)	$7,194.61	$1,228.00	$5,967.00	$98,771.99
Year 2 (13-24)	$7,194.61	$1,304.00	$5,891.00	$97,468.24
Year 3 (25-36)	$7,194.61	$1,384.00	$5,810.00	$96,084.07
Year 4 (37-48)	$7,194.61	$1,470.00	$5,725.00	$94,614.53
Year 5 (49-60)	$7,194.61	$1,560.00	$5,634.00	$93,054.36
Year 6 (61-72)	$7,194.61	$1,656.00	$5,538.00	$91,397.95
Year 7 (73-84)	$7,194.61	$1,759.00	$5,436.00	$89,639.39
Year 8 (85-96)	$7,194.61	$1,867.00	$5,328.00	$87,772.35
Year 9 (97-108)	$7,194.61	$1,982.00	$5,212.00	$85,790.17
Year 10 (109-120)	$7,194.61	$2,104.00	$5,090.00	$83,685.72
Year 11 (121-132)	$7,194.61	$2,234.00	$4,960.00	$81,451.48
Year 12 (133-144)	$7,194.61	$2,372.00	$4,823.00	$79,079.44
Year 13 (145-156)	$7,194.61	$2,518.00	$4,676.00	$76,561.09
Year 14 (157-168)	$7,194.61	$2,674.00	$4,521.00	$73,887.42
Year 15 (169-180)	$7,194.61	$2,839.00	$4,356.00	$71,048.84
Year 16 (181-192)	$7,194.61	$3,014.00	$4,181.00	$68,035.19
Year 17 (193-204)	$7,194.61	$3,200.00	$3,995.00	$64,835.66
Year 18 (205-216)	$7,194.61	$3,397.00	$3,798.00	$61,438.79
Year 19 (217-228)	$7,194.61	$3,606.00	$3,588.00	$57,832.40
Year 20 (229-240)	$7,194.61	$3,829.00	$3,366.00	$54,003.59
Year 21 (241-252)	$7,194.61	$4,065.00	$3,130.00	$49,938.62
Year 22 (253-264)	$7,194.61	$4,316.00	$2,879.00	$45,622.93
Year 23 (265-276)	$7,194.61	$4,582.00	$2,613.00	$41,041.06
Year 24 (277-288)	$7,194.61	$4,864.00	$2,330.00	$36,176.59
Year 25 (289-300)	$7,194.61	$5,165.00	$2,030.00	$31,012.09
Year 26 (301-312)	$7,194.61	$5,483.00	$1,712.00	$25,529.05
Year 27 (313-324)	$7,194.61	$5,821.00	$1,373.00	$19,707.84
Year 28 (325-336)	$7,194.61	$6,180.00	$1,014.00	$13,527.58
Year 29 (337-348)	$7,194.61	$6,561.00	$633.00	$6,966.14
Year 30 (349-360)	$7,194.61	$6,966.00	$228.00	$0.00
Totals	$215,838.19	$100,000.00	$115,838.19	

Experience Talks...

Interest Can Be A GOOD Thing

Candice uses a credit card that pays her 2% cash back. Every month she sees cash transferred into her account. Candice is using this program as one of her strategies for saving. Candice then transfers the money into a second account that generates interest.

Moral of the story: Lock for interest in all the right places, find a way to have your money make you money.

Experience Talks...

Read And Question The "Fine Print"

J ake had a home to sell. It was 1998. Jake listed his property with a real estate broker and agreed to purchase his next home from the same broker. Jake agreed to pay the real estate broker a 4% commission to sell his house…. A large discount from the going rate of 5 -6%, the average commission rate realtors were charging at the time. At the time he listed his house, Jake received a Seller's Disclosure of fees he would be charged at the time he sold his house. So, the 4% was noted in writing on this document.

It took several months for Jake's home to sell. Finally, the day of closing came, and Jake went to the title company's office to sign the contracts. As Jake was signing the contracts (and there was a mound of paperwork) he actually took the time to read them. He paid special attention to the HUD statement which outlined the fees and 'pre-paid fees.' During the review of those documents Jake noticed that the realtor commission seemed to be higher than he had remembered… so he re-calculated the commission amount and pointed out the difference.

Instead of letting what he thought might be a 'mistake' go unchallenged, and paying the higher fee, Jake called the discrepancy to the attention of the title officer. The real estate broker's commission had been calculated at a rate higher than the agreed-upon 4%. Of course, the title office had no authority to change the figure, only the real estate broker could authorize a change in his own commission. Since the real estate broker was not present, Jake called the broker. Right then the real estate agent said that he had 'forgotten' that he had agreed on the 4% commission but authorized the change. It was an honest mistake.

Jake calculated that he saved about $ 5,000.

Moral of the story: Review and calculate your fees, know what you expect to pay… don't rely solely on others.

Experience Talks...

Are Credit Scores Friend or Foe?

Credit scores can be your best ally, or your worst enemy....as Curtis found out firsthand. Curtis went through a divorce and relates that he was left with all of the debt and few of the assets from his marriage. Curtis spent the next 10+ years of his life attempting to pay off his debt and get into 'the black' financially.

Through this process Curtis learned a few key points: Before his divorce he was not organized financially. Curtis admits that he had not paid enough attention to his financial life. He was a small business owner and had focused on the everyday management of his business. However, Curtis had made a good living and, at the time, did have money in the bank. Like others, Curtis had a mortgage and some family credit card debt; but Curtis had not been attentive enough about monitoring his bills, and he didn't realize the amount of 'late-pays' he and his wife were allowing on the home-front. Curtis neglected to review the house-hold credit card charges and payments carefully and missed the fact that his partner had begun to charge large-purchase items just prior to the divorce. Later he became responsible for the large credit-card balances.

Curtis hadn't grasped the impact of these actions on his new financial situation. These over-sights lowered his credit score and he was about to understand the far-reaching affect that his now lower credit score would have on him going forward:

1. When Curtis applied for a credit card, a new mortgage for his house, and a business loan, he either was denied the loan, or offered an interest rate that was higher than the rate he had been awarded just a few years earlier.

2. The credit card companies were also anxious for Curtis to pay-down the credit card balances he now had responsibility for, and they were not willing to issue new credit to Curtis. Curtis was unable to keep up the credit card payments, causing him to fall behind and worsen his financial picture.

3. Curtis also found out that even Insurance Companies run credit reports when you submit an application for most types of insurance. These credit reports also hurt him financially, as lower credit scores can cause higher insurance premiums.

Moral of the story: Keep a keen eye on your re-payment schedules for your loans – watch your outstanding loan balances on ALL fronts.

Experience Talks...

When 'FREE' Can Actually Cost You Money

Tina is a credit counselor. She mentioned to me that few of the individuals who make purchases with terms of 'no interest for X months' actually adhere to the re-payment schedule and get the 'no interest feature.' Many individuals do not realize that if they don't pay a monthly amount to keep the terms of the 'free interest' from becoming voided, the original contract is terminated, and another interest rate is then assessed on the total purchase amount.

For example: If you buy a TV on a 'no interest for 24 months' schedule, the store will require you to pay something each month toward the cost of the TV. So, if the TV costs $600, your monthly payments may be about $25 for the 24 months. While you do not pay any interest for the TV, you do have to keep up your payments and pay on time. If you do not pay according to the payment schedule, then you void the contract and an interest charge may be assessed on the total cost ($600) of the TV. As Tina reported, about 80% of people who enter into this type of no interest arrangement default on the contract and end up paying much more for the item than they had planned.

Moral of the story: Contracts can be difficult to understand, don't enter into a contract without fully grasping your responsibility to perform, and the ramifications if you fail to perform.

CHAPTER 3

An Introduction To Investing

LEARNING OBJECTIVES:

After completing Chapter 3, you should be able to:

a.   Describe an 'asset.'

b.   Explain what the 'stock market' and 'exchanges' are; and elaborate on how they operate.

   • Describe volatility in relationship to how the stock market behaves.

   • Name some of the attributes of a *Bear* and *Bull* market.

c.   Describe how investment products are the same or different from savings products.

d.   Identify the characteristics and differences between a stock, bond, and cash equivalent investment product; and provide examples of each.

e.   Identify the characteristics of a mutual fund:

   • Describe the differences between *'share classes'* discussed in the text;

   • Identify some of the *fees* associated with mutual funds;

   • Define and express the differences between **size** and *style*;

   • Clarify what a *'value'* vs. *'growth'* equity product is;

   • Give an explanation of what a *prospectus* is; how you might utilize it;

   • Briefly describe how you might use a mutual fund *index*.

f.   Articulate the differences between an *Investment/Brokerage Account* and a *Retirement/Custodian Account*.

g.   Demonstrate your understanding of how risk tolerance and time horizon impact you as an investor.

h.   Define *diversification and asset allocation;* how are they alike or different? Provide examples to illustrate your point(s).

Experience Talks...

Investing Is NOT For Dummies

My parents didn't invest in anything other than CDs and real estate property. My father didn't really understand the stock market or the world of 'investing.' However, on occasion my father loaned money out to individuals he knew well so they could purchase a home. Dad collected a small interest amount on the money he loaned. He made these loans using the home as collateral. Some of those individuals were not able to qualify for the loans without my Dad's help. My Dad also bought a house and kept it as an investment property once or twice, collecting rent to add to his income. These activities constituted his investment strategy.

As I mentioned in an earlier section, my Granddad also liked to invest in real estate property. My guess is that both of these men were conservative enough to keep their everyday expenses in line with their incomes. They certainly would guard against the possibility of needing to sell a real estate property at an inopportune time. Real estate property can be difficult to sell and is considered to be an 'illiquid' investment product. Noted in the following chapter, some investment products are liquid (easy to sell), and like real estate property, some investment products are illiquid (meaning you cannot access the investment principal –cash- within a few days).

My Uncle on my Mom's side understood the stock market, and he was very knowledgeable about the various investment products that were bought and sold in the market. My Uncle managed my Grandmother's money (the money my Granddad left her when he passed away) by investing a portion of my Grandmother's money in the stock market. Fortunately, my Uncle was a competent and intelligent investor. He invested the money in the stock market during some very lucrative market growth years – the 1980s and 1990s, and My Uncle's prudent money management provided income for Nana to live on.

As I indicated previously, investing in the stock market was not an activity that my parents knew much about. They were not risk-takers and viewed the stock market as too 'risky.' I was not introduced to the stock market until I was married in 1981. So, sometime between 1981 and 1983 I became a 'stock market investor.' Over the course of the next several years I watched as our financial advisor worked to buy and sell different types of investments with us. Some investment vehicles did really well, and others (like a Real Estate investment we owned – probably a REIT – in Austin, TX in the mid-1980s) lost a lot of money. I learned about the ups and downs of the market, firsthand.

Most months, when the account statements came in, I opened the envelopes and conducted a quick review of the holdings. I put the statements neatly in a binder for safe keeping. Over the years I began to become interested in learning about the investment world and the different product offerings… and after my divorce, I had the responsibility of managing my portion of the investments that I received in the settlement, and I then became a more active investor. This experience led to me becoming a Financial Advisor. After about 30 years of monitoring and managing my personal investments, including 18+ years of helping others to understand and navigate the 'complicated' world of the stock market, I embrace the responsibility to continuously educate myself and others.

Navigating The World Of 'Investing'

I have listened to many individuals recount their 'investing' stories/experiences. Some experiences have been very positive; other investors have had negative experiences. There also is quite a disparity regarding the experience levels of the investors themselves. While some of the investors are quite savvy, others, even some individuals who have been investing for years, are still novices. I have noted that it isn't the amount of time someone has been investing that dictates the sophistication of the investor, it is the individual's quest for knowledge and understanding that is important. .If you plan to invest in the stock market, I strongly suggest that you begin with some education. Therefore, the following information will begin to acquaint you with some of the terms associated with investing in the stock market. The data will provide a springboard for you to initiate your research on this topic so that you can begin to devise your own investment opinions.

One of my favorite sayings is,"10 Financial Advisors in a room, 10 perspectives for how to invest. There is NOT just one approach! And in my opinion, there is NOT only one BEST way! Investing looks different for each of us."

Chapter 3

An Introduction To Investing

Investing 101

One status symbol Americans use to measure our success is our ability to accumulate wealth. Of course, wealth has a different meaning to each of us, but in general, one dimension of wealth is the accumulation of material things. At the heart of this paradigm is the pursuit of 'money,' or assets.

The Coveted Asset

Remember, there are a myriad of definitions that may describe an individual's perception of 'Wealth.' However, we will start with a description of some of the types of 'assets' that sometimes define wealth in various settings. Ultimately, we will study assets against the landscape of investing.

Let's start with description of what an asset is. Assets are more than cars, homes, jewelry and bank accounts.

To explain assets, the Dictionary offers us the following definition of 'as-set:'

> *"noun*
>
> plural noun: **assets**
>
> • - *a useful or valuable thing, person, or quality,*
>
> • - *property owned by a person or company, regarded as having value and available to meet debts, commitments or legacies."* (61)

In economics an asset can be identified as:

> *"Any form in which wealth can be held."*
>
> https://books.google.com (62)

One of the most accepted accounting definitions of asset is presented by Wikipedia: (62)

> *"In the **financial accounting** sense of the term, it is not necessary to be able to legally enforce the asset's benefit for qualifying a resource as being an asset, provided the entity can control its use by other means.*
>
> *The **accounting equation** is the mathematical structure of the balance sheet. It relates assets, liabilities, and owner's equity:*
>
> *Assets = Liabilities + Capital (which for a corporation equals owner's equity)*
>
> *Liabilities = Assets − Capital*
>
> *Equity = Assets − Liabilities*
>
> *Assets are listed on the balance sheet.*
>
> *Assets are formally controlled and managed within larger organizations via the use of asset tracking tools. These tools monitor the purchasing, upgrading, servicing, licensing, disposal etc., of both physical and non-physical assets."*

The International Financial Reporting Standards® (IFRS) Framework states that,

> *"An asset is a resource controlled by the enterprise as a result of past events and from which future economic benefits are expected to flow to the enterprise." (62)*

Plainly stated, assets are 'stuff' with a value. Assets are any goods or tangible item to which we can assign a value, like: a car, jewelry, a home, investment products, cash in checking or other types of accounts, boats, etc. and future income of same, or intangible products such as good will, trademarks, copyrights, etc.

Current assets are classified as cash and other assets that are anticipated to be converted to cash, sold, or consumed within a short period of time. Here are six different types of current assets:

1. **Cash and cash equivalents** are liquid assets like currency, deposit accounts, and negotiable instruments like money orders and checks.

2. **Short-term investments** are securities that are bought with the anticipation of selling them within a one-year period to generate a gain.

3. **Receivables** are payments due for the sale of products or services and are net of allowance for uncollected accounts.

4. **Inventory** are the items held and reported as value, either on a company or individual's balance sheet.

5. **Prepaid expenses** are expenses that are paid in advance and are recorded as assets before they have been collected or used.

6. The phrase **net current assets** (also called working capital), refers to the total of current assets, minus the total of current liabilities.

Long-term assets are investments that are to be held for many years. This group usually consists of four types of investments:

1. **Investments in securities: such as bonds, common stock, or long-term notes.**

2. **Investments in fixed assets not used in operations (e.g., land held for sale).**

3. **Investments in special funds (e.g., sinking funds or pension funds).**

4. **Different forms of insurance may also be treated as long term-investments.**

Fixed assets are referred to as *Property and Equipment*. This type of inventory is bought by the business for use in the operation of the business and to assist in the generation of profits. These fixed assets can include land, buildings, machinery, furniture, tools, and certain wasting resources e.g., timberland and minerals. These types of assets are depreciated expenses for the business (with exception of land). These fixed assets are also called capital assets in management accounting.

Intangible assets include items, like: patents, copyrights, franchises, goodwill, trademarks, trade names, etc. and, with the exception of goodwill, and are amortized to be expensed over a 5 to 40 year period. Websites are treated differently in different countries and may fall under either tangible or intangible assets.

Tangible assets are assets that have a physical matter: such as equipment and real estate. (63)

What assets do you have?

_____

_____

Life

Growing up my family's assets were simple to identify: a car, a house, furniture, savings/checking accounts. No investment or retirement accounts. My parents saved by using CDs. There were few business assets to inventory and no insurance policies to account for.

My husband and I have two cars and a motorcycle, a house, insurance policies, interest in a small business, and Investment and Retirement Accounts. While the value of these assets is not large, the responsibility for managing the assets today, and planning for the distribution of those assets tomorrow, is a responsibility that my husband and I take very seriously. Knowing how to take care of our family from a conscientious financial standpoint is critical.

Individuals can also face the challenge of managing their parent's assets. For example: One of my clients suddenly found both of his parents with critical health conditions and was obligated to assume the responsibility for not only his parents' everyday living expenses, but he had to manage and dispose of the family business as well.

As the client began to unravel his parents' 'financial picture,' he found that the family business was in serious debt, that his parents were dramatically outspending their income and depleting their investment and savings accounts. Difficult decisions regarding his parents' healthcare had to be made immediately, and a financial plan had to be instantaneously developed as well. My client also had his own, immediate family to take care of. The strain of the situation was apparent.

The process of transition took about three years to resolve. The business was sold and both parents were moved to a retirement community. And he solved the biggest hurdle of all, reducing his parent's expenses to correspond with income flow.

Being exposed to this process can prompt you to reevaluate your own financial position.

While you may have a short list of personal assets today, tomorrow may bring you a different scenario. Like my story, you may have investment assets, either yours, or your family's, that you will manage in the future. So, in this section of the handbook we are going to focus on 'investment' assets. We will examine a few investment product choices; review some investment account options; provide some general information on the stock market and how the stock market has behaved in the past; consider some of the investor terms - risk tolerance, diversification, asset allocation; and review what an Investor Profile is. Use this section of the handbook as a reference and resource; it is not designed to offer specific investment advice.

What Is Investing?
How Is It Different From Saving?

Investing is generally perceived to be quite different from *saving*. When you invest, you can put your money at greater risk. When you invest you 'may sustain losses.' (64) **Investing** is not the same as **'saving.'** Saving is generally considered to be a **shorter-term proposition, employs safety measures, and typically delays spending.** Whereas **investing has a longer-term time horizon, involves risk, and anticipates an increase in value.** (65)

Let's begin with a discussion about the investor. Who is this investor?

- An **investor** is anyone who buys and holds property to achieve some form of gain.

Another definition, from https://www.chegg com/flashcards/ is:

> *"An individual who commits money to investment products with the expectation of financial return. Generally, the primary concern of an investor is to minimize risk while maximizing return, as opposed to a speculator, who is willing to accept a higher level of risk in the hopes of collecting higher-than-average profits." (66)*

Will You Ever Invest In The Stock Market?

> *"October: This is one of the peculiarly dangerous months to speculate in stocks. The others are July, January, September, April, November, May, March, June, December, August and February."*
>
> Mark Twain

You may associate the term 'stock market' with how people speculate that they can make money by investing in stocks and bonds, and other types of investment vehicles/products.

Individuals are often baffled by the concept of the *stock market*. Exactly what is the *stock market*? What do the numbers mean on the television channels? How can you understand the behavior and activity of the *stock market* better? How is money actually made by investing in the *stock market*? How is money lost when it is invested in the *stock market*?

The *stock market* is a term that can be broadly interpreted. Read the varied definitions for the term that are on the following page and then contemplate, what is your OWN definition….

Write your own definition of what you think the *stock market* is:

_____

_____

Definitions of stock market taken from internet sources:

- ☒ *"The stock market refers to the collection of markets and exchanges where regular activities of buying, selling, and issuance of shares of publicly-held companies takes place. Such financial activities are conducted through institutionalized formal exchanges or over-the-counter (OTC) marketplaces which operate under a defined set of regulations."*

  - ○ https://www.investopedia.com/terms/s/stockmarket.asp

- ☒ *"A stock market, equity market of share market is the aggregation of buyers and sellers (a loose network of economic transactions, not physical facility or discrete entity) of stocks (also called shares), which represent ownership claims on businesses; these may include securities listed on a public stock exchange, as well as stock that is only traded privately."*

  - ○ https://en.wikipedia.org/wiki/Stock_market

- ☒ *"The stock market refers to public markets that exist for issuing, buying and selling stocks that trade on a stock exchange or over-the-counter. Stocks, also known as equities, represent fractional ownership in a company, and the stock market is a place where investors can buy and sell ownership of such investible assets."*

  - ○ https://corporatefinanceinstitute.com/resources/knowledge/trading-investing/stock-market/

- ☒ *"... These markets streamline the purchase and sales activities of investors by allowing transactions to be made quickly and at a fair price."*

  - ○ https://opentextbc.ca/businessopenstax/chapter/securities-markets

Before you plunk down your hard-earned money, it is critical for you to understand some of the basics of investing. Let's start with a description of what the DOW® and S&P® numbers represent, several types of investment accounts, and some of the basic investment product choices.

The Dow® And S&P®

Although you may not have paid much attention to the financial channels in the past, the terms *Dow Jones Industrial Average®* *(DJIA or the DOW)* and *S&P 500®* *(Standard and Poor's®)* are somewhat familiar terms for many Americans. The *Dow Jones®* and *S&P 500®* *numbers* are presented on the news and financial channels on days when the stock market is open. By merely watching the financial news, you learn whether the "Dow® and S&P 500® are up or down" that day. The rise and fall of the *Dow Jones Industrial Average®* and *S&P 500®* *numbers that are recorded and presented each day* is one indication of the overall volatility of the markets. For example: Higher numbers represent a gain in value for the index (and the average of their holdings); lower numbers indicate a loss in value for the index.

However, what is important to understand is the fact that the Dow Jones Industrial Average (DJIA)® is an INDEX. The DJIA® is made up of only 30 stocks (30 individual companies). **So, if you don't own any of those 30 stocks, your stocks may be performing quite differently than what the "Dow Number" (which is only those 30 companies) indicates.** On-the-other-hand, the S&P 500® is comprised of the five hundred companies that have their common stock included in this INDEX. The numbers displayed for both represent a composite indicating how the company's stock prices are fluctuating. You will notice that the numbers go up and down, indicating that the *average prices* of the stock holdings are either appreciating or losing market value. A third barometer, the NASDAQ®, is a computerized market trading and surveillance network that provides daily quotes on equities. All three of these market indicators can be viewed each trading day on several of the news channels and the 'market channels;' the numbers provide you with a gauge of where the general markets are moving that day.

Individuals question how the stock market works, how they can participate in the stock market, and how they can 'make money' in the stock market. We will explore the answers to these questions here. However, one thing is readily apparent, on the whole: *Investors tend to expect to make money if they invest in the stock market.* I am afraid to say, that expectation may, or may not, come to fruition. Here's some perspectives provided by the U.S. Securities and Exchange Commission regarding 'making money' and 'losing money' with investments in the stock market.

Making money:

You make money when...

- Your investment appreciates (has a **gain in value**) because:

  1. 'Consumers perceive that the company you invest in performs better than others in the same type of business, increasing demand for the products or services;

  2. The company you invest in is currently experiencing higher profits, either through cost cutting efforts, higher sales volume, price increases, etc.;

  3. Other investors believe the company you invest in will make greater profits in the future; and

  4. Other investors are eager to buy your investment; the demand causes your investment to appear more attractive.' (67)

Losing money:

You lose money in the stock market when...

- Your investment experiences a **decline** in value because:

  1. 'The company you invest in produces inferior products or services, compared to competitors;

  2. Demand for the company's products or services declines;

  3. Company managers make decisions which negatively impact the profits/bottom-line;

  4. Company personnel commit fraud: deceptive business practices;

  5. Market brokers manipulate the stock price through unethical business practices; and

  6. You sell your investment when stock prices are depressed.' (67)

"When stocks are attractive, you buy them. Sure, they can go lower. I've bought stocks at $12 that went to $2, but then they later went to $30. You just don't know when you can find the bottom."

Peter Lynch

How You Begin

Whether you begin to invest on your own, or with the help of an advisor, you will want to understand:

a. The mechanics of opening an account and what type of an account you should open;

b. The importance of knowing who you are as an investor, i.e. your risk tolerance level and your time horizon so you can select appropriate investment products for you, etc..; and

c. What the characteristics and costs are for each investment product type.

Let's begin by reviewing some legal requirements for opening an account.

Opening Accounts

In 2001 Congress passed the Patriot Act. The Patriot Act requires the financial institution to verify your identity when you open any type of investment account. Not all of the following information is required by the Patriot Act, however, by providing the information noted below, you will help to satisfy this requirement. The questions may include, but are not limited to providing:

1. Name

2. Date of Birth

3. Address

4. Phone Number

5. Social Security or TIN (for business) number

6. Information about your spouse if you are married

7. Employment history

8. Assets you hold

9. Investment Experience

10. Current banking relationships

Before you can invest in the stock market you will open an account to hold your investments/money. For simplification we will refer to just two types of investment accounts: either an Investment/Brokerage Account or a Retirement/Custodian Account.

Types of Accounts

Please note, I am NOT a Tax Advisor, but the type of investment account you open may be dictated by the 'Tax Treatment' of the money you place into the account. There are several types of *after-tax* accounts, however, we will focus on two types here; and there are also several types of *before-tax* accounts that we examine in this section:

A. **After-Tax Investment/Brokerage Accounts and Roth Retirement/Custodian Accounts**

    a. The Investment/Brokerage Account is an account that you place money AFTER you have paid ordinary income taxes on it. This type of account offers you the flexibility to move money in and out of the account at any age without incurring an IRS penalty. However, buy and sell activities can trigger other tax and fee consequences. Also, this type of account allows you to put as much, or as little, money into the account each year without violating any 'contribution limits.' The gains realized from money placed in an Investment Account are not tax deferred.

    b. Roth Retirement/Custodian Accounts also accepts money AFTER ordinary income taxes have already been paid on your contributions. However, with Roth Retirement/Custodian Accounts there is an annual contribution limit, and you will pay an IRS 10% penalty if you withdraw funds prior to being age 59 ½ (other withdrawal rules can also apply). Withdrawals you make after you have met the 5 year holding period, and you are age 59 ½, are NOT taxed at ordinary income tax rates. (Rules can change.)

B. **NON-Roth Retirement/Custodian Before-Tax Accounts**

    • For NON-Roth Retirement/Custodian Accounts, contributions are made PRE-TAX. Annual contribution limits apply, and withdrawal of funds before the age of 59 ½ triggers IRS penalties. Typically, you cannot move money out of the account without tax consequences. When you withdraw money from these types of accounts, you are taxed at your ordinary income rate (at the time the funds are withdrawn).

    ☒ We will review some of the varieties of Retirement/Custodian Accounts in the next section.

Titling & Beneficiaries - A Place to Start

What type of account you will open can be a direct result of a minimum of three things:

1. The **tax-status** of the money you plan to place into the account,

   - **The tax status identifies the fact that either you have, or have not, paid ordinary income taxes already on the money before you place it into your account.**

2. Do you want your money to be readily **assessable for near-term withdrawals without IRS penalties?**

3. **Contribution Amounts:** Custodian/Retirement Accounts have annual contribution limits.

CHECK WITH A TAX ADVISOR.

The Investment/Brokerage Account

There are some other characteristics to consider when you plan to open any type of Investment/Brokerage or Retirement/Custodian Account. Among other distinctions it is important to address how the accounts are 'titled,' and how 'beneficiaries' for each account are designated.

1. How you **Title** your Investment/Brokerage Account:

Your account can be titled in several ways. Here are three common ways you can title the account:

- ☒ In a **single name** (yours) (i.e.: Joe Smith Investment Account);

- ☒ The account might be **titled jointly with another person**. There are various kinds of joint account arrangements, we will review three here:

  - ○ **Joint Tenants with Rights of Survivorship (JTWOS):** Upon the death of one of the account owners, the assets pass to the other account owners.

  - ○ **Tenants in Common (TIC)**: The assets are held in 'shares'/separate interest for each of the account owners; at death the shares pass to the heirs of the owners.

  - ○ **Community Property (COMM):** Assets acquired after marriage are considered joint property;

- ☒ You might title the account in the name of your Trust (for example: Joe Smith Revocable Trust dated 09/08/2014).

2. Beneficiary considerations for your Investment/Brokerage Account:

Beneficiary designations should also be addressed when you open the account.

- **If you have a <u>single name account</u>, you might add a TOD (transfer on death) to add a beneficiary (MAY BE A SEPARATE FORM).**

  How this works: If you have added/designated a TOD to your Investment/Brokerage account, then *the assets will pass to whomever you have named as TOD beneficiary when you die (the TOD will <u>not be in effect if you are incapacitated</u>)*. There is one point to remember here: If the person(s) you have named as TOD also pass(es) away, either before you die, or at the same time you die, there are then no other beneficiaries designated on the account. This means that you no longer have a valid TOD designation on your account; so be sure to keep your beneficiaries updated. Check with an Estate Planning attorney to determine if this is the best option for you.

- **Another titling option that DOES (more directly) provide you with the option to name one or several beneficiary designations is: Titling your account in a Trust.** If your account is titled in a Trust, and you die, <u>or become incapacitated</u>, the account held in **Trust** will be managed or will pass according to the directives outlined in your Trust to your beneficiaries. Check with an Estate Planning attorney to determine if this is the best option for you.

BE SURE TO CHECK WITH YOUR ADVISORS.

A Retirement/Custodian Account

Remember that the tax status identifies the fact that either you have, or have not, paid taxes already on the money you place in the account.

1. If you have NOT paid taxes already on the money you are placing into the Account, then the money is placed into a *'pre-tax' Retirement/Custodian Account.***

2. If you have paid taxes already on the money you are placing into the Account, then the money is placed into an *'after-tax' Retirement/Custodian Roth Account.****

** Examples: Individual Retirement Accounts, 403B, SEP, SIMPLE, Rollover, etc. – discussed in the next section. *** These examples may allow for Roth versions.

How accounts are titled, and the beneficiary considerations differ by type of Investment Account.

1. How you **Title** your Retirement/Custodian Account:

   A Retirement Account is titled uniquely. The Retirement Account will be held in custody by the financial institution you invest with, for your benefit.

   - For Joe Smith's Retirement Account, the account may be titled:

   - ABC Financial Institution For Benefit Of (FBO) Joe Smith, followed by the type of Retirement Account you have (Traditional IRA or Roth or Rollover IRA, etc.). Here is one example: ABC Financial FBO Joe Smith Traditional IRA.

2. **Beneficiary** considerations for your Retirement/Custodian Account:

   For your Retirement/Custodian Account you **DO specifically designate a beneficiary on the Retirement/ Custodian Account documents.**

   - It is a good idea to name both a primary and contingent beneficiary. [If your primary beneficiary(s) pass(es) away, the Account will be awarded to whomever you have named as your contingent beneficiary(s)].

Reviewing what we discussed here about titling and beneficiaries, note 2 differences between Investment/Brokerage and Non-Roth Retirement Accounts here:

_____

_____

Now that we have reviewed how to determine what type of investment account you might consider, before you proceed: it makes sense to familiarize yourself with some basic information about the stock market; identify some basic investing terms; review Investor Profile information and types of Risk; and examine various types of investment products. Let's begin with a review of *How the Stock Market Behaves.*

How Does The Market Behave?

> *"The financial markets generally are unpredictable... The idea that you can actually predict what's going to happen contradicts my way of looking at the market."*
>
> *"Markets are constantly in a state of uncertainty and flux and money is made by discounting the obvious and betting on the unexpected."*
>
> George Soros (73)

In the 1960s Mr. Soros was a stock trader and philanthropist. His quotes capture the general uncertainty of how the stock market behaves. During the history of the stock market there have been many downturns, or periods of loss. Downturns, or market pullbacks, can occur for a variety of reasons, causing investors to react in a potentially negative fashion. Consumer fear or panic can take hold after some 'initiating event;' for example: a banking crisis, a weather incident, or a terrorist attack, can all prompt a change in investor behavior. Additional consumer concerns can range from, Trade-war worries, recession fears, a 'corporate earnings' downturn, war, a banking crisis, a 'housing decline,' etc. These and other significant events can make it difficult for investors to remain confident and focused on the long term.

As a financial advisor I helped educate investors regarding risk and market behavior. Communication between an advisor and client is very important, and generally centers around topics such as these listed here. To begin with, as the financial advisor works with a client, they should, **at a minimum**, record the following information

- understand and document the risk tolerance and investment profile of an investor;

- carefully determine each investor's objectives and financial circumstances;

- discuss investment products that are appropriate for each investor's risk tolerance, time-horizon and objectives;

- share information around the history of how the market behaves, market performance;

- discuss historical returns of a specific asset allocation model, both positive and negative; (at no time will a financial advisor predict, or guarantee returns);

- develop a diversified asset allocated portfolio tailored to each individual investor's objectives and needs;

- provide focus on a long-term strategy recommendation, if appropriate;

- give support to the investor regarding discipline to adhere to the pre-stated strategy unless there is a change in the investor's objectives, risk tolerance, or circumstances;

- work with the client to modify the asset allocation, and re-balance a portfolio when a change in the market dynamics, investor's risk tolerance, circumstances, or objectives occurs;

- set up a schedule to review account and product performance with the client, revise as appropriate.

Research where the Dow Jones Industrial Average® closed on the following dates:

12/31/2003 _____

12/31/2005 _____

12/31/2007 _____

12/31/2008 _____

12/31/2012 _____

12/31/2019 _____

Don't Start If You Can't Handle The Volatility and Risk

Individuals struggle to understand the dynamics of the markets, especially the volatility aspect of the market. Anyone who has ever invested in the stock market, or just watched from afar, probably has heard about the 'volatility' of the markets.

Volatility can be defined as:

- ○ The standard deviation of the return of the investment; a measure of the variation in an investment's price.

- ○ In simple terms... volatility is the constant variation of an investment's offering price.

Volatility is price movement, calculated over time:

- ○ Fluctuation in stock prices occurs and is reported every few minutes if the stock is publicly held and reported on one of the *Exchanges*.

- ○ *Daily* value of the stock is reported at the 'open' and at the 'close' of the stock market exchange.

- ○ To calculate the volatility of the stock, the mathematical formula for the standard deviation of the value of the investment is applied, and a volatility calculation number is produced and reported. That number represents the volatility of a specific investment product over time.

So, volatility is merely the fact that the value of your investment will go up and down over time. It is the *down* that investors have trouble with. The *down* means a loss in value for the investment.

Life

I began investing more than 35 years ago. As an investor, I know that when I put a portion of my money in the stock market, and elect 'non-guaranteed-principal or rate-of-return' investment products, I sign up for volatility; and risk is part of the contract. This means that when I invest in stock market investment products, like individual stocks and mutual funds, I have absolutely no guarantee that I will get my principal back. Nor can I rely on achieving a gain on my principal (what money was originally invested.).

Therefore, although the stock market can be a very exciting place to invest money, with the ups and downs of the stock market, investing can also be intimidating. If you are considering putting your money into the stock market as an investment strategy, understand that you may lose some or all of your money. Here is a chart that depicts the concept of volatility... if you started with an investment of $ 1,000 at a particular point in time, as the chart illustrates, your investment may lose value, gain value, and do so at various points in time over a longer timeframe. While this chart looks like you could have increased your investment, the reverse is also true. The chart is for illustrative purposes only.

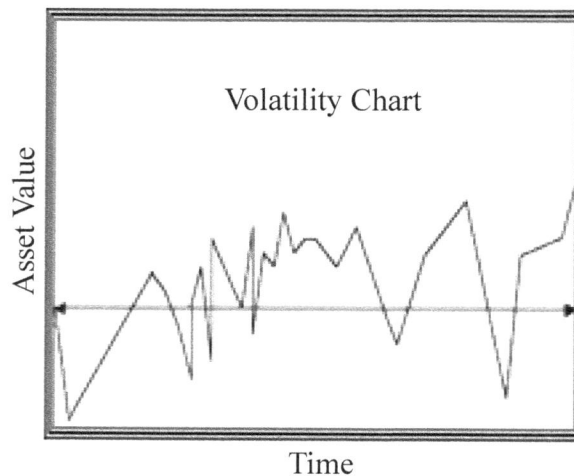

Volatility Chart

Asset Value

Time

Life

An example: In February 2008 the stock market declined dramatically in one day, losing @ 1,032 points! ! And recently, (2020) February 24th and 25th, the DOW® declined @ 1,031 and 879 points, respectively.

Now that is volatility!

https://en.m.wikipedia.org/wiki/List_of_largest_daily_changes_in_the_Dow_Jones_Industrial_Average,

"Sizzlers and Fizzlers". us.spindices.com. Archived from the original on 2018-03-16. Retrieved 2018-03-16.

Life

Another example of Volatility:

- If I buy HHH stock for $10.00 (cost basis) and one day it is worth $11.00, it is up 10% from what I paid for the stock.

- If the next day its value drops to $9.00, the stock value is down about 10% from what I paid for the stock.

HHH Stock's Volatility

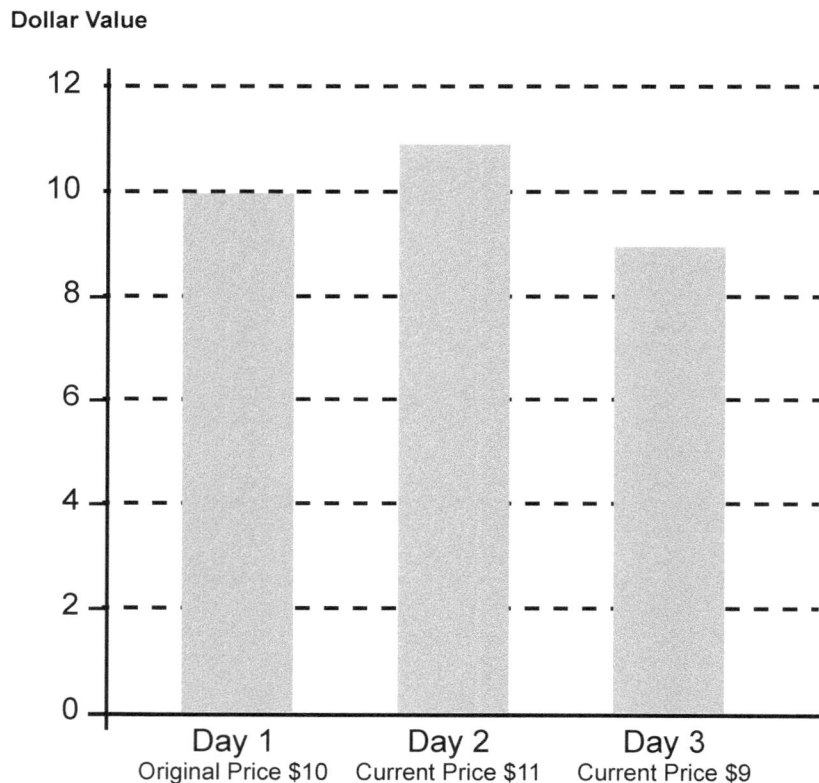

Dollar Value

Day 1	Day 2	Day 3
Original Price $10	Current Price $11	Current Price $9

How Do You Determine Your Investor Profile And Risk Tolerance?

When a new investor sits down with a financial advisor it is typical protocol for the Advisor to ask the investor a series of questions to help quantify the investor's *risk tolerance* and *investor profile*. The Investor Profile Questionnaire helps you define your investment style. Stating, "I want my money to grow, grow, grow," is not an adequate description of your investor profile.

Answer the following questions to help you formulate and clarify which type of investor you might be.

Answer these questions yourself, it will help you determine/become apparent to you as to what your risk tolerance is. When you are required to quantify your losses and objectives, you will note a trend in your answers.

1. How much loss can you accept in your investment or retirement account?

   • No more than a small decline.

   • Occasional losses might be okay if there is opportunity for my account to grow over time.

   • Some losses are fine if I have an opportunity for my account to realize higher gains over time.

2. In relationship to 'keeping up with inflation:'

   • Safety is the ultimate goal, even if I do not keep up with the pace of inflation.

   • I want my investment gains to at least keep pace with inflation, even if I have an occasional short-term loss.

   • My investments should grow much faster than inflation; I am willing to risk a considerable short-term loss in order to outpace inflation over time.

3. Thinking in terms of realizing LOSSES in 1 year, quantify what amount of loss you would be willing to accept before you would make a change in your portfolio: (Circle One)

   • Less than 5%   15% - 25%

   • 5% to 10%   more than 25%

   • 10% to 15%

4. Determine your Time Horizon: I plan to keep my money invested; I do not plan to withdraw money for income needs for: (Circle One)

   • 1- 5 years   10- 20 years

   • 5- 10 years   More than 20 years

To objectively determine what your investor profile is, it is imperative for you to answer the questions the advisor poses. Remember that as an investor you must be ready for a downturn in the market if it arrives, like in 2001 and 2008. So, now that you have answered the Investor Profile Questionnaire, which of the 5 categories below do you fall in?

For the purpose of this discussion we will use 5 Investor Profile/Risk Tolerance categories:

- **Capital Preservation** - Keep what I have – NO risk please; I realize I might not keep up with the rate of inflation.

- **Income** - I need to generate income each month so I can withdraw it to pay expenses; I can withstand a little risk, but I have a shorter time horizon; I would like to keep up with the rate of inflation.

- **Moderate** - I want both income and growth; I can withstand a moderate level of risk; I have a longer time horizon; I want to outpace inflation.

- **Growth** - I don't need the income now, I primarily want my money to appreciate, but don't go too aggressive please; I have a longer time horizon before I need to access any money to cover expenses; I absolutely want to outpace inflation; I can withstand some short-term losses if there is potential to gain over time.

- **Aggressive Growth** - I want to rock and roll - give me all growth potential; I am a risk taker and believe over time my investments will appreciate at a greater rate with this type of investment strategy; outpacing inflation is a must; I can withstand short-term losses for the potential to realize gains over time.

These investor categories are offered as examples only and, as you can see, each investment category carries a different set of risk factors with it. As you meet with your advisor, he or she will discuss those risks with you in detail. Be sure you ask about them. You probably will employ several 'buckets' (strategies) at the same time. There is no such thing as 'one size fits all' in investing… each client will have different goals, risk tolerance and time horizon.

Which type of investor are you? Why?

_____

_____

Types of Risk

Understanding your personal risk profile will be helpful as you select your investment products. At first glance it is apparent that investment risk will center around 'losing' money. However, there are several reasons, or risk categories, which affect 'losing' money. We also know that employing investment products as part of your long-term investment strategy normally involves a higher level of 'risk.' Be sure you fully understand the differences between the types of risk each product carries before you invest. Ask your advisors what type of risk is associated with the investment products you are considering. A brief description is offered here of the different types of investment risk:

☒ **Principal Risk** is the type of risk that is most equated with investing risk—loss of your money – your 'principal' (original money you invested) investment. For example, if you invest $1,000 in a stock and when you sell that stock you discover that the stock's share price has declined in value, you have lost money if you sell it at that time;

☒ **Inflation Risk** is the risk that your investment returns do not keep up with the rate of inflation. For example, if you invest in a Certificate of Deposit or bond issue that pays 2.9%, and inflation during the same period is 3.2%, you are losing purchasing power – your money is worth less (in the future);

☒ **Foreign-exchange Risk** is a result of a negative exchange rate between U.S. currency and the non–U.S. currency to which the investment is exposed;

☒ **Interest-rate Risk** is risk that is associated with the prevailing interest rates. Interest-rate risk occurs when an investment's value changes because there is a shift in the 'absolute level' of interest rates; or a change in the spread between two rates; or the shape of the yield curve varies; or there is a change in any other interest rate relationship. Your investment return will be affected, either positively or negatively as rates fluctuate;

☒ **Liquidity Risk** is the danger that you will need to sell, or liquidate, an investment at an unfavorable time. For example, if you need to pay for something and your money is 'invested,' and you do not have 'ready cash' available; you probably will need to sell an investment holding to satisfy your debt. If the investment product that you own is 'depressed,' or is valued at less than you originally paid for the product, you have incurred liquidity risk (owning Real Estate is a good example of Liquidity Risk **because it could take a while to sell the real estate and get cash);**

☒ **Credit Risk** occurs when the companies with which you hold bonds cannot make interest or principal payments. If this happens, you lose money because you will not be paid your interest payments. Loss of interest affects your investment performance/gains;

☒ **Reinvestment Risk** can occur when you sell an investment that produces a specific income stream and then find that cannot be replaced due to the current market conditions;

☒ **Market Risk** is produced because of the economic and political impact upon your investments. When there is a shift in the economy or political arena that affects the sector or industry in which you have invested, market risk occurs;

☒ **Call Risk** is the risk that the maturity of your investment will be accelerated, meaning your original investment (principal) is returned to you, and then you may not be able to reinvest that same principal at the same or a higher rate as you enjoyed with your original investment;

☒ **Volatility Risk** is inclusive of any of the other types of risk. When risk occurs, volatility results. (74)

For example, in 2008 The U.S. stock market investors experienced **Market Risk** because of the economic and political impact. There was a shift in the economy in the financial arena that affected not only the financial sectors but impacted the market as a whole.

(https://www.investopedia.com/terms/r/risk.asp; https://www.getsmarteraboutmoney.ca/invest/investing-basics/understanding-risk/types-of-investment-risk/)

Which type of investment risk do you view as the most risk important to YOU? WHY?

_____

_____

Let's take a minute to describe a few examples of the various risk associated with investment products.

Product	Types of Risk
CDs	Inflation/ Liquidity
Callable Municipal Bond	Reinvestment/ Inflation/ Liquidity
International Stock	Market/ Foreign Exchange/ Liquidity
Stocks	In some cases most risk categories

Understanding the product types, volatility, and the risk associated with each, is a good place to start. But something else to keep in mind... just because a particular investment has done well in the past does not mean that the performance of that investment will repeat its performance in the future. Looking at history is a good place for us to start. We might first consider the historical trends in order to give us some perspective, or indication, of the potential of what could occur in the future.

Past Performance Does Not Guarantee Future Results

The Macrotrends® *"Dow Jones – DJIA – 100 Year Historical Chart,"* pictured below indicates "the current price of the Dow Jones Industrial Average® as of October 22, 2019 as 26,788.10." (Chart courtesy of StockCharts.com, 68)

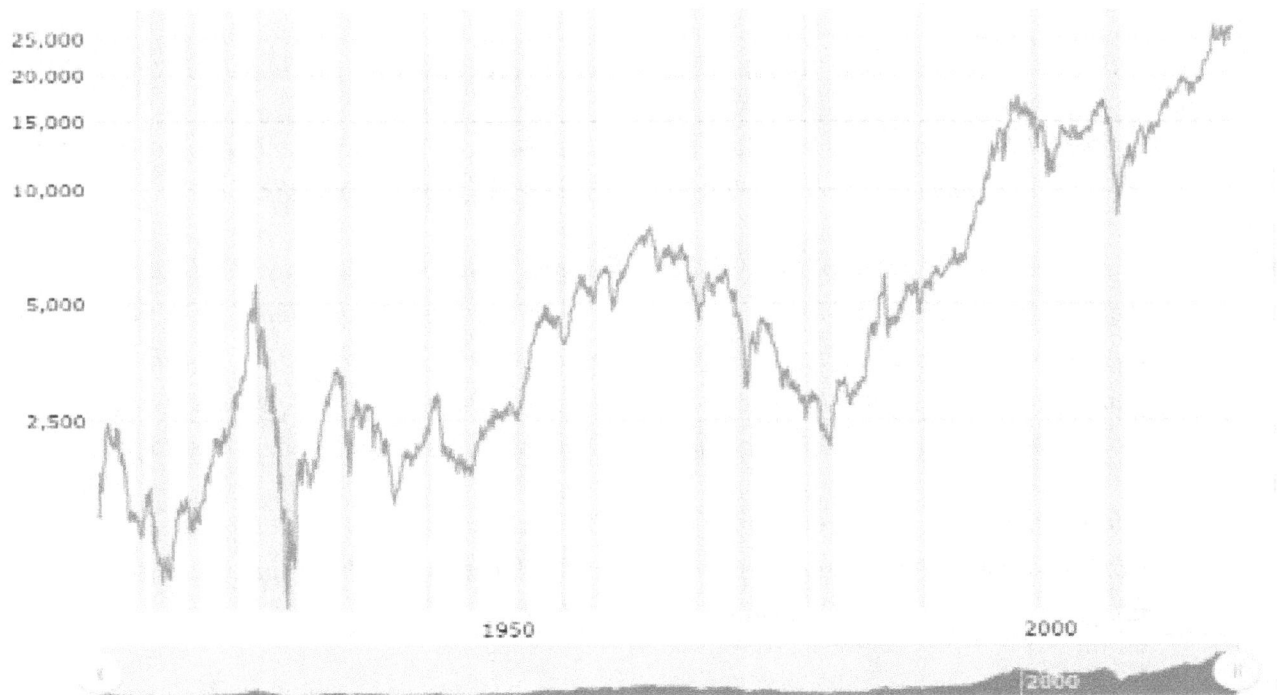

Wow, on the surface it looks like purchasing 'stocks' is what you would naturally want to do with your money. But if you take a moment and step back you also see that during those years the Dow Jones Industrial Average® had some fairly traumatic declines. When we review the S&P 500® Index... we find that this Index posted positive calendar returns 74% of the time, and negative S&P 500® market returns were reported 26% of the time. Don't forget how painful the down-markets can be. Expecting volatility is essential as an investor (68), read on for historical proof.

Where is the Bear?

In a moment we will move on to a discussion of investment products, but first let's review a little more about the ups and down of the stock market itself. Let's start with the down markets, or "Bear Markets." **A Bear Market is generally defined as a stock market decline of 20% or more from peak to trough.** Not all of the experts agree on the number of bear markets we have historically experienced. Here are what some sources report:

☒ *Since the last day of 1946 the S&P 500® has had 8 Bear Markets through 11/6//2014. (68)*

☒ *"For those old enough to remember, in the 1970's the market dropped 48% over 19 months and in the 1930's dropped 86% over 39 months. The most recent U.S. bear market occurred in 2007-2009 when the stock market dropped 57% over 17 months. (69)*

☒ *Declines of -20% or more have occurred about once every 3 ½ years since 1900 (through June of 2009). (70)*

☒ *CBSNEWS® 12/26/2018, "What's a bear market, and how long might it last?" reveals...*

   o *"On average, bear markets have lasted 14 months in the period since World War II, while market corrections have lasted an average of five months." (71)*

☒ *A 2003 Leuthold Group LLC Study presents: "The study traces 22 bear market lows over the past 100 years in the US, with a bear market being defined as a peak to trough decline in the market averages of 20 percent or more. The study points out that the average peak to trough bear market decline over the last 100 years is 37 percent, with the median decline being 34 percent. Eight of the 22 bear markets declined by more than 45 percent." (71)*

☒ *Dana Anspach, 1/5/2020, reports in 'the balance®.com') article: "U.S. Stock Bear Markets and Their Subsequent Recoveries:" (https://www.thebalance.com/u-s-stock-bear-markets-and-their-subsequent-recoveries-2388520)*

   o *"Bear markets are defined as periods when the stock market declines by 20% or more from the highest point to its subsequent lowest point. From 1900–2014, there were 32 bear markets. Statistically, they occur about once every 3.5 years and last an average of 367 days.*

   o *Despite the occurrences of bear markets, markets typically have been up more than they have been down throughout history. From 1950 through 2018, for example, the S&P 500 was on 53.7% of days and down 46.3% of days, and the number of up days exceeded the number of down days in every decade (1)."*

Beyond the number of pullbacks that the market has experienced, it suffices to say that no one has been able to predict when the market will experience a decline… or inversely, when the market will rebound.

American Funds® is a mutual fund company which offers investment choices. The company provides various commentaries for investors and advisors to consider. One such commentary, "What past market declines can teach us," elaborates:

> o   *"No one can predict consistently when market declines will happen.*
>
> -   *It's easy to look back today and say with hindsight that the stock market was overvalued at a particular time and was due for a decline. But no one has been able to accurately predict market declines on a consistent basis. In January 1973, a New York Times® poll of 8 market authorities predicted that the market would "move somewhat higher" in the future. The Dow Industrials proceeded to decline 45% over the next 23 months. Then, although almost no one predicted it, the Dow rose 38% in 1975." (72)*

Additionally, Austyn Whittenburg, CFP®, CBEC®, August 9/2019, presents a chart in his article: *"What Should You Do About Market Volatility?"*

A History of Declines (1949 - December 2018)

Type of Decline	Average Frequency[1]	Average Length[2]	Last Occurrence[3]
-5% or more	About 3 times a year	44 days	December 2018
-10% or more	About once a year	114 days	December 2018
-15% or more	About once every 4 years	270 days	December 2018
-20% or more	About once every 7 years	431 days	December 2018

Source: RIMES, Standard & Poor's.
[1] Assumes 50% recovery rate of lost value.
[2] Measures market high to market low.
[3] The average frequency and average length rows exclude the most recent decline in December 2018 because the 50% recovery of lost value occurred after 12/31/18.

https://www.whittenburgwealth.com/blog/what-should-you-do-about-market-volatility

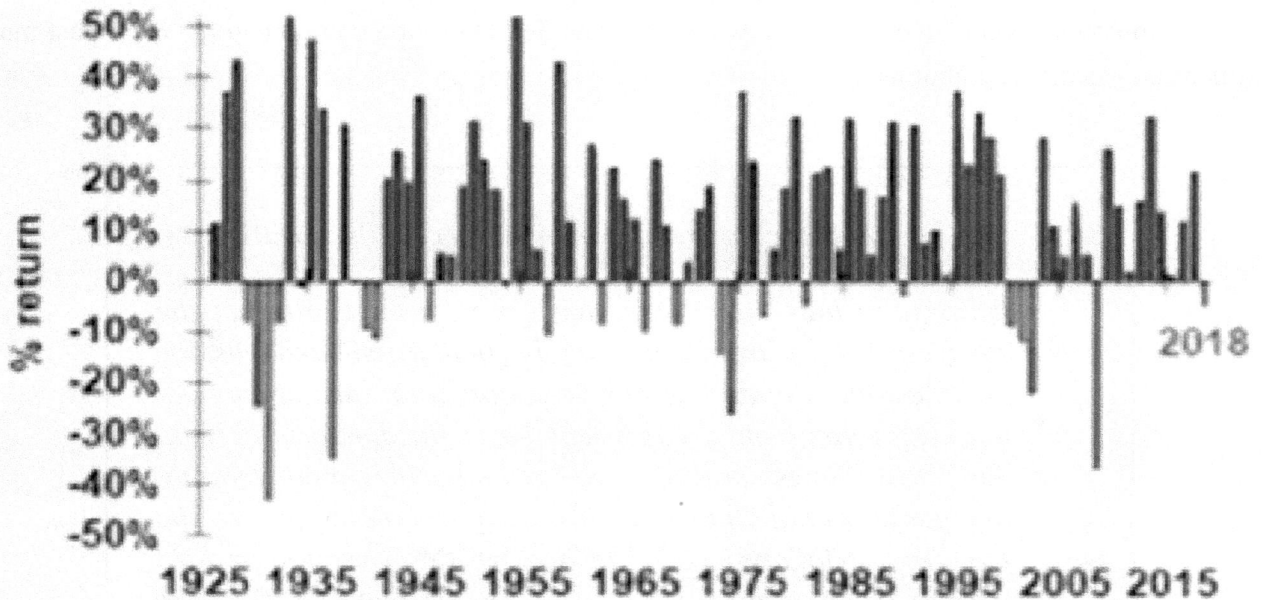

Stock market total returns, 1926-2018

DR. BILL CONERLY BASED ON DATA FROM STANDARD AND POOR'S
https://seekingalpha.com/article/4231716-stock-market-in-2019-last-years-decline-not-good-forecast

IN THE CHART ABOVE CAN YOU DECIPHER WHICH YEARS WERE BULL AND WHICH YEARS WERE BEAR MARKETS?

I Like The Bull

> *"The current bull market that started in March 2009 is the longest bull market in history. It topped the bull market of the 1990s that lasted 113 months (10/10/2019)."*
>
> *https://www.investopedia.com/market-milestones-as-the-bull-market-turns-10-4588903*

As we also have seen, historically the market also has had periods of gains. When the market is experiencing an 'upward trend,' investors are generally happy. A Bull Market is a market with an upswing in momentum: "Past performance does not guarantee future results, but since 1926 [through 2010], 'the good news is that for every two years that the market has lost ground, there have been three years with returns of 18% or more — a 3:2 ratio of great years to lousy ones!" (68) I am not going to provide lots of information regarding length and intensity of the bull markets. It is enough to say that if you look back a few pages, the overall performance of the stock market indicates that in the past we have had more positive inertia than negative. I would only caution that going forward; it might be wise to temper your expectations. It also is wise to manage expectations, so "expect less, and be pleased if your expectations are exceeded."

Life

Keeping the market down-turns in perspective is NOT easy. When you have a portfolio that holds investment products that fluctuate with the state of the market, and a dramatic decline occurs — reach out to your Financial Advisor for information and perspective.

While this information about the Bear Market can be down-right scary, it is important to be realistic about the possibilities of market decline, as history has demonstrated time, and time, again.

Don't be surprised by a market downturn… EXPECT IT!

Analysts, like Michael Markowski, ("*China's Tariffs on US Products is 19th Nail in Secular Bull's Coffin*") are constantly looking at economic factors in an effort to predict market behavior. As Mr. Markowski's chart below suggests, and as reported earlier, there have been 8 Bear Markets since 1802. Business cycles and policitical forces constantly are at play to influence how the market reacts.

Secular Bear and Bull Markets for period 1802-2018

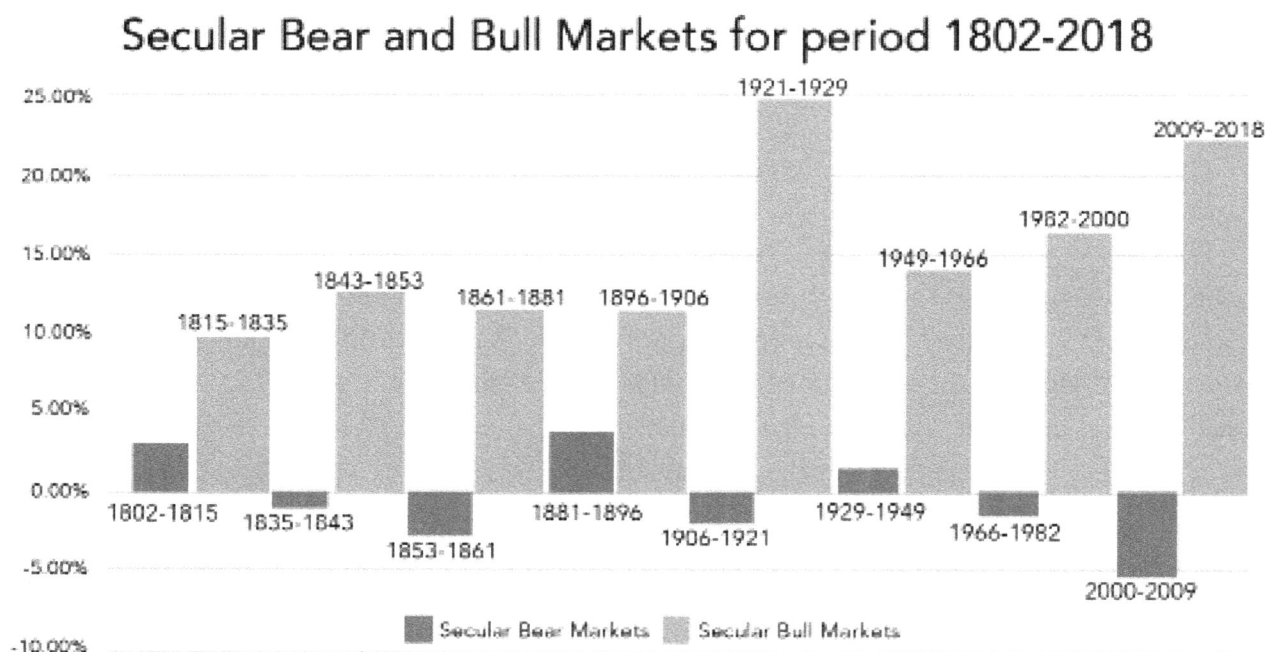

https://bullsnbears.com/2018/04/05/chinas-tariffs-on-us-products-is-10th-nail-in-secular-bulls-coffin/

As reported, analysts watch a variety of economic indicators in an effort to understand the market behaviors. One such indicator is where the economy/market is in relation to the '*Business Cycle.*' Understanding the Economic and Business Cycles can help any investor to make informed decisions. For example, in Kent Thune's Article, "*The Best Sector for Stages in Economic Cycle,*" (6/17/2021), Mr. Thune offers this commentary:

- "A new bear market for stocks can begin even as the economy grows, although at a very slow pace. This could be a good time to start putting more of your dollars back into stocks before the Federal Reserve announces that a recession has begun." (https://www.thebalance.com, 66)

Information should be gathered from a variety and sources, and investors might then discuss the data in detail with their Financial Advisor.

You might consider Mr. Buffett's words of advice:

> *I never attempt to make money on the stock market. I buy on the assumption that they could close the market the next day and not reopen it for five years.* " *(73)*
>
> Warren Buffet

Provide a brief comparison of the Bear and Bull Markets.

_____

_____

So, if we consider that a Bull Market is, "A prolonged period in which investment prices rise faster than their historical average. [And that] bull markets can happen as a result of an economic recovery, an economic boom, or investor psychology…." (66), we can be watching for economic and psychological indicators that might set the stage for a bull market. Before the 2019 Bull Market, "The longest and most famous bull market is the one that began in the early 1990s in which the U.S. equity markets grew at their fastest pace ever, opposite of bear market." (66) We should remember that we can pretty much count on two things:

1. the market going up (Bull) and then,

2. the market going down (Bear)…

when each event will happen is anyone's guess.

Time Horizon

As we have noted before, investment products are characteristically utilized when you have a longer **time horizon,** and you are expecting to capture a higher rate of return than a 'fixed' product may offer you. Your time horizon measures **the length of time you will be invested.** This means the length of time, in years, that you plan to leave your money invested, with no plans to withdraw the money from your account. Articulating your time horizon will be an important step in helping you and your financial advisor determine appropriate investment products for you.

Now let's consider the investment products themselves.

A Few Investment Products To Consider

People are becoming much more interested in the day-to-day mechanics of investing. Individuals are taking not only an interest in the investment products; they are also taking control of their investment accounts. The first step in this process is education. Through various reports individuals learn about the investment and banking product management process, the governance of those products, and the relationships between the oversight agencies. We are aware that those agencies continue to be under constant scrutiny. Americans deserve transparency regarding how their money and investments are being managed and safeguarded. It all starts with understanding the various choices of investment products.

How Investment Products Are Labeled

There are many, investment and banking products, and each are purchased/offered because they have different objectives. Understand the objectives of each of the investment products that you choose, the risks associated with each, fees related with each investment product, and the penalties that may be assessed if you initiate an 'early withdrawal' or sale of a product. Work with a trusted advisor to help you determine which investment products meet your goals, risk tolerance, and time horizon. Here are the investment products we will review in this section:

- ☒ **"Cash Equivalents"**

  - ○ Checking/Savings Accounts

  - ○ Money Market

  - ○ Certificates of Deposit

- ☒ **Bonds**

  - ○ U.S. Treasuries

  - ○ Municipal Bonds

  - ○ Government-sponsored Bonds

  - ○ Corporate Bonds

  - ○ International Bonds

☒   **Mutual Funds**

☒   **Stocks**

We will review annuities in our next section. Annuities are also investment products, but as you will learn later, they are somewhat unique.

Have you had experience with any of these investment products? If so, which ones?

_____

_____

FIXED RATE PRODUCTS

Typical investment products have inherent 'risk' because they generally do not offer a 'guaranteed' rate of return, nor do they guarantee the return of your investment money (your principal). Conversely, some products which are employed for 'saving' do offer a stated, 'fixed' rate of return, along with the return of your principal. Let's begin with a couple of examples of fixed rate investment products.

A fixed investment product can be employed for both 'saving' and 'investing.' Certificates of Deposits (CDs) and EE Bonds are two fixed rate products. When you purchase a CD FROM AN FDIC INSURED FINANCIAL INSTITUTION, you know what your expected interest rate, or 'return' on your investment is, and you also know the stated 'maturity' date' or 'call' date. The maturity date notes when you will get your principal (the money you originally invested) returned to you. The risk is lower because, <u>unless you purchase a CD that is over the FDIC insured limits</u> (discussed later in the next chapter), the U.S. government guarantees the return of your principal, along with the declared interest.

Life

For example:

Let's suppose that you purchase a $ 10,000 CD, with an interest rate of 1.3%, maturing in 1 year. The U.S. government guarantees* that you will get your **principal ($10,000) and the 1.3%** **interest** *on your money.... on the day it* **matures (in the event that the FDIC insurance pays accrued interest, the interest will be pro-rated).**

One additional note about a maturing CD: If you do not direct the bank or financial institution to do otherwise, many CDs may 'rollover.' This means the money will be automatically re-invested in another CD after the maturity date arrives. Typically, the bank will notify you that you have a certain number of days to advise them that you do NOT want your money to reinvest for another time period. If you don't let the financial institution know otherwise, the CD will usually reinvest for another term.

*Financial Institution must be FDIC insured.

While we are on the subject of CDs, there are a couple of different features to look for when you consider purchasing a CD. Many of these features also apply to certain types of bonds. Here are some areas to research if you are considering the purchase of a CD:

- Is the CD '**non-callable**?'

- Is the CD '**callable**?'

- Does the CD have a '**step-up**' feature?

Review these terms:

☒ A **non-callable CD** cannot be 'called away' or forced to mature early. The CD will pay interest as originally stated.

☒ A **callable CD** can be 'called away,' by the financial institution. When the CD is called away it matures, and your principal is returned to you early. You lose future interest payments.

☒ **A step-up CD** will have 'laddered' interest rates… the interest rates for a step-up CD will change according to a pre-determined schedule. Step-up CDs pay different interest rates for different years.

Here is an example of a 'step-up' CD:

Years	Interest Percent Paid
1-2	1.5 %
3-4	2.0 %
5-6	2.5 %

When you consider a CD, be sure to ask about the features.

Some fixed products may have risk. But, generally the risk of a fixed investment product is *lower* than a **non-guaranteed-rate-of-return** investment product. However, no blanket statement will apply to every situation or product.

So, do *investors* ever choose fixed products? Of course, they do. You will see that a certain percentage of 'fixed'- return rate products may be appropriate for even the most aggressive investor. But, for the purpose of explaining how saving is different from investing, we will focus on more traditional **'investment strategies'** and **investment products** that do not necessarily offer a 'fixed rate' of return. (As you will see, even bonds can fall into this category.)

For our purposes we will stick to some of the more common, investment product choices. After reading here about some of the traditional investment products, if you are interested in broadening your *investment product* horizon, seek out a guide about 'investing' on your own, then find an advisor to work with.

Equities or Stocks?

Often individuals interchange these terms, **'equities'** and **'stocks.'** But, 'equities' is a general term that can describe a variety of investment choices. For instance, the term 'equities' can refer to an **individual stock, a basket of stocks** (called Equity Mutual Funds), **a real estate investment trust, oil royalties,** etc. For the purpose of our discussion: equities will be classified as an individual stock.

Stocks

When you think of investing in the stock market, I bet you think of buying 'stocks.' But do you know what stocks are?

> *Common Stocks* are actual ownership stakes, or ownership shares of a company.
>
> *Preferred Stocks* are ownership in a public company and have no voting rights; generally issued with a stated dividend that is paid prior to dividend payment to common stockholders.
>
> https://www.investopedia.com/ask/answers/difference-between-preferred-stock-and-common-stock/

For example, if you buy 10 shares of ZAM Company, you own a small part of the ZAM Company. You are now a small stake holder in the profits and losses of the company.

If you choose to invest in a single company, be sure you gather as much information as you can prior to making your stock choice. Your financial advisor can provide research on a company to assist you in making your selection decision.

More about stocks...

a. Typically, investors purchase several shares of a company's stock, not just one or two shares. One reason? When you purchase or sell stocks you may be charged a 'commission,' or fee for handling the transaction. Therefore, it is generally cost prohibitive to purchase or sell a very small quantity of stock.

b. When you are a stock owner you have a vested interest in how the company is doing financially. You care about how the company is managed, especially the impact of the actions taken by management on the profit and loss of the company. It will be important for you to watch the share price go up or down in an effort to understand where the share price is moving... Is your stock appreciating, or growing, in value? Or, is the company performing poorly? ... and therefore, the stock's value is declining.

c. If you are a long-term investor you might hold the same stock shares for a long, long, time. We had clients that have had held a specific stock for 20 or more years and they have no plans to sell the stock. On the other hand, you might decide that the financial information upon which you made your stock selection has changed, so you might sell your shares. Or, maybe you just want to take your profits and do something else with your money. Watching the analyst stock research reports can be very helpful in watching your stock positions.

d. Some stocks yield returns in the form of 'dividends.'

e. In general, stocks can be volatile.

f. Stocks typically are more appropriate for longer-term investing.

g. Generally, stocks can be considered liquid, trades settle in an average of 2-4 days (there are some exceptions).

"In an incredible feat for a pizza company, Domino's share price growth has outperformed all of the world's largest tech companies so far this decade. An investment in Domino's at the start of 2010 has grown by more than 2,000% to date, leaving the likes of Amazon, Google, Facebook, and Apple in the dust."

"Domino's stock has outperformed Google, Facebook, Apple, and Amazon this decade" (7/18/18)*

Domino's stock price growth vs. Big Tech

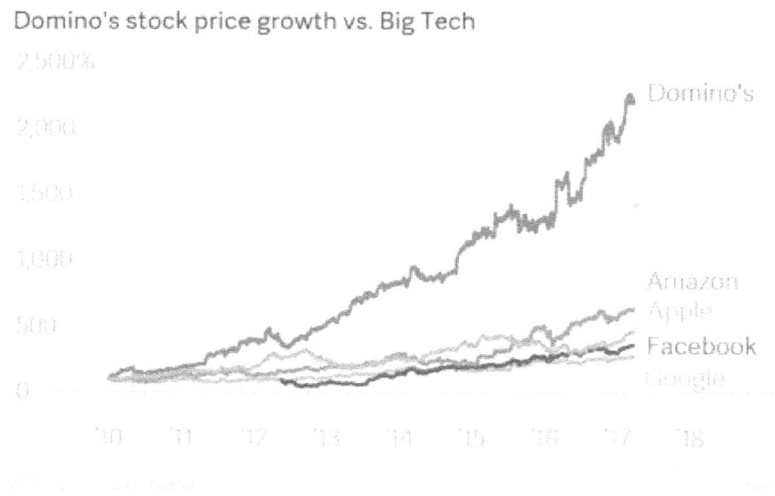

Life

March 22, 2017 an article by Chase Purdy, *"Domino's stock has out-performed Google, Facebook, Apple, and Amazon this decade,"* was featured in QUARTZ®. *The article provided the chart on the previous page which illustrated/'show-cased' Domino's Pizza® stock's performance this decade.*

I don't know anyone who actually bought any of these stocks and kept them for the years indicated (exact dates) ... it has been my experience that investors tend to sell their 'winners' too soon. Patience is hard to come by when uncertainty is knocking at your door.

Remember, past performance does not predict future earnings.

*https://qz.com/938620/dominos-dpz-stock-has-outperformed-google-goog-facebook-fb-apple-aapland-amazon-amzn-this-decade/   ATLAS Data Fact Sheet

Some stocks enjoy exuberant growth - Like Domino's Pizza® stock which rose + 2000% between 1/1/2010 and 7/18/18 (https://www. investopedia.com/news/how-domino-stock-has-risen-over-2000-2010-dpzaaplgoog/); and other Stocks - such as Sears Holdings® did not fare well, dropping 55% in 2016, as reported by Timothy Green (1/11/2017, https://www.fool.com/investing/2017/01/11/why-shares-of-sears-holdings-crashed-55-in-2016.aspx).

Mutual Funds

Many investors choose not to buy individual stocks but may invest instead in a **'basket' of stocks,** or **'basket' of bonds,** found inside a Mutual Fund. In contrast to a single stock or bond, one share of a Mutual Fund has a variety of stocks and/or bonds positions/holdings.

When you purchase a share of a **mutual fund you buy an undivided interest in the mutual fund portfolio, and you then own a percentage of the group of individual holdings in the mutual fund.** When you are in the possession of a mutual fund share, you own a small piece of several companies and/ or debt of several companies.

For the sake of our discussion we will focus on the *Open-ended Mutual Funds*. ***Open-ended* mutual fund shares do not have restrictions on the number of shares that are issued, and the shares can be redeemed at any time.** I like to think of the open-ended mutual fund as 'user-friendly;' they are easy to buy and sell…. If you own an open-end mutual fund, there is a ready market for you to sell your fund(s) when you are ready to do so. Open-ended mutual funds are also typically traded like stocks on some market exchanges. Conversely, a **closed-end mutual fund is issued by a publicly traded** *investment company.* **The investment company only issues a finite number of shares, enough to raise a pre-determined amount of capital. The shares are offered as an** *initial public offering* **(IPO). The closed-end mutual fund is then created, listed and traded like a stock on an exchange as well.**

Some ***mutual fund*** data to consider:

a.   You do NOT direct the selection of companies or products to be included in the mutual fund you choose to purchase. If you choose to purchase a mutual fund, **you will allow the mutual fund manager to make the individual stock, bond and investment selections to be held in the mutual fund.** In other words, you allow the fund manager 'discretion' to make decisions on your behalf.

In short, experienced mutual fund managers have discretion to buy and sell individual stocks, individual bonds, or other investment selections within a single fund; meaning they do not have to ask you for your permission to make a product change in the fund.

b.   If you are not an experienced investor, mutual funds may offer you an opportunity to access professional management/managers at a lower cost than hiring your own investment manager. Using a mutual fund manager to manage your account in this manner can prove to be invaluable.

c.   When you purchase shares of the mutual funds you get a predetermined ratio, or percentage, of the individual holdings within the mutual fund.

d.   A mutual fund provides you instant diversification because you are not purchasing just one stock or bond. For example; one share of the *BlackRock® Global Allocation Fund* at one time provided ownership of a percentage of about 500 different stocks and fixed-income products. Of course, these numbers change at the discretion of the mutual fund manager.

e.   The amount of money you want to invest sometimes drives the investment product decision. If you have a smaller amount to invest, you may want to start with purchasing mutual funds because you will be able to spread your risk with immediate diversification through the ownership of percentages in many stocks and/or bonds contained within one mutual fund.

f.   Open-ended mutual funds are fairly 'liquid,' if you want to sell and convert your mutual fund to cash it takes an average of 2-4 days.

g.   As mentioned, mutual funds are managed by a team of individuals, typically lead by one manager. The Manager has a set of guidelines, as well as the *pre-determined stated fund objective*s, to direct the selection of investment products that will be placed in the mutual fund. Both the financial advisor and the client rely on the manager to adhere to the mutual fund's stated objectives.

h.   Buying and selling a mutual fund may, or may not, cause you to incur direct or indirect costs; among other fees, administration and sales charges may apply.

i.   Mutual funds have share class options which can affect performance returns. (We will discuss this topic in detail later in this section.)

j.   Each fund is assigned a 'ticker' that identifies the fund and allows the investor to look up the fund on-line, on the fund website, or in some published periodicals.

k.   Mutual Funds are offered by Fund Families. Fund families may have several types of mutual funds; the funds hold the money in each mutual fund's separate account, invest the money as per the prospectus, and the accounts are monitored by the Security Exchange Commissions (SEC).

Haven't I Heard About These Mutual Funds Before?

Some investors are largely familiar with mutual funds if they are employed by a company that offers some type of retirement plan that provides for deferred tax savings. Those retirement plans commonly have a selection of mutual funds, or separately managed account funds, from which investors can choose. The employee makes his or her own fund choices, selecting the funds from a list offered in the plan.

There are several reports available to help you make prudent mutual fund choices. Among other reports, when you are considering which mutual fund to acquire, a financial advisor can provide performance and fund information in the form of: a) **independent research ratings** and, b) **a prospectus**. You can also call the fund family directly and get a prospectus and fact sheet. There is also a myriad of research sources for investors to access so they can learn about specific investment products. One such research source is https://www.Morningstar.com. The data provided offers critical information for you and your financial advisor to review and analyze before you make a purchase. *One of the most important features of the prospectus is the stated objective of the fund, historical information, fees, etc. The prospectus may be difficult to understand, ask an advisor for assistance.* It is important to understand the mutual funds features; we will review a few of the characteristics of mutual funds here.

Pricing

One comment here about how mutual funds are priced. You will see **NAV, or Net Asset Value**, utilized to describe the price of one share of a mutual fund. https://www.investopedia.com/terms/n/nav.asp notes that the per-share dollar amount of the fund is calculated by dividing the total value of all the securities, or holdings, in its portfolio, less any liabilities, by the number of fund shares outstanding (as illustrated below). 'The NAV per share is computed once a day based on the closing market prices of the securities in the fund's portfolio. Mutual fund managers buy and sell orders are processed at the end of the day.'

NAV = (Assets - Liabilities) / Total number of outstanding shares

Give Me Style And Size

For sake of discussion, we will focus on open-ended mutual funds. Mutual funds are sorted on various criteria, such as: **asset classes**, or '**styles,**' '**size,**' and '**sector**' categories. You will hear the terms '**size and style**' when you evaluate mutual funds. Independent research agencies, like *Morningstar*® and *Lipper Group*®, sort funds into **size and style** categories. These published reports provide valuable information regarding each fund. These reports rate and rank funds, identify historical performance information, identify holdings, sales charges, alpha and beta, and standard deviation, etc. This information provides data to help you to evaluate the mutual funds. I offer an explanation of the Lipper® rankings:

According to Lipper®:

"Lipper® *Leader ratings are derived from highly sophisticated formulas that analyze funds against clearly defined criteria. Funds are compared to similar funds, and only those that truly stand out are awarded Lipper*® *Leader status.*

Funds are ranked against their peers on each of four measures: Total Return, Consistent Return, Preservation, and Expense. A fifth measure, Tax Efficiency, applies in the United States. Scores are subject to change every month and are calculated for the following periods: 3-year, 5-year, 10-year, and overall. The overall calculation is based on an equal-weighted average of percentile ranks for each measure over 3-year, 5-year, and 10-year periods (if applicable).

For each measure, the highest 20% of funds in each peer group are named Lipper® *Leaders. The next 20% receive a rating of 2; the middle 20% are rated 3; the next 20% are rated 4, and the lowest 20% are rated 5." (75)*

Utilizing *Morningstar*®, *Lipper*®, reports, as well as other sources helps you to group 'like' funds for comparison on different levels. Grouping funds according to their 'size and style' is a good place to start. Why is this important? These reports help you and your advisor evaluate and select funds.

Life

When working with individuals that are interested in investing in some mutual funds, I utilized a Morningstar® or Lipper® report, with the prospectus, to help me educate the client regarding each fund.

These types of reports allow you to compare mutual funds more easily because each report illustrates the fund information based on the same criteria. What this means is:

You can compare 'like' funds against each other on a variety of benchmark measures. For example, you might review two reports on Large Cap Value funds to compare:

- Alpha: A measurement of investment product gain that is not credited to the market. Sometimes this measure is attributed to the fund management... i.e. if the fund does better or worse than its' index, did the management team contribute to this result? A higher number is good.

- Beta: A measure of a specific mutual fund's comparative volatility verses a specific market index. For example, if the Beta is more than 1.0, then the fund is more volatile than the market. A number less than 1.0 means the fund is lessvolatile than the index.

- Standard Deviation: A measure of the investment's historical volatility. A measure of the divergence of returns from their average. (Higher numbers indicate a higher volatility of the fund.)

- Performance: One/three/five- and 10-year gains or losses for each fund. Compare the fund performance against the performance of a couple of indexes.

Reviewing these reports is a good approach to becoming familiar with your investments and will help you learn about the fund that you are considering.

Size

The 'size' criterion is just that… the fund is sorted according to the size of the companies that the mutual fund holds. The size of companies is one determining factor that helps establish what the mutual fund manager may buy. The size of the company is also expressed as 'market capitalization.' **Market capitalization** refers to the **size of the company as expressed in dollars. Capitalization is calculated by multiplying a company's outstanding shares by the current market price of one share.** Here are a couple of 'size' categories:

- In a **Large Cap fund** the manager will characteristically include large companies with +$10 Billion capitalization;

- **Mid-Cap funds** may hold stocks of companies that have between $2 Billion and $10 Billion capitalization; and

- **Small-Cap funds** hold companies whose capitalization is less than $ 2 Billion. (76)

Style: Growth or Value?

Sometimes the mutual fund holds positions that are a specific investment style or size, and sometimes they hold multiples of a variety of size/styles and positions. For example, one mutual fund might hold only *Municipal Bonds*, or another mutual fund might hold only *Large Cap Growth* stocks.

Let's spend a moment talking about two styles: **growth** and **value**. There is not just one definition of either of these two terms. While we can agree that there is no hard and fast definition of growth and value stocks, most investors agree on some general criteria that defines these two terms. (77) Read on…

Growth

When I explain the difference between a 'growth' or 'value' stock I put it in these simple terms:

- A **growth stock** is a stock that the analysts, after careful review of the financials of a company, determines that it has a history of 'growing' and is likely to continue to grow.

Here are some of the characteristics of **growth stocks**, as presented by *https://www.investopedia.com/articles/professionals/072415/value-or-growth-stocks-which-best.asp* and other sources:

- Overall proven **track record of growth** – about + 10 % for smaller companies, and about + 5 % for larger companies within the past 5 years;

- A strong ROE (**Return on Equity**). The ROE identifies **how efficiently the company's assets are being employed to produce company earnings.** To calculate ROE – divide the Net Income by the Book Value of the company. A healthy ROE will fall between the 13%-15%; (78)

- A higher EPS (**Earnings Per Share**). The EPS is calculated by **dividing the net earnings by outstanding shares.** The higher the number, the more earnings per share have been generated. A higher EPS may be another indication that the company's management is doing a good job of controlling costs and translating sales into earnings. (79)

Life

So, for example, if XYZ stock is selling @ $ 7.00 a share, but the analysts forecast a growth in the share price to $ 8.25 a share in the near future, then the stock may be placed in the 'growth' category.

Value

Conversely, a **value stock** may be perceived as:

- **Undervalued:** analysts believe the **P&L (Profit and Loss)** for the company suggests a higher per share price than the stock is currently selling for;

- Lower P/E (**Price to Earnings**). P/E is calculated by **dividing the share price by the company's earnings.** The P/E indicates what the market is willing to pay for the company's earnings. A lower P/E may indicate that the company's stock is a 'sleeper' and has been overlooked (77);

- The PEG (**Projected Earnings Growth**) is another criterion to consider for value or growth stocks. The PEG is calculated by **dividing the P/E by the projected growth in earnings**. "The lower the number, the less you pay for each unit of future earnings growth." (80) Therefore, a lower PEG number may indicate a value stock.

Life

For example, if the ABC stock is selling @ $ 3.50 a share today, but the analysts suggest that the financials dictate that the stock is potentially worth $5.00 a share TODAY, the stock may be a 'value' stock. It's like the stock is on sale.

Warren Buffett, one of the most successful and now famous investors in the U.S., suggests:

> *"Price is what you pay. Value is what you get."*
>
> Warren Buffett

Sector Funds

A few words about **sector funds**… Arranging funds or investment choices into sector categories provides you with an easy way to identify a fund or stock objective. Like anything else, these groupings put companies and stocks together that are in the same industries, have similar characteristics, etc. Here is a chart that helps to illustrate my point:

Consumer Goods Cyclical	Energy	Transportation	Industrial
Automotive	Oil	Airlines	Factory Equipment
Manufacturing Clothing	Natural Gas	Railroads	Heavy Construction
Home Construction	Exploration Equipment	Trucking	Heavy Machinery
Hotels	Power Plants	Ocean Shipping	Waste Management
Restaurants	**Financial**	Airfreight Services	Containers and Packaging
Consumer Goods Non-Cyclical	Banks	**Utilities**	
Cosmetics & Personal Care	Insurance	Electrical	
Food	Securities Brokers	Telephone	
Medical supplies and Pharmaceuticals	**Technology**	Water	
Healthcare providers	**Communications**	Natural Gas Delivery	
Tobacco	Office Equipment		
Household products	Computers		
	Semi-conductors		
	Software		

Learning about the sector that your investment choice may fall into will provide you with another dimension for you to research and learn about. Understand how the characteristics of your sectors behave in all types of markets, and in the economic cycle.

More About Mutual Funds

> *"Our favorite holding period is forever."*
>
> Warren Buffett

What's All The Fuss About Share Class?

When examining the characteristics of a mutual fund, I mentioned that the open-ended mutual fund is 'fairly liquid.' I will now qualify that statement. **Mutual funds have share classes.** Each share class has different characteristics. **One of the characteristics of a share class is that it may have a** *'surrender,'* *or holding,* **schedule. This schedule identifies how long you must hold the mutual fund to avoid a** *surrender penalty.* **The penalty is tied to the timing of your withdrawal, or sale, of the mutual fund.** Different share classes have distinctive holding periods. As the investor, with the help of your financial advisor, you will designate which mutual fund share class you will purchase. To help you make the share class decision, one criterion you should consider is the length of your 'investment time horizon.' Remember, your 'investment horizon' is the length of time you plan to hold the fund. Why is your time horizon important? Because some share classes have restrictions on selling a mutual fund before a particular time period has passed, or you may incur a 'surrender penalty.' So, if you decide to sell your mutual fund prior to the stated 'surrender' time period, you may be assessed a penalty (fee). Avoid penalty costs if you can. You do not want to pay any surrender costs because of poor planning…. with proper planning you may avoid the penalty fees.

This topic is better illustrated through an explanation of the **most familiar share classes**, *A share*, *B share,* and *C share.* Of course, there are other classes, like: *I shares,* **Exchange Traded Funds (ETF s), R shares,** etc. that also vary in characteristics as well.

  o **A Share** mutual funds generally require up-front fees for a purchase.* The up-front fees are referred to as 'front-end-loads.' This means that you will pay a fee to purchase the fund when you invest (up-front). Typically, internal sales and 12b-1 fees are lower than some of the other share classes. Sometimes load fees can be reduced or eliminated for larger dollar purchases or purchases within a 'managed account.'

*'Breakpoint' purchases may waive these up-front fees.

- **B Share** mutual funds do not charge an up-front fee, however they have a 'back-end-load,' or 'deferred sales charge.' These types of fees are charged to the investor if the fund is sold before a **pre-determined diminishing-fee schedule. These back-end load fees are referred to as Contingent Deferred Sales Charge (CDSC).**

For example, a B Share might charge a fee of 5% in the first year, 4% in the second year, 3% in the third year, and so on if the fund is sold in the first 5 years. After the investor has held the fund for the length of the CDSC, in this case 5 years, then the -back-end- fees should no longer apply and the investor will not be charged a penalty to sell the fund. Internal sales and 12b-1 fees are usually higher than some other share classes of mutual funds.

- Typically, **C Share** mutual funds do not charge either an up-front or a back-end- load fee if the investor holds the fund for 1 year. If the fund is sold within the first year the investor generally pays a 1% CDSC surrender charge. Internal sales and 12b-1 fees can be higher than other share classes of mutual funds. (https://www.finra.org/investors/alerts/understanding-mutual-fund-classes)

Note: Consider **'exchanging'** your mutual fund before you sell it. For example: If you hold a mutual fund in a particular fund family that you want to sell, and you can identify another fund in that **same fund family** that you want to purchase, you can keep the same share class and transact an 'exchange.' **When you exchange a fund and maintain the same share class you will not incur a surrender penalty.** The original purchase date of your first fund will be honored. This can reduce fees for you. However, if you have capital or ordinary income gains (within an investment/brokerage account only), you could still realize the gains, or losses, for tax purposes. Again, consult your advisors.

Life

An example of this 'exchange' idea:

If you own **AGK Intermediate Bond** mutual fund, in a C share position, and there is a **AGK Government Bond** mutual fund in a C share position that you would like to own instead, you have an exchange option:

1. **Exchange** *all or part of the* **AGK Intermediate Bond** (C share) fund into the **AGK Government Bond** (C share) mutual fund.

2. Your exchange will continue to use the **initial purchase date** for the **AGK Government Bond** (C share) fund. The clock does not start again for the CSDC.

3. Remember, if this fund is held in an Investment/Brokerage Account, your **gain or loss on the amount you exchanged will be noted for tax purposes** for the year in which you make the exchange. (In other words, you may be charged either short-term or long-term capital gains or losses.) Consult your Tax Advisor.

I believe that most financial advisors go to great lengths to select the correct share class with their clients at the time of the fund purchase. The decision is based on your time horizon for holding the fund and other factors like fees and your trading history.

Fees

Fees are a given when you invest. Whether you purchase, or hold stocks, bonds, mutual funds, or other investment products, typically you will pay some type of purchase or account fee. Mutual funds have fees associated with them as well. When you review the prospectus for each mutual fund, ask about the 12b-1 and other fund fees. The **12b-1 fees are assessed to cover the cost of distribution** of the mutual fund; **expenses incurred for commissions and managing dealers, underwriters, brokers, registered representatives; and for advertising and sales literature costs, selling, promoting, or related fund**

marketing expenses. 'Expense Ratios' are calculated as a percentage/ratio of expenses that are subtracted from the fund value. The expense ratio fees are paid to the fund family that manages the mutual fund portfolio. The fees include the 12b-1 fee AND the management fee for the fund. Another fee consideration: the turnover rate. **_Turnover_ denotes the amount of buying and selling a manger does within the mutual fund.** A high _turnover_ rate generally can signal that taxes may be triggered. In an investment/brokerage account, the tax implications may affect you. Consult the prospectus for historical turnover rates of the funds in which you invest. For more information on the types of fees mentioned here, and other fees and how to calculate them, go to:

- https://www.nerdwallet.com/article/investing/mutual-fund-fees-what-investors-need-to-know

- https://investor.gov

- https://www.personalfund.com

Not only do these websites offer commentary on investing, they also elaborate on subjects such as: marginal tax rates, projected rates of return, 'cost of ownership,' transaction costs, fund distribution costs, tax costs for funds, expense ratios, NAV (Net Asset Value), dividend distributions, and a variety of other important investing subjects.

The details of share class costs and fund expenses and fees, as well as the fund manager's objectives and the legal details of the mutual fund are found in the mutual fund 'prospectus.' The prospectus is a legal document that provides all of the important information that the investor needs to be aware of regarding each fund. Your advisor will provide the prospectus to you and you should review the prospectus prior to purchasing any mutual fund. You will receive a prospectus from the fund family when you purchase a mutual fund as well. (You can generally opt to receive the prospectus my email.)

As you can see from the above explanation of share class, you should seriously consider your investment time horizon and commitment to the mutual fund you select before you purchase it. If you plan to initiate a lot of trading, you will also want to discuss these planned activities with your advisor. As an investor you must choose the share class of the mutual fund you plan to purchase, BEFORE you purchase it. Once you make your mutual fund purchase that is the share class you own. So plan carefully.

Please Note: When you cross a certain dollar threshold, your advisor may educate you regarding the benefits/costs of opening a 'Managed Account.' Managed accounts have a different fee structure, and alternative 'rules' regarding holding investments in them. However, sometimes they are more cost effective -- under certain trading/investment position scenarios.

If you were only going to invest your money for 2 years, in order to avoid fees and surrender penalties which of the 3 Share Classes that we have discussed would you consider? WHY?

_____

_____

Life

Financial Advisors will disclose the fees connected with your investment purchase with you. The discussion will include fees such as: account fees, transaction fees, wrap or advisory fees, mutual fund fees, insurance M&E fees, 'rider' fees, or other fees associated with investing. This discussion is essential. Do not be hesitant to ask about the fees. To be comfortable with your investment decision, understanding the fee structure of your product is critical.

A discussion regarding fees is important because *fees* impact your investment performance. At the end of the day, your ultimate concern is whether or not you are making, or losing, money in your account. Calculating your gains (or losses) is simple math:

- What you paid – minus – what the current market value is = gain or loss

Watch as your numbers go up and down!

Asset Allocation Meets Diversification

The difference between *Asset Allocation and Diversification* is sometimes difficult for investors to grasp.

- **Asset Allocation** is generally thought of as the proportion (percentage) of each asset class that an investor has in their portfolio. *"Asset allocation is an investment strategy that aims to balance risk and reward by apportioning a portfolio's assets according to an individual's goals, risk tolerance, and investment horizon"* (https://www.investopedia.com/terms/a/assetallocation.asp)   So much money is invested in stocks, so much in bonds, and so much in cash. Whereas,

- **Diversification** is a risk management practice to reduce the overall impact of any one investment choice within a portfolio. *"Diversification is a technique that reduces risk by allocating investments among various financial instruments, industries, and other categories."* (https://www.investopedia.com/investing/importance-diversification/) So, even if you have 50% in stocks or equities, within that 50% allocation, you may have 10% in *Large Cap Value* stocks, 10% in *Large Cap Growth* stocks, 10% in *International* stocks, etc.

Simple **asset allocation** is accomplished by dividing up the investment product purchases into the areas of:
- Stocks

- Bonds

- Cash or cash equivalents

In other words – *allocation* requires that you do not put all of your eggs in one basket. The asset allocation that is appropriate for you and your investor profile will vary. The percentage of stocks/bonds/cash that is right for you is determined by how you answer the Investor Profile questions.

There are many approaches to *asset allocation* and *diversification*. One approach to asset allocation and diversification is the purchase of **Balanced, Asset Allocated, Target**, or **Lifestyle** mutual funds, as these funds may be inherently diversified. For example, a *Balanced* fund may allocate 60% of holdings to stocks and 40% of holdings to bonds and cash and rebalance often to maintain this ratio range. Other types of *Balanced* or *Asset Allocated* mutual funds balance allocations between *U.S. and International* or *World* holdings.

Lifestyle, or *Target* funds are also *Asset Allocated* funds. Two of the characteristics that makes these types of funds a little different is that the mutual fund manager actively manages the portfolios through asset allocation and rebalancing activities, based on two primary criteria: a) the age of the investor, and b) a specific 'target date,' usually the investor's retirement date. These two characteristics tie together. For instance, if you will be close to age 65 in the year 2062, you might select a *Lifestyle* fund that is dated 2060. What happens is that the mutual fund manager will classically start out with a more aggressive asset allocation, and through the years the manager will modify the allocation, becoming more conservative over time. Obviously, every single fund will be managed differently. But these kinds of funds utilize the expertise of the fund managers to rebalance and make changes in the holdings and the allocations over time. These types of funds virtually do the rebalancing and asset allocation for you, based on industry norms, 'age-appropriate' asset allocations.

Explain the objective for asset allocation and diversification of an investment portfolio. Search for a fund on the internet and name it here.

_____

_____

Examples of *Diversification* could be to add both *growth* and *value* style investments to your asset categories; add different size company investment products; include a couple of different types of bond funds (like International bonds and Intermediate Bonds); maybe insert a sector fund (like Health Care or Natural Resources), etc. Making varied investment selections will help you diversify your portfolio to reduce the impact of any one investment choice.

According to Daniel Jark (Sep 30, 2020), in an Investopedia article, *"Portfololio Diversification Done Right,"*... *"Diversification is a great strategy for anyone looking to reduce risk on their investment for the long term. The process of diversification includes investing in more than one type of asset.... including bonds, shares, commodities, REITs, hybrids, and more in your portfolio.*

- *Investing in several different securities within each asset. A diversified portfolio spreads investments around in different securities of the same asset type meaning multiple bonds from different issuers, shares in several companies from different industries, etc.*

- *Investing in assets that are not significantly correlated to one another. The idea here is to choose different asset classes and securities with different lifetimes and cycles in order to minimize the impact of any negative conditions that could adversely affect your portfolio."*

https://www.investopedia.com/articles/investing/030116/portfolio-diversification-done-right.asp

Correlation

Another diversification idea is to own funds that **have not historically *'correlated,' or moved in the same direction*** (increased or decreased in value), **when the market moves up or down.** This approach incorporates investment choices that are **'uncorrelated,'** meaning that, "the price movement of one asset has no effect on the price movement of the other asset". (76) **Correlation** of assets refers to the **extent that investment product prices move in the same direction. (81) So, "uncorrelated" assets should have an inverse objective. Non-correlated investment strategies are employed to counterbalance, or neutralize, overall portfolio risk.** (81) Assets such as real estate, private equity, commodities, and 'hedge funds' are examples of 'alternative' investments which can be non-correlated to other types of investment products.

Life

Here is another example of diversifying a portfolio:

1. 15% in Large Cap Growth equities

2. 15% in Large Cap Value equities

3. 10% in International equities

4. 5% in Mid Cap growth equities

5. 3% in Natural Resources

6. 2% in Health Sciences

7. 20% in Intermediate Bonds

8. 10% in Global Bonds

9. 10% in Short Term Bonds

10. 10% in Cash

Remember: <u>This is not presented as advice for you</u>, each person's investment profile, risk tolerance, and objectives are different.

Asset allocation divides the investment products into what 3 areas?

_____

_____

_____

Another Diversification Idea

However, as an example, what happened in 2008 gave investors a wake-up call. Typical diversification approaches seemed to come up short. In other words, the diversification approach did not work, because, with the exception of cash and treasuries, and a sector here and there, many '*main-stream*' sectors declined overall. What did this mean? The '*non-correlation*' approach of diversification let us down. If most of the sectors decline, then there is no '*opposite behavior to the market*' to be experienced. For example, if, both *Growth* and *Value*; both *International and Domestic; Stocks and Bonds; Large and Small Cap positions; sectors like Health Sciences and Natural Resources*; all decline in the same year, diversification alone will not protect you from loss. So, placing some of your money in each investment category *was not sufficient enough to protect investors* to the extent that was historically typical/ expected. Remember, market declines happen, and they happen often.

What can the managers of the mutual funds to do protect you if the market experiences a decline like it did in 2008? If you have your money in a mutual fund, or it is managed by a professional money manager, **those managers are required to invest your money according to the stated investment objectives noted in the prospectus. Even if the manager would like to pull out of the market in a time of decline, they probably cannot.** They must stay invested according to what is *stated in their fund prospectus*. What this means… they do not have the opportunity to change the fund objectives mid-stream…. If they manage a '*Large Value*' fund, they must continue to stay invested in 'Large Value' positions, period. Do you have an alternative strategy?

Options?

I hesitate to introduce the subject of **Options** *(another, but very complex investment strategy)*; however, I offer this discussion in order for you to explore the topic of *Options* <u>much later</u>, when you become a more sophisticated investor. **'Options,'** offer an additional investment strategy to consider. Purchasing *Options* can also offer a potential *non-correlation* opportunity for investors to explore. (82) The subject of *Options* can be very, very complicated, and there are several variations. For our purposes here we will briefly describe two types of Options; a *Covered Call Option* and a *Put Option*.

Both the **Covered Call** and **Put Options** are traded on the exchanges just like stocks and bonds, meaning they can be bought and sold. Like other investment choices, you will have VERY specific objectives for adding these positions to your portfolio... In VERY simple terms:

- Selling a **Covered Call Option** can help you generate cash into your portfolio, (however, your position may be 'called/sold' out of your portfolio);

- The **Put Option** can be used in structuring a risk management strategy to help you lessen the risk in your portfolio by **protecting the downside**.

To utilize 'Options' strategies you will require the assistance of an experienced financial advisor who has the track record and the 'platform' to use 'Options.' Working with 'Options' can be costly (the fees may become quite steep) if your advisor is not qualified and/or does not have the appropriate platform for buying and selling 'Options.' Investors need to carefully research 'Options' to understand how they may help them diversify their portfolio. Here is a website to visit, when, and if, you decide to explore these types of investment products: http://www.investorwords.com/.

Remember: "... options are very complex and require a great deal of observation and maintenance." Be sure to check with your financial advisor to understand each type of investment to determine which investments offer non-correlated performance and protection choices to satisfy your specific objectives.

Are Bonds for Income?

Bonds are loans that you make with your money. You loan your money to corporations, municipalities, governments, or other issuers when you purchase a bond. In return you are typically paid 'interest' income over some stated period of time. Bonds represent an obligation or debt that the issuer has to you.

Bonds are unique in the fact that they have a **stated maturity date and a stated 'interest rate.'** On the maturity date your original investment, or principal, should be returned to you. During the time you 'hold' the bond you receive the interest payments according to the pre-determined schedule identified at the time of your purchase. When you buy a bond, you do not purchase a share or a portion of any stock or company. Unlike equity purchases, where you own a share or a portion of a company, when you buy a bond you *lend* your money for a stated, fixed interest rate, or 'coupon.' Additionally, there is no dividend payment for bondholders, you receive a 'stated rate of return,' the interest payment, paid to you in cash.

Some of the reasons that issuers offer bonds to investors are to raise money for projects or for expansion; to finance specific programs; or to pay operating expenses. Here is a brief review of some **features of bonds** (unless the issuer defaults):

a.   Bondholders (you) receive **interest** on the money you lend. The interest is paid according to the schedule set at issuance.

b.   The bondholder's **principal** (amount originally invested) is returned to the bondholder 'at maturity' (pre-set date in the future), or when the bond is called.

c.   The bond could have a **'call date.'** A **call date** is a **stated date upon which your principal can be returned to you, and the interest payments stop. The call date is** *earlier* **than the stated maturity date.** Therefore, you may not receive the bond interest for as long as you might have expected.

One of the most important aspects of a bond...is , of course, the **YIELD**…. The yield is what money you will receive in 'interest.' https://www.investopedia.com/terms/y/yield.asp describes yield as:

> *"The income return on an investment...the interest or dividends received from a security and is usually expressed annually as a percentage based on the investment's cost, its current market value or its face value."*
>
> https://www.investopedia.com/articles/investing/121015/yield-vs-total-return-how-they-differ-and-how-use-them.asp

To make it simple, we will review the most common bond yield terms you should be familiar with:

a. **Coupon** – The percent interest rate the debt issuer pays you for an explicit time period; paid on a specific pre-determined schedule.

b. **Yield** – The rate of return on your investment; rate of interest paid on a bond or note.

c. **Yield to maturity** – The performance of an investment, measured from the time of purchase to the maturity date.

d. **Yield to call** – The performance, or rate of return, of a callable investment, measured from the time of purchase to the first call date.

e. **Modified duration** - The measurement of how much the value of a bond will change, given a change in interest rates in the marketplace.

f. **Yield to worst** - Identifies the yield that will be paid if the bond is called on the earliest stated date. When you purchase a callable bond, this yield percentage should be communicated to you.

The **form** that you purchase a bond determines the bond's pricing, impacting the 'rate of return,' or the yield, which you, the bond holder receives. You purchase bonds either:

a. **'At par'** – New bonds are issued at a **par price of $1000 increments.**

b. **'At a premium'** – The **Secondary market** offers investment products for a second time. The products are **not an original issue, they are not purchased from the issuer.** A bond that is offered 'at a premium' is *above* par, * **meaning you pay more than the 'at par' price, and therefore your interest yield is reduced, vs. what the 'par' stated interest rate is.**

c. **At a discount'** - On the secondary market, a bond can be offered *below* par,* **meaning you pay less than the 'at par' price and therefore you get more yield than you would realize when you purchase the bond at the 'at par' rate.**

So, if you purchase a bond that was originally issued 'at par' ($1,000) for $1,200, you are paying 'a premium.' If the coupon of the original bond was 5%, because you paid more for the bond, your yield will be reduced (divide $ 50 coupon by $ 1200 premium price). On-the-other-hand, if you paid $950 for the bond (purchased the bond at 'a discount') you will realize a slightly higher yield than the 'at par' coupon of 5% (divide $ 50 coupon by $ 950 discount price). The concept of purchasing a bond either **'at par,' at 'a discount,' or at 'a premium,'** is not an easy one to grasp. However, understanding that there is a difference is the important piece here. If you are purchasing a bond investment product, ask about the yield.... Find out in what form you are purchasing your bond and discuss how the form impacts the yield with your advisor

*The secondary markets buy and sell investment products after they have been issued. The primary market initially issues the products.

The bond **yield** will be affected by the price paid for the bond.

- For example, if the bondholder pays a premium for the bond, even though the coupon for the bond is 5%, because a **premium** was paid, the net effective yield would be less than 5%. If you purchased the bond **at a discount**, your yield will be greater than the 5% coupon.

(https://www.investopedia.com/terms/b/bond-yield.asp;
https://www.dummies.com/personal-finance/investing/bonds/what-is-the-yield-of-a-bond/)

Research two bond offerings, note if they are: at par, at a discount, at a premium.

_____

_____

Life

Sometimes clients know just enough to be dangerous about bond yields. What I mean by that is this: they ONLY focus on the yield; clients are sometimes not interested in the details. Be sure you don't fall into the category of, "Just give me the big picture... what is the yield, and how long will I get that income?"

*Be sure to review all of the details of the bond you are considering. For example, if you are considering a bond that has a long maturity date, please understand if the bond is **callable**. If the bond has a call feature, how early can the bond be called? And, if it is called, then what is the **yield to call?***

Here's an example of what can happen:

1. *Bond JKL has a 10 year maturity at a 4.26% yield to maturity.*

2. *Bond JKL has call dates beginning in year 2; at the 2 year mark the yield to call is 3.45%.*

3. *Not only do you have a potentially lower yield, but you may incur reinvestment risk as well. **Reinvestment Risk** occurs when you hold an investment that produces a specific income stream (the yield), and the income stream or yield cannot be replaced due to the current market conditions when your bond is called.*

4. *This means that after 2 years your bond gets called and you cannot find a similar investment that is paying your original 4.26% yield to maturity.*

Remember the insurer must remain solvent for the investor to receive the yield.

Types of Bonds

Just like equities, all bonds are not created equal. There are several types of bonds. The type of bond is, in essence, the type of entity to which you are loaning your money. We will review a few of the most common types of bonds here: Government, Municipal, Corporate, International, and Savings Bonds.

A. When you purchase a **Government bond** – you are **loaning money to the U.S. government.**

Government Bonds are issued by the U.S. government and are fully backed by 'the full faith and credit of the U.S. government.' In other words, the bond's principal and interest will be paid back to you unless the government ceases to exist. Here are some definitions of different kinds of government bonds:

- **T-Bills** are sold at a discount and mature in **one year or less** (1, 3, or 6 months); T-Bills do not pay interest prior to maturity; T-Bills are sold at a discount of the par value to create a positive yield to maturity.

- **A T-Note** is issued in terms of 2, 3, 5, 7, and 10-year maturities; T-Notes pay interest semi-annually.

- **T-Bonds** are debt obligations that have maturities of ten to thirty years; T-Bonds pay interest semi-annually.

- **Government Federal Agency bonds** are sponsored by government federal credit agencies. These bonds are fully backed by the U.S. government guarantee. But **GSE** (Government Sponsored Enterprise) **Agency bonds** do not carry the same 'full faith and credit' protection. Typically, these debt instruments are issued for the purpose of loaning money to specific groups of borrowers. An example would be loans made by Fannie Mae to homeowners. Agency issue maturities range from overnight to 30 years.

B. **Municipal bonds** are issued by state or local government or U.S. territories or authorities. Municipal bonds are typically issued to fund public projects, like building schools or highways. These types of bonds are typically purchased by investors that are in higher tax brackets because the interest paid on these types of bonds is generally exempt (can vary depending on income bracket) from federal income tax; and these bonds are usually purchased in an Investment Account (not purchased in a Retirement Account). If you can find a municipal bond that is also issued in the state you live in, then you may not be required to pay any state income taxes on the interest received as well.

There are two common types of municipal bonds:

- **Revenue bonds** fund projects that produce revenue. This revenue generates income for the issuer (like an airport or toll road).

- **General Obligation bonds** (G.O.s) are bonds that are supported by the tax revenues generated by the issuing municipality (fund public works projects).

When you purchase a Municipal bond, you should inquire about two additional details:

- *The Municipal bond ratings:* Unlike U.S. government bonds, municipal bond principal is not guaranteed to be repaid by the federal government. So, you can check the rating on the municipal bond. Municipal bond ratings are generally provided by two independent sources: Moody's® and Standard and Poor's®. The ratings are offered to help you evaluate the strength of the bond — the likelihood that the bond issuer will be able to repay you your principal, along with the stated interest.

- **Municipal bonds can also be insured by an insurance agency.** Insurance can further strengthen the bond quality, but the insurance is only as good as the insurance company that is providing it.

C. **Corporate bonds** are issued by **corporations**. With the purchase of a **Corporate bond** you loan money to a specific company or corporation, like GE® or Citigroup®. These corporations can then use your money for acquisitions, expansion, operating expenses, etc.

There are two types of Corporate Bonds:

1. **Secured** – the issuer names a specific asset to be held as collateral

2. **Unsecured** – no collateral

Here is a definition of a **secured bond**
(http//www.thebalance.com/secured-bonds-vs-unsecured-bonds-417067):

> *"Secured bond: Secured bonds are those that are collateralized by an asset, such as property, equipment (especially for airlines, railroads, and transportation companies), or by another income stream."*

Here is the definition also provided for **an unsecured bond**
(http//www.thebalance.com/secured-bonds-vs-unsecured-bonds-417067):

> *"Unsecured bonds are not secured by a specific asset, but rather by "the full faith and credit" of the issuer. In other words, the investor has the issuer's promise to repay but has no clainm on the specific collateral."*

D. **International bonds** are debt instruments that are issued by a foreign government or corporation. An International Bond is issued by a borrower in a foreign country. The category can include foreign bonds, parallel bonds, and Eurobonds. An investor who is interested in gaining a diverse exposure to foreign securities may invest in international bonds.

E. **Savings bonds** stand alone. President Franklin D. Roosevelt introduced savings bonds to the American public when he 'placed the first order for a $500 Series EE Savings Bond in a radio broadcast on April 30, 1941.' (83) At one time buying Savings bonds was very popular in the U.S., but, as CNN® Business reported (6/14/2014), this behavior has changed: " Americans bought over 40 million of the most popular savings bonds in 2000. Last year [2013], the U.S. sold a mere 400,000 of them ". (84) Like other types of bonds, a savings bond is a type of certificate that signifies an individual has loaned money to the U.S. Government for a 'return of your principal' at a later date, along with a stated 'interest payment.' Because savings bonds are backed by the U.S. government, they are considered to be one of the safest ways to invest.

There are two popular types of savings bonds:

1) **I bonds (indexed for inflation); and**

2) **Series EE bonds.**

I bonds are designed to offer a rate of return that moves with inflation. The objective of these types of bonds is to ensure the holder a 'real rate of return' which is higher than the current rate of inflation. Therefore, the interest rate is calculated in two parts: a) a fixed base rate, plus b) a semi-annual rate calculated based on the rate of inflation as measured by the Consumer Price Index. *I bonds* are sold at face value in denominations of $50, $75, $100, $200, $500, $1,000, $5,000 and $10,000. An *I bond* can earn interest for as long as 30 years. The interest on an *I Bond* is added every month and the interest is compounded semiannually. *I bonds* are state and local income tax exempt. The federal income tax on *I bond* earnings can be deferred until the bonds are cashed in or when they stop earning interest after 30 years. Investors cashing in an *I bond* before five years are subject to a 3-month earnings penalty. Interest rates for *I bonds* change every May and November, based on either current market rates or inflation.

Conversely, the **Series *EE Savings bonds*** purchased after May 2005 now earn a fixed rate of return. Rates are based on interest rates set by the large government bond trading market. **Series *EE savings bonds* are bought at only half the denomination that they will eventually be valued.** So, if you purchase a $25 Series *EE savings bond,* when the bond matures, it will be worth $50.

Life

When my children were younger they received Savings Bonds as birthday and holiday presents. The idea was for them to let the bonds mature and then they could use them towards their college education costs.

Please recognize that we have just scratched the surface here in our discussion of bonds. Further research will lead you into a discussion of **'investment grade', finance bonds, industrial bonds, utility bonds and transportation bonds, 'high yield'** corporate bonds, and other types of bonds. Investigate and expand your knowledge prior to making a bond purchase.

Like most investment options, bonds can be complicated and certainly require you to do more research. Be sure you do your due diligence and ask questions. Again, a trusted advisor should be consulted.

Research one tax free bond and one corporate bond to identify coupon and yields:

Note: the coupon identifies the interest rate that the bond paid when it was issued; the yield identifies what the interest rate will be in the *future, depending on the new bond price.*

_____

_____

(https://www.thestreet.com/markets/rates-and-bonds/the-different-kinds-of-bonds-229831; http://www.buschinvestments.com/What-Types-of-Bonds.c71.htm; https://www.thebalance.com/what-is-a-bond-356068)

Indexes Are Just Average

We cannot move away from the investment product topic without a brief discussion about *Indexes*. Lipper®, Inc., a research firm that monitors market returns states, "indexes are unmanaged and do not take transaction costs or fees into consideration." (68, 75) There is a 'corresponding index' for most stock market size and style products. The *Index* **presents a base-line performance average for investment products.** Each major index category has a management firm that publishes 'index performance.' The performance numbers are used by investors and financial advisors to *compare performance of investment products.*

There are many, many indexes, so for the purpose of our discussion I will list seven indexes that are regularly utilized by stock market investors, for your review.

- ☒ **Large Growth** – represented by the **Russell 1000® Growth Index**

- ☒ **Large Value** - represented by the **Russell 1000® Value Index**

- ☒ **Small/Mid Growth** - represented by the **Russell 2500® Growth Index**

- ☒ **Small/Mid Value** - represented by the **Russell 2500® Value Index**

- ☒ **International** - represented by the **MSCI® Index** (Morgan Stanley Capital International®)

- ☒ **Bonds** - represented by the **Barclays® Capital Aggregate Bond Index**

- ☒ **Cash** - represented by the **3-month Treasury Bill, published by the Federal Reserve.** (68)

Remember, there are also the DOW Jones Industrial Average®, S&P 500® and the NASDAQ® Composite indexes.

- The Dow Jones Industrial Average® is an index that indicates how 30 large, publicly owned companies based in the United States have traded during a standard trading session, usually one day, in the stock market. (https://www.investopedia.com/terms/d/dija/asp)

- Since 1957 the S&P 500® Index has published the prices of 500 large-cap common stocks which are actively traded in the United States. (https://www.investopedia.com/terms/s/sp500.asp)

- The NASDAQ® composite index is a stock market index of all of the common stocks and similar securities which are listed on the *NASDAQ®*. The NASDAQ® is the market capitalization-weighted composite index and has over 3,300 common equities. This index is one measure of the performance of stocks of technology companies and growth companies. Both U.S. and non-U.S. companies are listed on the NASDAQ® stock market. (https://www.fool.com/investing/stock-market/exchange/nasdaq/)

Compare your fund or investment product's performance to the indexes as another tool for evaluating your investment selection. Use the index as ONE of several criteria for your evaluation.

Life

In the world of investing, understanding that there is a corresponding index against which you can compare your investment, is a big deal. Work with your advisor to really understand how you read the research report that is relevant to your investment (i.e. provides information for the 'type' of investment you hold).

My bet is that once you get comfortable with reading such reports and are familiar with the index you should use to compare your investment; it will help make your investment decisions easier for you.

Performance Simplified

Investors are - bottom-line - interested in the **performance** of their investment accounts. *"How much money am I losing or making?"* To fully understand how your portfolio is performing, be sure you compare performances of specific investment products to their appropriate indexes, and that you comprehend the components of performance. The performance of your portfolio will be comprised of one or more of the following in some combination:

- **Yield:** The interest rate paid on an investment product, calculated with the price you bought the investment product for. (Remember if you buy a bond at a *discount* the yield is greater than the interest rate; the reverse is true if you paid a *premium* for the bond). In addition, Bond Mutual Funds have many holdings, so the yield is calculated on each of those holdings and is then averaged.

- **Capital appreciation:** The difference of what your investment products are worth, minus what you paid for them. The difference is your gains (appreciation).

- **Total return:** Add up both the yield and the capital appreciation of the investment product.

- **Dividend:** The earnings that are paid, either in cash or in stock, by an equity investment product.

By understanding each of the components of the performance of your investment products, you are better able to monitor your portfolio and make product selections. Some investors calculate their returns and then deduct tax implications. Conducting this step adds another measure to help you calculate your end-result performance. (https://www.nasdaq.com/glossary/c/capital-growth; https://www.visualcapitalist.com/40-stock-market-terms-every-beginner-know/; https://www.tmxmoney.com/en/investor_tools/glossary.html)

AMT

Although I am not a tax advisor, you should be familiar with the impact of potentially incurring **Alternative Minimum Tax (AMT)** because AMT can also impact your investment decisions. While only some individuals in the higher income brackets will be affected, you should be comfortable with the term. The AMT **imposes a tax on specified exclusions, deductions, and credits so that higher income tax bracket taxpayers may not totally erase income taxes.** The AMT is typically linked to bond income and is a complicated subject. If you are eligible and find yourself in a higher tax bracket, your tax advisor will calculate the AMT tax for you on your investments and explain how the AMT works in detail.

Dollar-Cost Averaging Over Time

You'll often hear the phrase, 'dollar-cost average into (or out of) the fund or investment product.' Here's how **dollar-cost averaging** works:

☒ Because prices of investments fluctuate, an investor can devise a plan to make **periodic, systematic investment purchases** of an investment product over time. The purchases are made on a pre-determined schedule; no matter what the cost for your investment product is on that day.

Life

For example:

If you want to dollar cost average into an investment product, you might:

- *Determine a day of the month... set up a schedule to invest on X day;*

- *Give direction for which investment product should be purchased;*

- *Specify the dollar amount to be invested;*

- *Designate what account the investment will be purchased in.*

This process sets up an automatic system for you to invest... generally no monthly investment fee is assessed, and you do not have to provide the same direction to your advisor over and over again.

What this strategy does: You buy shares of the product when the shares are either high or low. "Dollar cost averaging (DCA) is an investment strategy with the goal of reducing the impact of volatility on large purchases of financial assets such as equities. ... Dollar cost averaging is not always the most profitable way to invest a large sum, but it is alleged to minimize downside risk." https://en.wikipedia.org/wiki/Dollar_cost_averaging

Obviously paying less for an investment product provides you with a greater opportunity for an upside gain.

Cash is King

Checking Accounts, Savings Accounts, Money Markets, and Certificates of Deposit are terms used for 'cash-like' money. Corporate Finance Institute® provides this definition:

> *"Cash includes legal tender, bills, coins, checks received but not deposited, and checking and savings accounts. Cash equivalents are any short-term investment securities with maturity periods of 90 days or less. They include bank certificates of deposit, banker's acceptances, Treasury bills, commercial paper and other money market investments"* (86)

These types of investment products are typically utilized for 'savings' objectives. However, it may be appropriate to position a portion of your investment money in one or more of these types of cash equivalent products. Placing your money in any one of these investment products can provide quicker access to your money for withdrawal or income purposes, and some of those products might still offer you some appreciation opportunity in the form of interest. While the interest rate or return for some of these types of investment products is commonly lower than with higher risk investment products, as we have reviewed, those higher risk products can also decline in value. With a few exceptions, the cash investment products should not lose any, or very little of, their value. (Assuming solvency of the insurer.)

Life

Even the most aggressive of investors tend to have some money set aside for emergencies. How much cash you want to keep available will be a very personal choice. Your short-term goals may play a part in helping you decide what the right percentage or amount of cash to have 'on-hand' should be. Note: a prudent investor plans for a rainy day.

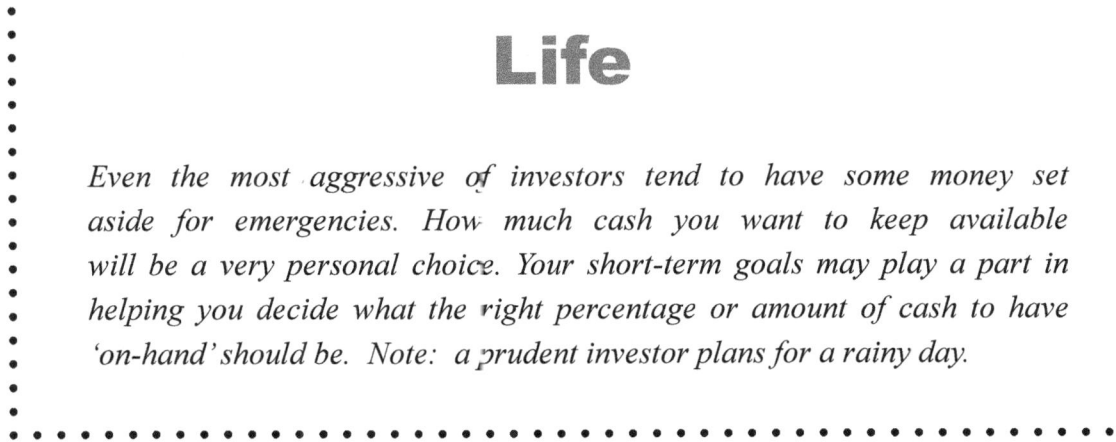

Conclusion:

When you begin to invest your money for longer-term growth objectives, ensure that you take an active role in the process with your advisor. Communication, education and understanding are critical ingredients to the success of your investing experience. **Remember, it is wise to set your objectives and to identify your risk tolerance and investor profile prior to investing. Subsequently:** Monitor your objectives and risk tolerance and convey any attitude or objective changes you have to your advisors on a timely basis. Build a cash reserve to cover six months (minimum) to a year of your living expenses; and ear-mark additional savings for your 'emergency fund.' If you decide to invest, seek out and work with a professional who can educate you and advise you in the area of investing. Be sure your investment choices take into consideration what we have discussed in this section.

It is easy to get bogged down in all of the data. Admittedly, there is a lot to know, but with the help of a professional financial planner and tax advisor you will be able to make sense of most of the information.

Here are a few items presented by various sources to keep in mind to help you avoid investment mistakes. (85)

- ○ *Do not focus on the minutia:* fees, expenses, or small losses should never drive your decision.

- ○ *Avoid making decisions when you are emotionally charged.*

   For example, market volatility in 2008 prompted reminders to financial advisors to counsel investors to avoid making decisions when the investors are in an emotional state.

- ○ *Do not make decisions that are counter to your plan and the strategy you developed with your financial advisor.* Investment decisions need to be based on your long-term objectives, risk tolerance and time horizon. If there is a change in any one of these areas notify your financial advisor immediately.

- ○ *Do not overreact to a specific 'event.'*

- ○ *Attempting to time the market is probably not possible.* Moving in and out of the market is ill-advised.

After thorough thought and investigation, if you have made the decision to start investing, you may want to also consider how you will react if the market becomes volatile (remember the Investor Profile Questionnaire). Read on....

o Pippa Stevens, 3/24/2021 article, "*This chart shows why investors should never try to time the stock martet,*"

> • "*Looking at data going back to 1930, the firm found that if an investor missed the S&P 500's 10 best days each decade, the total return would stand at 28%. If, on the other hand, the investor held steady through the ups and downs, the return would have been 17,715%.*" (87)
>
> • *Drew Housman 8/2019, The Simple Dollar® also supports that statistic,* "*Missing the five best days when you're otherwise fully* invested drops your overall return by 35%." (88)

The Importance of staying invested
The growth of $10,000 invested from July 1, 2006 - June 30, 2016

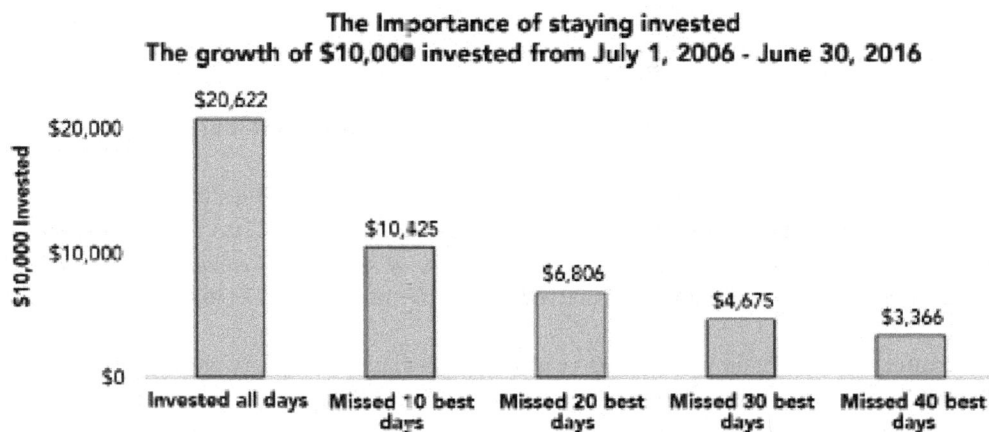

https://russellinvestments.com/us/blog/market-timing-tricky-ever

Source: Russell 1000® Index. Indexes are unmanaged and cannot be invested in directly. Returns represent past performance, are not a guarantee of future performance, and are not indicative of any specific investment. This hypothetical example is for illustration only and is not intended to reflect the return of any actual investment. Investments do not typically grow at an even rate of return and may experience negative growth. Exhibit n, etc. is reproduced here courtesy of Russell Investments® and is © 2016 Russell Investments. All rights reserved.

☒ My old partner put it this way, "do not chase the hot dot." This means do not purchase what you 'heard' is 'a hot pick,' rather **base your decisions on valid economic research and fundamentals**.

☒ ***Do not neglect to diversify.*** Asset allocation, diversification, and rebalancing are critical to your overall success as an investor.

☒ ***Create a 'protection strategy.'*** Work with your advisor to understand what outcomes may be possible, given recent history and seek out protection strategy solutions.

☒ ***Active management*** of your portfolio can be key.

AGAIN… CHECK WITH AN ADVISOR… THIS IS INFORMATION IS NOT INTENDED TO BE SPECIFIC INVESTMENT ADVICE FOR YOU.

Sources

(61)   Online dictionary.

(62)   International Accounting Standards Board®, IASB; <u>The Study of Economics: Principles, Concepts,</u> https://books.google. com, Turley Mings/Matthew Marlin (1999) p. 267; https://en.wikipedia.org/wiki/Asset, *"Asset."*

(63)   https://corporatefinanceinstitute.com/resources/knowledge/accounting/types-of-assets/, *"Types of Assets.;"* *"and Classification of assets – BISI."*

(64)   https://www.finweb.com/financial-planning/saving-vs-investing.html, home → Financial Planning→ Saving → *"Saving vs. Investing,"* The Independent Financial Portal - Financial Web; www.investoreducation.org. *"Answers to Test Your Money$marts."*

(65)   https://www.wellsfargo.com/goals-investing/saving-vs-investing/,' *"Saving vs. Investing."*

(66)   https://www.chegg.com/flashcards/business-bac045dd-8795-4654-aad1-b3c4d3b43681/deck.

(67)   *"Six Good Reasons to Stay Invested,"* https://russellinvestments.com/-/media/files/ca/en/insights/investor-education/ investor-insights/six-good-reasons.pdf?la=en-ca&hash=E91B1E455F1DA6810A1A0DBOEF89AA3159229605; John Hancock®, *"A special focus on volatility and the financial markets: Reasons to stay invested,"* (3/2009), https://static.contentres.com/media/documents/abbcd1b7-7ebc-410e-bf9c-2416937d4683.pdf.

(68)   https://www.macrotrends.net/1319/dow-jones-100-year-historical-chart;   https://www.thebalance.com/major-market-indexes-list-2466397,   https://seekingalpha.com/article/2650925-bear-markets-corrections-and-benchmarks, *"Corrections, And Benchmarks,"* Kendall Anderson, 11/2014; https://www.icmarc.org/prebuilt/apps/downloadDoc.asp, *"Market Returns: Positive vs. Negative Years U.S. Stocks: 1926-2017;"* Hancock®, *"A special focus on volatility and the financial markets,"* 2011. (68a) 31, 2011, Bank of America's® Merrill Lynch® Affluent Insights Quarterly.; 'Wall Street Journal® Market Beat' (9/26/11), *"Bear Markets Bottom Not Might Come Until Mid-2012";* *"10 Things You Should Know About Bear Markets,"* Hartford Funds(r), Ned Davis, (8/31/2020), https://www.hartfordfunds.com/practice-management/client-conversations/bear-markets.html.

(69)   American Funds® (2009), *"What past market declines can teach us,"* https://americanfundsretirement.retire. americanfunds.com/basics/volatile-market/market-declines.html.

(70)   https://www.investopedia.com/a-history-of-bear-markets-4582652, *"A History of Bear Markets,"* Mark Kolakowski, 9/2019; American Funds®, *"What past market declines can teach us,"* (2009).

(71)   https://www.business-standard.com/article/opinion/market-recoveries-historical-perspective-103090401106_1.html, *"Market recoveries - historical perspective,"* AP 1 New Delhi, 1/28/2013, https://www.cbsnews.com/news/whats-a-bear-market-and-how-long-might-it-last/, "CBSNEWS® *"What's a bear market, and how long will it last?,"* 12/2018.

(72)   https://www.hepburncapital.com/ready-for-some-growth/, *"Ready for some Growth?"* https://www.capitalgroup.com/ individual/planning/market-fluctuations/past-market-declines.html, American Funds®, *"What Past Market Declines Can Teach Us."* American Funds® (2009), Types of risk: a review of the basic kinds of risk, including inflation, liquidity and credit; American Funds® (2008), *"Dealing with Declines."*

(73)   h t t p s : / / w w w . b r a i n y q u o t e . c o m / q u o t e s / w a r r e n _ b u f f e t t _ 1 4 9 6 8 2 ; https://www.brainyquote.com/quotes/george_soros_173296.

(74)   https://www.getsmarteraboutmoney.ca/invest/investing-basics/understanding-risk/types-of-investment-risk/, *"9 types of investment risk."*

(75)   https://lipperalpha.refinitiv.com/lipper/thomson-reuters-lipper-leaders/#, *"A sophisticated approach to finding funds that fit your needs,"* Refinitiv Lipper Leaders®, Lipper® Alpha Insight; https://www.investopedia.com/articles/investing/091015/lipper-rating-system-explained.asp, *"The Lipper® Rating System Explained."*

(76)   https://www.investopedia.com/articles/financial-theory/09/uncorrelated-assets-diversification.asp, *"Protecting Portfolios Using Correlation Diversification,"* Manoj Singh, 3/2018; https://financialengines.com/education-center/; *"Market capitalization: large-cap, mid-cap, and small-cap stocks,"* *"Small Cap Stocks vs. Large Cap Stocks: What's the Difference?"* Sean Ross, (8/27/21), https://www.investopedia.com/terms/m/marketcapitalization.asp.

(77)   https://www.investopedia.com/articles/professionals/072415/value-or-growth-stocks-which-best.asp, *"Value or Growth Stocks: Which Are Better?"*; https://www.investopedia.com/articles/investing/080113/income-value-and-growth-stocks.asp, *"Income, Value, and Growth Stocks."*

(78)   https://corporatefinanceinstitute.com/resources/knowledge/finance/what-is-return-on-equity-roe/, *"Return on Equity (ROE)."*

(79)   https://www.thebalance.com/fundamental-analysis-understanding-earnings-per-share-3141099, *"Fundamental Analysis: Understanding Earnings Per Share,"* (6/2019).

(80)   https://www.thebalance.com/fundamental-analysis-understanding-the-peg-ratio-3140796, *"Understanding the PEG Ratio in Fundamental Analysis,"* (6/2018).

(81)   https://www.investopedia.com/terms/c/correlation.asp, *"Correlation Definition,"* 6/2019, Adam Hayes.

(82)   OIC The Options Industry Council – (1998-2009) *"Options Strategies: Covered Call, Options Strategies: Protective Put;"* Definition." https://www.optionseducation.org/.

(83)   *"Fun Facts About Savings Bonds,"* U.S. Department of the Treasury, Bureau of the Public Debt. https://www.econedlink.org/?s=fun+facts+about+savings+bonds; *"A History of the US Savings Bonds Program,"* https://www.treasurydirect.gov/indiv/research/history/history_sb.pdf.

(84)   https://abcnews.go.com/GMA/SaveInMay/find-savings-bond/story?id=1962435, *"Find Out If You Have a Savings Bond,"* ABC NEWS, 5/2006, https://money.cnn.com/2014/06/14/investing/savings-bonds/index.html, *"U.S. savings bonds, a graduation gift staple for nearly a century, are on the verge of extension,"* CNN Business®, 6/14/14, Heather Long.

(85)   2006 The American Institute of Certified Public Accountants®, ISO 9001 Certified AICPA® 10/29/2019, *"Common Investing Mistakes You Need to Avoid,"* Peter Leeds 5/31/21, https://www.thesimpledollar.com/20-common-investment-mistakes-and-five-simple-steps-to-avoid-them/; William Artzberger, 6/2019, *"Avoid These 8 Common Investing Mistakes;"* https://www.investopedia.com/articles/stocks/07/beat_the_mistakes.asp.

(86)   https://corporatefinanceinstitute.com/resources/knowledge/accounting/cash-equivalents/.

(87)   https://www.investmentnews.com/article/20150108/BLOG09/150109953/how-to-manage-your-clients-emotions-when-market-volatility-spikes, *"How to manage your clients' emotions when market volatility spikes,"* Scott E. Couto; https://www.cnbc.com/2021/03/24/this-chart-shows-why-investors-should-never-try-to-time-the-stock-market.

(88)   https://www.thesimpledollar.com/investing/stocks/tempted-to-sell-missing-just-a-handful-of-the-best-stock-market-days-can-tank-your-returns/?platform=hootsuite, *"Why Mistiming The Market Can Be Disastrous,"* Drew Housman, 8/2019, The Simple Dollar®.

Chapter 3
Check For Understanding

For a chapter review, read and complete the following follow-up activities.

- ☒ Create a list of your assets.

- ☒ Organize a chart to capture your understanding of some of the investment choices in these three categories: Equities/Bonds/Cash.

- ☒ Evaluate your answers to the Investor Profile Questionnaire. Does the evaluation accurately describe your current investment philosophy?

- ☒ Estimate what the return percentage is for an investment that you purchased for $400, and now has a market value of $482 two years later.

- ☒ In your own words define 'risk,' as it relates to investing.

- ☒ Name some of the differences between A, B and C Shares of Mutual Funds.

- ☒ Explain the differences between 'Small, Medium and Large Cap' stocks.

- ☒ Identify three mutual fund sectors.

- ☒ In simple terms interpret the differences between correlated and non-correlated investment products.

- ☒ Design a hypothetical portfolio for a moderate investor.

- ☒ Describe what the 'market indexes' are, and how you might utilize the index information.

- ☒ Identify a list of your 'trusted advisors.'

- ☒ Consider why it is imperative to use 'trusted advisors' to navigate the investing process.

About
Experience Talks...

Investing is a very individual decision. The following scenarios are narratives that friends of mine or clients have shared with me. As I have indicated before, the names have been changed to protect the identity of the individuals who have shared their stories. Read each story to help you learn a little more about how 'investing' can be so varied from person to person.

Experience Talks...

Here Today...Could Mean Gone Tomorrow

J oe told me this investing story:

Joe announced to me that he was a 'conservative' investor. He worked for a manufacturing plant. Joe also said that his dream was to buy a house... so he had saved his money over the course of several years and had saved a nest-egg of about $ 50,000 for his down-payment on his house.

Joe also had a friend who was NOT a conservative investor. This friend (let's call him Rick) continuously told Joe about his personal investing experience with his own financial advisor. Rick touted that his advisor had doubled his money for him in a very short period of time.

Upon further investigation, Joe learned that Rick's financial advisor was a 'day-trader.' A day-trader is a broker, or investor, that typically has discretion to take the money investors entrust to him... and invest that money in a very aggressive manner. Typically, day-traders do just that, buy and hold investment properties for short periods of time... only 'days' in some cases... hoping that the investment will appreciate very quickly. The day-trader then sells the investment and moves on to the next investment product. The strategy is considered to be very risky.

Initially Joe was not interested in allowing Rick's day-trader financial advisor to invest his money in this manner, but after a few conversations, Joe decided that, based on his friend Rick's track record, he would go ahead. After all, Joe was only going to invest in this manner until he doubled his down-payment money for his house. Joe had decided he would then take his $ 100,000 (double the $ 50,000) and go ahead and buy his house.

According to Joe, everything went very, very well in the first several weeks. Literally it seemed as if his account grew overnight to @ $80,000 and Joe was extremely pleased.

A few years later when I met Joe and he told me this story; he was not so happy about the experience. What Joe recounted to me was this: 'One day my account was about $80,000... and then, poof, the money was all but gone.'

With that experience, Joe was reluctant to invest a second time. Who could blame him?

Moral of the story: Most likely if it sounds too good to be true, it is too good to be true.

Experience Talks...

How Can They Tax "A Liquidation Event?"

Doris was a woman in her mid-sixties. Several years before I met Doris her mother had passed away and Doris had been left a sizeable inherited investment account.

Doris had little investing experience, so when she was invited to attend a "Lunch and Learn" event sponsored by a financial advisor, she went to gain some information.

When I met Doris a few years later, through a friend, she was very skeptical of financial advisors… and when I heard her story, who could fault her for being so? Doris had met with the financial advisor that sponsored the Lunch & Learn event and the financial advisor had offered to help Doris manage her inherited account. Doris agreed that she needed help, so she signed the paperwork to liquidate (sell) and transfer her account to the new financial advisor's management.

However, there was a fly in the ointment… Either Doris didn't understand, or she 'forgot,' or she really hadn't listened fully, or …the consequences of her 'transfer' had not been explained in full to her; because Doris reported to me that at the end of the year Doris received a $ 50,000 tax bill!

Obviously, there was some type of 'taxable' event created by the liquidation of the account and subsequent transfer. After that experience, Doris was more than cautious when it came to 'investing.'

Moral of the story: Ask your trusted friends, advisors, and family members for referrals. Interview your advisors carefully; ask an experienced colleague to attend the interviews with you; consult a tax-advisor before you incur 'liquidation' consequences.

Experience Talks...

Somebody Could Pay YOU Rent

Scott is a real estate developer. Over the past 25+ years Scott has built various real estate projects: private homes, retirement housing, and condominiums. When I met Scott he had been in the construction business for a number of years and owned a variety of properties.

One time he told me he owned, either alone or with one of his partners, over 80 rental properties.

Scott's retirement strategy was to have all of the property mortgages paid in full prior to the time he retired; and to collect rent to add to his income and social security benefits during retirement. As long as the properties are rented, his strategy has merit.

Moral of the story: There is more than one way to produce income for your retirement.

Experience Talks...

The Little Piggy Goes To Market, But Sometimes He Stays 'Home'

In September of 2008 Linda and Paul, a retired couple, became nervous about the stock market.

They called their financial advisor and discussed revising their current investment plan. Upon long deliberation, Linda and Paul decided they would liquidate a sizeable portion, about 25% or 30% of their Retirement Account assets, and keep that money in cash until the market straightened out.

When the market began to recover in 2009, they probably missed some of the up-swing, but all-in-all; they were satisfied with their decision.

Moral of the story: When investor's objectives change, so should their investment allocation; understand what your 'comfort zone' will be.

CHAPTER 4

An Introduction To Retirement Planning

LEARNING OBJECTIVES:

After reading Chapter 4, you should be able to:

a. Articulate and demonstrate your understanding of the advantages and disadvantages of utilizing a *retirement account*.

- Describe the characteristics of a retirement account;

- Explain a strategy for utilizing a retirement account early in life;

- Create both a short-term and long-term retirement plan.

b. Describe the differences between an Individual Retirement Account and a group retirement account; provide examples for how you will use both types of accounts.

- What are some of the group retirement plan options?

- Be able to articulate the differences between a *defined benefit* and *defined contribution* retirement plan;

- Be able to illustrate the *'matching'* feature of a retirement plan;

- Explain a *'vesting'* schedule.

c. Consider what the challenges and risks that you might face when you retire are; be able to list some of those challenges.

d. Define *'tax deferral'* and tax implications of retirement account contributions and withdrawals.

e. Understand what an *annuity* (investment product) is; provide clarification to describe under what circumstances an annuity might be an appropriate product to purchase.

- Describe the *advantages* and *disadvantages* of both a *fixed* and *variable* annuity.

Experience Talks...

This Isn't Your Grandfather's or Your Dad's Retirement Now

My father passed away at the age of 78… he was still working. Selling real estate afforded my father the opportunity to keep working as long as he was able. Even when he became ill, my father was still listing and selling houses, and managing property (collecting rents) for clients. On-the-other-hand, my husband John's father retired at the age of about 60, with two 20-year retirement pensions. One pension was from the Army, and his second pension was from a city in Alabama where he was a Fire-fighter for 20 years. Not only did John's dad have two pensions, his medical needs were also subsidized by the government because he was a Veteran.

My husband, like his father, was able to 'retire' from one career early in life, and he is receiving his first pension. Because he has started a second career, he is working towards building a retirement savings account to supplement his retirement income as well. And several of my Uncles were fortunate enough to retire with pensions and/or retirement accounts. They had either worked for the government, or they worked for large companies that offered a retirement plan option.

Navigating Retirement

During the past several years I have counseled many individuals regarding their personal retirement plans. Just as individuals are unique, so are their approaches to how they will live in retirement, and how they will pay their expenses when they are retired and are no longer drawing an income. While some individuals plan to work a long, long, time (like my father), others are anxious to retire 'as soon as possible.'

Whatever your retirement plan will be when you approach retirement age, my guess is that you will begin to prepare your plan many years in advance. The following section will introduce you to some 'Retirement' concepts. As you go forward and plan for your retirement someday, use this information as a reference.

Chapter 4

An Introduction To Retirement Planning

What Are Your Retirement Goals?

> *"Retirement at sixty-five is ridiculous. When I was sixty-five, I still had pimples."*
>
> George Burns

Not Ready To Retire? It's Never Too Early To Start Planning

A recent report from the Federal Reserve, "Report on the Economic Well-Being in U.S. Household in 2018" (May 2019), found "that a quarter of Americans have no retirement savings at all." And....

☒ *"Many adults are struggling to save for retirement. Even among those who have some savings, people commonly lack financial knowledge and are uncomfortable making investment decisions."* https://www.federalreserve.gov/publications/files/2018-report-economic-well-being-us-households-201905.pdf

The following chart used with permission of Bloomberg L.P. Copyright©2017. All Rights reserved.

https://www.bloomberg.com/news/articles/2019-06-28/financial-worries-keep-most-americans-up-at-night (89)

Tossing and Turning Over Financial Concerns
Money problems keeping Americans up at night.

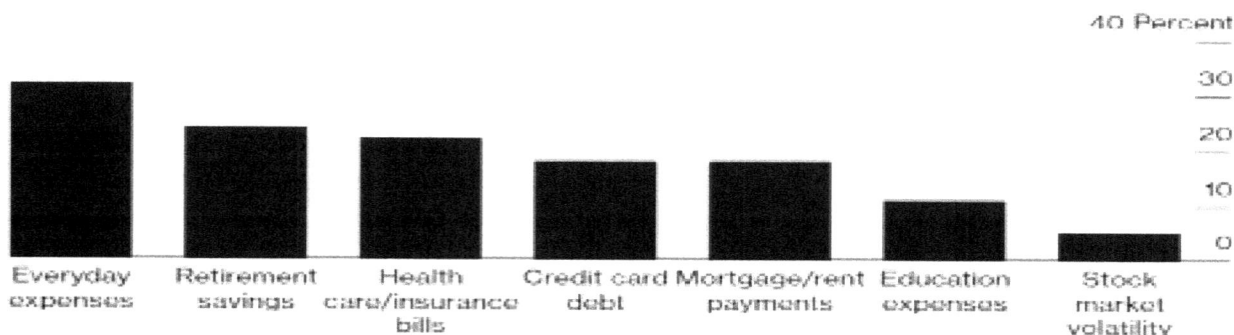

Source: Bankrate

An article published in the January 31, 2011, *"Boomers Anticipate a Different Retirement than Their Parents,"* sited survey data taken from Bank of America's® Merrill Lynch Affluent Insights Quarterly® and is a good read. The survey presented respondents' perceptions regarding lifestyle changes, attitude shifts regarding timing of their retirement, gender differences, concerns they face in retirement, etc. In addition, the article, *"Boomers Tout Benefits of Using Financial Advisors,"* reported that 78% of the Boomer respondents "recommended that individuals begin to plan financially for the life they want to lead in retirement no later than in their 30s, and 57% recommended starting this planning process in their 20s." (89/89a)

Financial planning encompasses a broad range of financial topics. In a previous section we discussed how a financial advisor can assist you in your budgeting and financing processes; and how your advisors can help you make decisions regarding investment strategies. Now we will discuss some strategies you may employ to help you plan for your retirement years. Here are some behavioral points to consider:

1. Be fiscally responsible,

2. Think long-term — save money every day to prepare yourself financially for your future and your retirement,

3. Live within your means – don't spend more than you earn,

4. Plan for a rainy day – save for emergencies,

5. Continue to abide by these principles when you are in retirement – don't outspend your retirement income, and,

6. Consider protection solutions along the way.

The Terms Of Retirement

> *"The question isn't at what age I want to retire, it's at what income."*
>
> George Foreman

While you may be a long, long, way from even thinking about retirement… once you start your career, you will more-than-likely grasp the concept that working full time is probably how you will spend a good part of your next 40 or 50 years! It won't be long until you will understand why *older folks* focus on getting ready for *retirement*.

The term *'retirement'* can conger up an image of white sandy beaches, a golf course, or lying back lazily in a hammock. Most people strive to prepare for retirement so that they can live comfortably in retirement and maintain their current lifestyle. Yet, besides raising children, caring for loved ones, juggling work and home responsibilities, managing your time and money, I believe one of the most complicated topics that you will wrestle with is developing a plan for your retirement.

- When can you retire?

- How much money do you need to save for retirement?

- How will inflation affect you in retirement?

- How will medical expenses impact your expense projections?

- Where should you invest your money now to maximize potential growth?

- When should you rebalance to help insure you maximize your income for retirement?

- How exactly will you distribute/withdraw your money in retirement?

- How will you plan for the impact of paying taxes?

- What protection measure should you have in place to prepare for retirement and beyond?

These are all important questions that deserve your time and attention. They are a call to action to develop your retirement plan strategy. Having a good financial plan in place for your retirement years can possibly add to your overall life enjoyment. I was at a conference recently and one of the speakers spoke about ways that individuals can be more satisfied in retirement. The speaker had conducted research and found that the two most stressful times in a person's life was the first year of marriage, and year one of their retirement. The speaker suggested that you can reduce stress in retirement if you are financially prepared.

> *"Before everything else, getting ready is the secret of success."*
>
> *Henry Ford*

Are we prepared? On March 12, 2019, CNBC® article titled, *"Here's how many American don't have access to a 401(k) plan,"* outlines the retirement plan picture: (99) (https://www.cnbc.com/2018/03/12/how-many-americans-dont-have-access-to-a-401k.html)

Access to Employer-Sponsored Retirement Plans Rises with Age (89a)

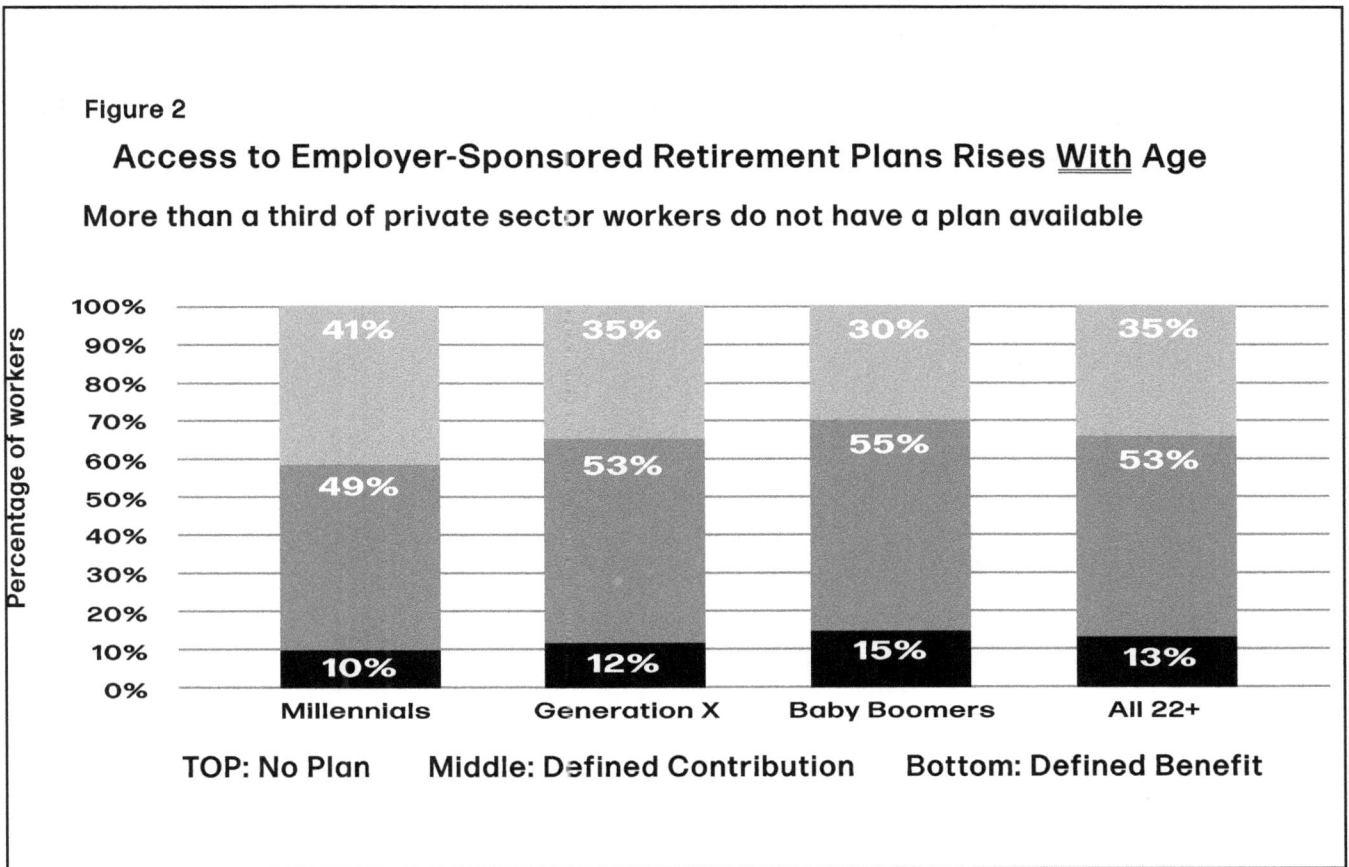

Figure 2

Access to Employer-Sponsored Retirement Plans Rises <u>With</u> Age

More than a third of private sector workers do not have a plan available

	Millennials	Generation X	Baby Boomers	All 22+
TOP: No Plan	41%	35%	30%	35%
Middle: Defined Contribution	49%	53%	55%	53%
Bottom: Defined Benefit	10%	12%	15%	13%

Percentage of workers

Note: Percentages may not total 100 percent due to rounding.
Source: Pew Analysis of 2012 Census Bureau Survery of Income and Program Participation data
© 2017 The Pew Charitable Trusts

On August 8th, 2008, USA Today® published, *"Retirement pop quiz! How well do you know your finances?"* Here is one of the questions the quiz posed:

- *"If you start at age 25 and want to accumulate $1 million dollars by the time you turn age 67, earning 6% on the money you save over those years, how much money will you need to save each month to accomplish your goal?*

- *The answer was:*

  - *If you are 25 years old, you need to put aside $440 a month to accomplish this goal.*

- *If you start earlier, the amount to save each month is slightly less: $319 a month for a 20-year-old, and*

- *If you wait until you are 50 years old, you will need to put $2,831 a month away for the 12 years." (100)*

What Retirement Plan Is Right For You? Retirement Plans Defined

Wading through the maze of retirement account choices takes time. In this section we are going to review a few of the types of retirement plans that you might run across, specifically: *employer-sponsored retirement plans* and *individual retirement plans.* I suggest you read through the following information, but focus on the section that applies to you, or might apply to you in the near future. *Keep the rest of the information for your reference as your income circumstances change.* Read through the information and consult both a tax advisor and a financial advisor before you decide which of the account types are right for you.

What do you think you can afford to set aside for your retirement savings each month? Even $20 or $25 is a start.

_____

Are You Alone, Or Part Of A Group?

All *retirement* accounts must be funded with *earned* income. This means that the money you can put into a retirement account will come from your paycheck. You can either open a retirement account *by yourself - alone*, or you can open an account *that is offered through your place of employment (if one is available) - group.* With both types of plans, you have a couple of tax-options to consider (other choices may be available). For example:

1. In a Traditional IRA or 401k account you set **pre-tax** money aside in a *'tax-deferred'* account. The money you place in these types of accounts grows tax-deferred until the time of withdrawal; which should be after you are at least age 59 1/2 (to avoid IRS penalties). At the time you withdraw the money, you will then pay taxes at *your ordinary income tax rate on the withdrawal amount.*

2. In a ROTH IRA or Roth 401k account **you pay the taxes FIRST**, then you place the money in your account. The investments in these types of account grow tax-free; but you must wait until you are 59 1/2 (and have held the account for a minimum of 5 years) to be able to withdraw the money without penalties; after which you do NOT pay taxes on withdrawals.

I wish I had been told about putting money away for retirement when I was in High School. I started working at a Fortune 500 company in 1972. Two years later, in 1974 the Employee Retirement Income Security Act (ERISA) was passed. ERISA created the tax-deferred **Individual Retirement Account** (IRA). The original IRA account was created to help *individuals save for retirement*. Initially you could only put $1500 a year away into an IRA **if you were not already covered by an employer retirement plan**. (90) Through the years the regulations and contribution limits for IRAs have been revised several times, and they can change each and every year.

Another important aspect of saving is "*The Magic of Coupounding*," which is further explained by the U.S. Department of Labor, Employee Benefits Security Administration. Visit their websight @ https://www.dol.gov to research this topic in depth. Dave Ramsey's commentary, "*How Teens Can Become Millionaires*," (https://www.daveramsey.com/blog/how-teens-can-become-millionaires/) further illustrates how compounding can work:

"Let's consider the case of two investors, Luke and Walt, who would like to become wealthy...

Luke:

a)   put $2,000 per year into the market between the ages of 19 and 26 (only) 8 years (total of $ 16,000),

b)   earned a 12% after tax return, and

c)   continued to earn 12% per year until he retired at age 65.

Walt:

a)   also invested $2,000 per year,

b)   earned the same 12% return,

c)   (but) waited until he was 27 to start investing, and

d)   continued to invest $2,000 per year for 39 years (total of $ 78,000).

Result:

In the end, both men would end up with about $1 million. However, Luke had to invest only $16,000 (i.e. $2,000 for eight years), while Walt had to invest $78,000 ($2,000 for 39 years) or just about six times the amount that Luke invested. Seems like Walt was severely penalized just for waiting eight years to start his investing."

A word of caution: Don't expect an average 12% return in today's **investing environment.**

https://www.daveramsey.com/blog/how-teens-can-become-millionaires

Traditional Individual Retirement Accounts (IRAs)

Individual Retirement Accounts (IRAs) are just that – for individuals. The purpose of a Non-Roth IRA* is for you to be able to:

a. Set aside money today for tomorrow's expenses, those expenses incurred in retirement;

b. Reduce your current gross income, dollar for dollar—to potentially pay fewer taxes on the money you make today; and

c. Postpone paying taxes on your 'deferred money' until a later date when you withdraw the **money — after you are age 59 ½ — to let a larger nest-egg grow.**

Remember, the money that can be contributed into your IRA can only come from earned income (exception is a Spousal IRA).**

Please complete: To avoid an IRS penalty…

In my Investment Account: I can move money in and out of the account at any age and not incur a 10% IRS penalty.   **True /False**

In my Retirement Account: I can move money in and out of the account at any age and not incur a 10% IRS penalty.   **True /False**

Much of the following discussion will focus on tax treatment of your money. Since I am not a tax advisor, please be sure to check: 1) how the tax and other important laws change, 2) with a tax advisor for final advice.

*A Roth IRA has different features.

** Age and other requirements may change through legislation.

Life

Here's an example of how to reduce your current taxable income* by placing your money in a retirement account, while putting money away in your Traditional IRA account:

What this means to you:

Without the IRA:	
Your Gross Salary:	$30,000
Minus Taxes @ 25%	$7,500
Net Income (Take Home Pay)	$22,500
With a traditional IRA contribution:	
Your Gross Salary:	$30,000
Your IRA Contribution	$3,000
Net Income	$27,000
Minus Taxes @ 25%	$6,750
Net Income (Take Home Pay)	$20,250
Money in Your IRA Account	$3,000
Your Total Net Income (Including the IRA amount)	$23,250
The TAX Difference: IRA value may fluctuate depending on investment product selection	**($750) less**

1)   You have started a retirement savings account.

      -   Your take-home pay is $ 250.00 less a month before taxes.

      -   You are paying taxes on $ 250.00 a month less.

2)   You saved money TODAY by paying LESS TAXES for now, you will pay taxes later (non-Roth) . (Tax savings depends on the difference in tax rates at the time of withdrawal.)

3)   And next year you can contribute more money to your account. It adds up.

*Consult a Tax Advisor

Provide your own example here:

_____

Traditional IRAs, continued

A discussion of the different types of retirement accounts will sound repetitive because they possess several of the same characteristics. Here are some important points to remember for your …..

TRADITIONAL IRA:

A. The IRS sets limits on how much you can contribute to an **Individual Retirement Account (IRA)** each year based on your age, so consult your tax advisor for those amounts.

B. As shown in the previous example, all of your contributions to your IRA are deducted from your reported gross income within the same year you contribute. This makes your contributions 'pre-tax' because you have not paid taxes on the contributed money yet.

C. Once you put money in an IRA [account] (cash only can be contributed) you can invest the money in investment products like stocks, bonds, mutual funds, etc. (not items like cars, jewelry, etc.). The idea is to invest and let your investment values grow (no guarantee) over time; and reduce your payment of income taxes now.

D. IRA money should not be withdrawn until you are 59 ½ years old because taking the money out early imposes an IRS 10% penalty.

E. After you are age 72 (current proposed legislation changed this age requirement 1/1/2020) you will be required to take out **Retirement Minimum Distributions (RMDs)**. (Except in instances when the government waives withdrawals in a particular year or changes the ruling.) The RMDs are simply money withdrawals that you will be required to take, and pay taxes on, after you turn 72 years old. The amount that you will be required to take out will typically be calculated for you by the financial institution where you have your account (remember Retirement Accounts are held in custody by the financial institution). When you take the money out of your account, you will pay your taxes at your **current income tax rate**.

> ○ **Like your RMDs, money withdrawn from your (non-Roth) retirement account is taxed at *ordinary income rates for the year in which it is withdrawn*. If you are paying taxes at a lower rate in retirement, then you should be ahead… However, if you find yourself in a higher tax bracket than when you contributed to this *before*-tax account, when you reach retirement age and begin withdrawals, then of course, you might not be ahead.**

Life

For example:

If Jim's IRA grows to $ 289,000 over a 40-year period, and he is in a 25% tax bracket when Jim begins taking withdrawals when he is 65 years old, he will pay taxes at a rate of 25% on his withdrawals:

$ 1,000 a month withdrawal = $ 250 a month payment in taxes.

F. With IRA accounts you should name a primary (and contingent) beneficiary as a part of the opening account documents. Therefore, In the event of your death, your assets will be distributed to your beneficiary.

G. Accounts are also held in custody by the financial institution where you hold your account.

H. For IRAs, income and participation in a group-sponsored retirement plan can affect deductibility and contribution amounts.

Roth IRAs

The Roth IRA is similar to a Traditional IRA. However, there are a couple of critical exceptions which are important to note here. Remember, the IRS can change, and does change, legislation… however, under today's legislation:

- Contributions are made with 'after-tax' dollars (you pay taxes first before you contribute);

- Once the money is invested, you must have been invested for a minimum of 5 years to realize the tax-free compounding growth benefits for your withdrawals;

- You NEVER pay taxes on the gains when you withdraw the money in the future, assuming you withdraw that money after age 59 ½ (and have waited 5 years from the date of your first contribution); and

- When you reach age 72* you are NOT required to take RMDs (Retirement Minimum Distributions).

   *Age and other requirements may change. I am NOT a Tax Advisor, consult yours for clarification.

If you are able to start a Roth IRA, it may be an avenue you should consider. Tax-free income in retirement will be very valuable. If you are not required to pay taxes on the money you withdraw from your Roth account in retirement, or if you are able to pass the money tax-free to your heirs, the benefit may be substantial.

Please Complete:

	Traditional IRA		ROTH IRA	
1. Pay taxes pre-distribution	Yes	No	Yes	No
2. To avoid penalties, you need to be 59 ½ to withdraw your money	Yes	No	Yes	No
3. At age 72, you MUST take RMD*	Yes	No	Yes	No

*The distribution age for RMD requirement may change.

Note: Spousal IRAs can be established for a non-working spouse by the working spouse who is eligible themselves for an IRA. Check again with your tax advisor.

Converting A Traditional IRA To A Roth IRA

In some cases, it may be smart to **convert a Traditional IRA to a Roth IRA**. Remember, when you do, you will be taxed at an ordinary income tax rate (both for federal and state, where applicable) for the money you convert; the amount you convert will be *added to your income for the year in which you convert. ("Roth IRA Conversion Rules,"* Greg Daugherty, 1/16/2020, https://www.investopedia.com/roth-ira-conversion-rules-4770480) For example, if your income is $ 45,000 and you convert $10,000 from your Traditional IRA to a Roth IRA, your taxable income for that year will be $55,000. Consider the consequences of a higher tax payment before you decide to convert!*

Historically, there have been income limits set by the IRS that you needed to consider in determining whether you could convert your traditional IRA to a Roth IRA. However, a new tax law, passed in 2010 allows individuals to convert a Traditional IRA to a Roth IRA, regardless of their income (there are no income limits). This special tax treatment is granted through a provision in the Tax Increase Prevention and Reconciliation Act of 2005. (90) No matter what year you might consider a conversion, consult your tax advisor to determine if you are **eligible**; ask about *other features and limitations* that may apply. Explore the consequences carefully **BEFORE** you convert.*

*Laws can, and do, change. Consult a Tax Advisor.

Employer-Sponsored Group Plans

When you are young and are just beginning to enter the work force, you may have a wonderful opportunity to set the stage for your future. When you start working ask if your employer provides a retirement plan. If there is an employer-sponsored retirement plan, CONSIDER TAKING ADVANTAGE of it, sign up to participate. However, (remember) if you work somewhere that does not offer a plan, you can still start putting money away by starting your own personal retirement plan (for example: an IRA).

Believe it or not **employer retirement plans** were first established in the late 19th century, although those early plans did not have any tax-deferred advantages. The government added the tax-favored status to the employer retirement plans in the 1920s. By 1935 (with the establishment of the Social Security system) the employer-sponsored plans gained in popularity. Today we will focus on two categories of employer-sponsored group plans: The Defined Benefit Pension Plan, and the Defined Contribution Retirement Plan. The United States Department of Labor®. (3/2018) reports: '55% of workers participate in a civilian workplace Retirement Plan.' Bureau of Labor Statistics, National Compensation Survey for 2017. (91/92)

1) Defined Benefit (pension) Employer-Sponsored Plans

Between 1940 and 1980 the number of private-sector employees who were covered by a pension plan grew from 15% of the American workers to 46% of the workers. However, a decline in the percentage of workers covered by a pension plan [Defined Benefit (DB)] is noted beginning in 1990. The Department of Labor reported that in 1985 there were 170,000 Defined Benefit plans, contrasted to 47,600 Defined Benefit plans in 2005 and 46,300 in 2016. (93) American workers just are not offered these types of pension plans today like they had been in the past. In fact, (2008) The U.S. Bureau of Labor Statistics reported that, "From 1980 through 2008, the proportion of private wage and salary workers participating in DB pension plans fell from 38 percent to 20 percent." (94)   Additionally, in November 2019, Barron's® reported, "Just 13% of people working for Corporate America have a defined-benefit pension plan these days, down from 76% in the mid-1980s, according to data from the Bureau of Labor Statistics." (91, 93, 94)

Retirement benefit access, participation, and take-up rates for union and nonunion civilian workers, March 2019

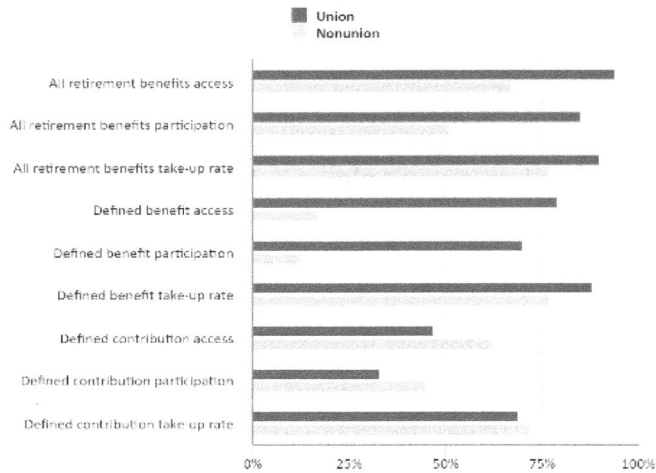

Click legend items to change data display. Hover over chart to view data.
Source: U.S. Bureau of Labor Statistics.

A **defined benefit plan** is an employer-sponsored retirement plan. A defined benefit plan is also referred to as a Pension Plan. These plans are different from other types of employer-sponsored retirement plans because they generally provide an 'income for life' feature. The defined benefit pension plan commits the employer to provide the qualifying employee with a specified monthly benefit (income) at retirement, based on a predetermined formula. This formula is based on the employee's salary history, length of service, and age. The employee's benefit is NOT determined by the performance or earnings of the investments in the plan. The way the plans are funded can also be unique.

Life

For example:

My husband, John, was employed by a police department in a city in Kansas and he has a pension plan. Money was involuntarily taken out of John's check each week and put into a pooled account managed by the city's Plan Administrator.

John worked a certain number of years and was a certain age to be able to receive benefits when he retired. So, when John met the criteria set out by the retirement pension plan document, John retired and receives a set amount of money each month for the rest of his life. He also had other withdrawal options at the time of his retirement. The amount John receives each month was periodically calculated for him prior to retirement using the current actuarial tables.

This type of plan allowed John to be able to plan what his retirement income was from this one income source.

2) Defined Contribution Employer-Sponsored Plans

With the reduction in the number of pension plans in the U.S., Americans now find themselves in the position of planning and saving for their own retirement. The Pew Chartiable Trusts, "*Employer-Sponsored Retirement Plan Access, Uptake, and Savings*" 2016 chartbook states that, "two-thirds [67%] of full-time workers have access to an [employer-sponsored retirement plan]." (94) Also, the "*Retirement Savings and Household Wealth in 2007*" report, published by Patrick Purcell, a Specialist in Income Security (94), stated that "49% of workers under the age of 65 participated in an employer-sponsored retirement plan ... about the same as in 2004."

A (Non-Roth) **Defined Contribution** employer-sponsored plan qualifies for special tax handling under Section 401(a) of the Internal Revenue Code. Money placed in a non-Roth employer-sponsored pre-tax retirement plan is also referred to as 'qualified' money. There are several types of qualified (pre-tax) Defined Contribution employer-sponsored retirement plans that employers can offer. Defined Contribution plans do not offer a stated 'end benefit' like a Defined Benefit plan. Characteristically, a Defined Contribution Plan will allow you to decide how much you will contribute. Your Non-Roth contributions are deducted from your reported gross income, thus lowering your taxes for the year you make the contribution. Typically, investment choices are offered by the retirement plan, and you select the options in which you want to invest. Some plans offer a 'match' on specified employee contributions. Each year the IRS determines the contribution levels for these types of plans. Vesting schedules generally apply for the employer 'match.' And again, to avoid IRS penalties, you should be 59 1/2 years old before you plan to withdraw the money from these types of accounts.

The features and characteristics of a **Non-Roth Defined Contribution employer-sponsored retirement plan** are similar to Individual Retirement Accounts (IRA), see the general features noted here*:

- in exchange for the tax advantages, you are expected to leave your money in your retirement accounts until you are 59 ½ years old; early withdrawal (prior to age 59 ½) could mean a 10% IRS penalty;

- the money is held in a custodian account;

- each account holder names a primary (and you also can name a contingent) beneficiary;

- if your account is not a Roth IRA or Roth employer-sponsored retirement account, Retirement Minimum Distributions (RMDs) should be taken after you turn age 72* (age requirement just changed for 1/1/2020, /except in years with the government changes the rules);

- the plans have contribution limits; contribution limits for these plans can change annually;

- certain plans require 'testing' to meet IRS regulations; special IRS document filing may also be required;

- contributions are made 'pre-tax;'

- taxes on Non-Roth contributions and investment gains are paid at ordinary income tax rates at the time the money is withdrawn;

- vesting schedules document when employees receive the employer's contributions (if employers do contribute);

- some types of group retirement plans protect your assets from creditors;

- eligibility requirements apply. (94, 95)

*Other restrictions may apply; specific plan features are detailed in the Plan Document.

More Retirement Plan Options For You

If you are already working, you may be familiar with a 401k, a SIMPLE or SEP IRA, a 403(b), or a Profit-Sharing Retirement Plan. These plans are additional employer-sponsored retirement plans. The following is a brief (general) overview of some of the employer-sponsored retirement plan more common options.

- ☒ **The 401k Retirement Plan (Non-Roth)** is one of the most well-known types of employer-sponsored retirement plan choices. The plan allows you to defer taxes on the money you put in your account. 401k accounts are fully protected by federal law from creditors. 401k Retirement plans are offered by **for-profit companies and corporations; however, it is reported in 2019 that only 50% of Americans have access to a 401k** (3/2019) (99), however, the US Census Bureau reports that 59% of the employed Americans have access to a 401k plan today (4/1/2021). Determine the amount you will contribute each year. Your contributions are deducted from your reported gross income in the year you contribute to your 401k, thus lowering your taxes for that year. 401k investment choices are offered by the retirement plan, and you typically select the options in which you want to invest. (However, some plans can have pooled investment accounts; the employer directs the investment selections for the employees.) An employer-sponsored 401k has a Plan Document that specifies how the plan is administered and outlines when withdrawals can be made.

401k plans can offer these additional features:

- ○ An employer 'match' on specified percentage limits of employee contributions.

- • Not all plans offer a match, and if the plan does offer a match, each plan's match percentage may be different.

- ○ Vesting schedules generally apply for the employer 'match.'

- ○ Participants may be able to access loans from their account.

- ○ Hardship withdrawals may or may not be allowed.

- ○ Annual nondiscrimination and participation tests must be met.

    ☒ Participation discrimination between different types, or classes, of employees might be allowed under certain circumstances (for example leased employees may be excluded); however, discrimination of other types is generally prohibited. *

- ○ May also offer Roth option.

    *This comment does not constitute legal advice, and a lawyer should be consulted to clarify, if necessary.

☒ A **403(b)** is an employer-sponsored retirement plan that is offered by **Not-for-profit organizations. public schools and certain associations**. Most of what is true for a 401k plan also applies to a 403(b) plan. These types of retirement plans may also be referred to as *Tax Sheltered Annuities*. There can be additional restrictions regarding the types of investment products held in these 403(b) retirement accounts.

☒ A **Profit-Sharing Plan** is the sharing of company profits, re-calculated annually, with employees. A Profit-Sharing plan can stand alone, or can be a second-tier, or overlay plan, added to a 401k plan. Vesting schedules generally apply. The Plan Document outlines the criteria for participating, and the specifics of what the plan offers.

☒ A **SEP IRA Retirement Plan** is typically offered by smaller businesses. Businesses that have variable profits may choose a Simplified Employee Plan (SEP). These types of plans must be filed and funded by a business' tax filing deadline, including extensions. A SEP plan allows employers ONLY to contribute to the plan. Eligibility requires that plan participants be a minimum of 21 years old, and have earned income of a minimum of $600,* indexed for inflation, during the year, and have worked for the employer in any part of at least 3 out of the last 5 years.* There are a couple of contribution formula choices. Contributions are treated as business deduction expenses.

> * With a SEP plan, the employer can decide year to year whether or not to contribute to the plan. Some owners may use this type of retirement plan as a 'bonus,' or profit-sharing option. Contribution limits exist (no more than 25% of compensation). Remember, the owner may contribute differently each year. All contributions made by the employer are owned (vested) by the employee immediately. The employee is responsible for managing the account. No special IRS filing or testing is required.

☒ **Owner-only 401k plan**s (also known as a Solo 401k) are for single owners and their employed spouses (spouses who also work in the business). The business cannot have any other full-time employees. These plans must be established by the end of the business' fiscal year. Other features to this type of plan are similar to 401k plans, however contribution levels are different/higher:

a. the participants can contribute as an 'employee,' and

b. the business can make additional contributions so the total contribution amount is much higher for the participant (owner and/or spouse).

☒ **SIMPLE (Savings Incentive Match Plan for Employees) IRA Retirement Plans** are for smaller businesses, who have one hundred or fewer employees that earned $ 5,000 or more in the previous year; and for businesses who want a lower cost retirement program in exchange for easier administration. These plans have lower contribution limits for the employee than some of the other plans; these plans are not subject to nondiscrimination and top-heavy testing and have less filing requirements; and these plans can offer a 'match' feature as well. **The employee is responsible for managing their own account, and sometimes they also pay for the annual account fee.**

  ○ No money can be transferred out of the account (it must remain as a SIMPLE account) for a minimum of 2 years from the date of opening the account or the IRS will impose a 25% penalty.

  *Criteria, qualifications, and IRS Regulations can change annually for Retirement Accounts.

Check with a tax advisor to determine plan opening rules and deadlines for each type of plan; and note other restrictions. For example, a 401k cannot be opened in the same year a business has contributed to a SIMPLE retirement plan. Carefully review the options with your financial and tax advisor.

When you invest in your retirement account, understanding the ramifications of your choices is very important.

Retirement Plan Questions. Circle True or False.

A 403b is appropriate for a not-for-profit organization or association?	True	False
A vesting schedule is used for every plan?	True	False
Non-Roth retirement plans generally tax-defer gains?	True	False
All retirement plans are kept in custody accounts?	True	False

I Want Free Money!
Does Your Plan Have A 'Match?'

Some retirement plans offer a ***company 'match' for your contributions, up to a specific, stated percentage.*** If the company you work for does *offer* a match, carefully determine what **percentage you can defer from your salary to enjoy the full advantage of the match.** For example, the formulas for what a company will match (if they do match) can vary greatly. One company may match dollar-for-dollar up to 4%, while another company may match 100% of the first 3% and then 50% of the next 2%. In order to get the full match for the second company, you will need to defer 5%. See the table below for two examples (95):

Life

In the following example, both companies' 'match' is 4%.
(Your company could match a greater percentage, or a lower percentage.)

This means that in Scenario A you will need to contribute 5% to get the full 4% employer match; and in Scenario B your total match is dollar for dollar up to a maximum match of 4%.

Check with your employer, each plan document will identify the match calculation if there is one.

	Scenario A		Scenario B	
	You Defer	Company Match	You Defer	Company Match
	3.0%	3.0%	4.0%	4.0%
	1.0%	0.5%	0.0%	0.0%
	1.0%	0.5%	0.0%	0.0%
	1.0%	0.0%	0.0%	0.0%
TOTAL	6.0% deferral	4.0% match	4.0% deferral	4.0% match
More Deferrals		0%		0%

When Do You Get The Vest?

We just discussed the point that some retirement plans have a feature called a 'company match.' If the plan has a company match, the plan can also have a vesting schedule for the 'match.' A vesting schedule is stated clearly in the retirement plan document. The vesting schedules can vary, according to each plan design. The **vesting schedule outlines the number of years the employee must be employed by the employer to receive the funds that the *employer* sets aside for the employee match.** These schedules outline the timeframe for shifting the **ownership of the employer 'match' money, or profit-sharing contributions made by the employer, from the employer to you, the participant.** That means that the employee has 'length of service' requirements to receive ownership of the employer 'match.' In-other-words, you may not be awarded your 'match' money until you have completed X years of employment with that company. This arrangement, or scheduling, protects the employer from providing what is perceived as a bonus, or benefit, to the employee who does not stay with the company and might take the match money and leave. This arrangeWnt also encourages the employee to remain employed with that employer.

> Note: Some Defined Contribution plans can transfer 100% of the match to you when the match is initially made. These types of plans have special rules, they are called 401k **Safe Harbor** Retirement Plans. These types of plans have no vesting schedules for the 401k company match.

> Additionally, **money you contribute is always 100% vested** immediately upon contribution. What this means: You always own the money in your account that you have deferred from your salary. **It is only the employer's contribution that can have a vesting schedule. (95)**

The matching schedule for a 401k defined contribution retirement plan can be different than the matching schedules for other types of retirement plans, like a Profit-Sharing Plan. In addition, ***defined benefit*** retirement plans (pension plans) typically also have a vesting schedule. The vesting schedule for a defined benefit plan can be dramatically different than the schedules for defined contribution retirement plans, as noted on the next page.

Life

Here are the two commonly used vesting schedules for *Defined Contribution Employer Retirement Plan contributions.* *

Graded vesting: With this vesting schedule, the vesting begins after the 2nd anniversary date of your employment. After year 2, you are 20% vested, and then you vest an additional 20% each year thereafter. Therefore, if you are with your employer for 6 years and 1 day you are fully vested on all past and future employer contributions. (95)

Years of Employment	Percent Vested
2	20%
3	40%
4	60%
5	80%
6	100%

Cliff vesting: With this vesting schedule no benefit is offered until after the third year of employment, and then the employee is 100% vested.

Years of Employment	Percent Vested
1	0%
2	0%
3	100%

*As previously noted, some retirement plans do not require a vesting schedule for employer contributions to your account. Additionally, the money you defer from your salary is always 100% vested to you upon contribution (no waiting period).

Be sure you know your plan's vesting schedule. Changing jobs is commonplace today but timing those changes can impact your retirement account. If you are close to a 'vest' date you may want to plan to wait until after you 'vest' to change jobs. Check the plan document to determine what additional 'vesting' prerequisites might also be required.

Answering The "How Much?" Question

Once you have determined which type of retirement plan is appropriate for you, you will then need to develop your deferral and savings plans. How you determine how much you should be putting away for retirement is a very individual decision. The Social Security Administration, in 2006, suggested that Americans have taken on a 'greater responsibility for financing their own retirement.' 'Social Security, once the foundation of retiree income, provides about 38% of the average household's retirement income.' (97)

Consider the 2019 Social Security Report findings, *"Understanding the Benefits"*:

"The amount of your average wages that Social Security retirement benefits replaces varies depending on your earnings and when you choose to start benefits. If you start benefits at "full retirement age," this percentage ranges from as much as 75 percent for very low earners, to about 40 percent for medium earners, to about 27 percent for high earners. If you start benefits after full retirement age, these percentages would be higher. If you start benefits earlier, these percentages would be lower." (97)

An AARP article, *"Planning for Retirement: How Much Money Do You Need To Retire?"* John Waggoner, 1/6/2021, (https://www.aarp.org/retirement//info-2020/how-much-money-do-you-need-to-retire.html) suggests the answer is predicated on 4 variables:

"Factor 1: How much you will spend.

Factor 2: How much you will earn on your savings.

Factor 3: How long you will live.

Factor 4: How much you withdraw from your savings each year."

Figuring out how much you should be saving, and how much you will be receiving from Social Security, along with WHAT ADDITIONAL COSTS may be looming in retirement, are daunting. If you have a difficult time imagining how much you will need in retirement, Peng Chen, Ph.D. (98) reports in his 2007 article, *"Take the Guesswork Out of Retirement Savings,"* that a study suggested that about 80% of your pre-retirement NET income is a good rule-of-thumb goal for retirement income. Work backwards – use the 80% rule-of-thumb calculation… factor in an inflation rate, and then determine how much you should be putting away for retirement to provide the income you project you will need later. Plan for your 'Desired Annual Retirement Income.' Fidelity® provides a wonderful commentary in their 2021 article, *"How much should I save for retirement?"* The article also provides some excellent tips on how to make 'Saving' a priority. (https://www.fidelity.com/viewpoints/retirement/how-much-money-should-I-save).

Use on-line Retirement Calculators to help you plan as well.

The Challenges, Are You Ready?

People often dream of the day they will retire. People speculate what they will do in retirement, where they will live, how they will spend their day, how much money they will have to spend, travel, work on their hobby, etc. I would guess that the majority of individuals, when asked, are excited about the day they are able to retire. Just ask your parents or older co-workers. I bet they are planning for their 'transition' day.

Remember the earlier comments by the Boomers... individuals who retire today are facing many, many challenges.

Bank of America®'s Better Money Habits® 2019 reported The Top 4 retirement concerns:

a) "Paying for health care,   c) Saving enough money, and

b) Maintaining an income stream,   d) Having too much debt"

https://bettermoneyhabits.bankofamerica.com/en/retirement/top-retirement-concerns

---

- *"Nearly six in 10 Americans worry about paying costs of a major illness/accident"*

- https://news.gallup.com/poll/233642/paying-medical-crises-retirement-lead-financial-fears.aspx

Here are some common concerns for current and future retirees:

- ☒ What are the investment strategies you need to employ to help ensure you can achieve your financial long-term goals?

- ☒ What additional costs might you incur in retirement? How can you plan for those costs now?

- ☒ Will you be able to retire on schedule and live in the manner you expect?

- ☒ How can you plan to manage taxes and, if appropriate, minimize estate taxes when you pass assets others? (95, 96)

List here the financial risks that you think others face now, or may face later in life when you retire.?

_____

_____

Planning for retirement can be daunting, especially if you read some of the many publications concerning the 'risks' for retirees. Of course, **running out of money** is the primary concern. Listed below are five risks that have gathered a consensus concerning the reasons for running out of money in retirement. (95, 101)

Risk #1: The potential to outlive your money by underestimating your life span.

Today, as everyone already has heard, people are living a lot longer. Here are a few statistics the Social Security Administration represents (*"Probability of a 65-Year-Old Living to a Given Age, by Sex and Year"*):

- ☒ "…a man who reaches age 65 in 2015 [has] a 90% chance of reaching age 70, a 62% chance of reaching age 80, and a 22% chance of reaching age 90."

(https://www.hamiltonproject.org/charts/probability_of_a_65_year_old_living_to_a_given_age_by_sex_and_year)

The Social Security Administration's *"Life Expectancy in North America 2019"* notes the expected changes over the years (https://www.ssa.gov/oact/STATS/table4c6.html); and their calculators, provided at https://www.ssa.gov/planners/lifeexpectancy.html, present:

"According to data we compiled:

- A man turning age 65 on April 1, 2019 can expect to live, on average, until age 84.0.

- A woman turning age 65 on April 1, 2019 can expect to live, on average, until age 86.5.

And those are just averages. About one out of every three 65-year-olds today will live past age 90, and about one out of seven will live past age 95."

Life

My grandmother lived to be 96, and my Mother passed away at age 97.
One of my clients died at the age of 101. FACTS!

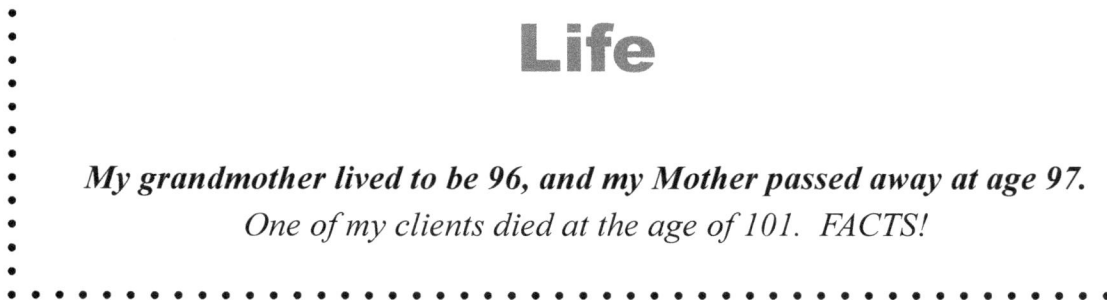

The Organization for Economic Co-operation and Development, **"Average US Life Expectancy Statistics by Gender, Ethnicity, State,"** (2017), reported that:

(https://www.simplyinsurance.com/average-us-life-expectancy-statistics/#section-1):..."in America the average life expectancy for women is 81 years [old] and 77 years [old] for men."

WHAT IS THE LIFE EXPECTANCY OF AN AMERICAN MALE OR FEMALE?

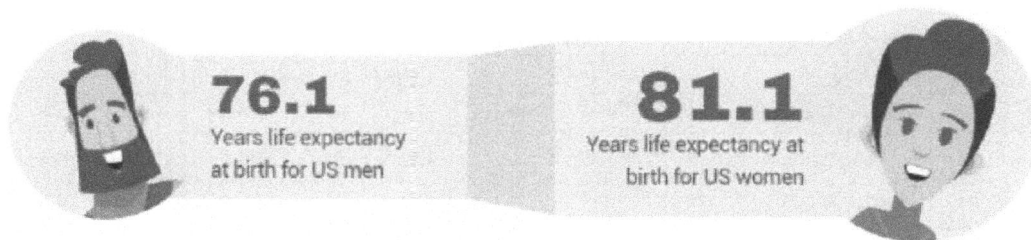

76.1
Years life expectancy
at birth for US men

81.1
Years life expectancy at
birth for US women

Gender Specific Figures:

- **Male: 76.1 years -** Average life expectancy of a US male (at birth).

- **Female: 81.1 years -** Average life expectancy of a US female (at birth).

- **5.0-year difference** between average US female and male lifespan expectancy.

Last available data is from OECD/2017/Average US Life Expectancy Statistics by Gender, Ethnicity, State. https://www.simplyinsurance.com/average-us-life-expectancy-statistics/

Additional sources: Vital Statistics Rapid Release Report No. 010 February 2021 Provisional Life Expectancy Estimates for January through June, 2020 Elizabeth Arias, Ph.D., Betzaida Tejada-Vera, M.S., and Farida Ahmad, M.P.H. Vital Statistics Surveillance Report 2/2021, presented the following longevity reports: (https://www.cdc.gov/nchs/data/vsrr/VSRR10-508.pdf)

U.S. Department of Health and Human Services • Centers for Disease Control and Prevention
National Center for Health Statistics • National Vital Statistics System

Table. Expectation of life by age, Hispanic origin, race for the non-Hispanic population, and sex: United States, 2020

Age (years)	All origins			Hispanic[1]			Non-Hispanic white[1]			Non-Hispanic black[1]		
	Total	Male	Female	Total	Male	Female	Total	Male	Female	Total	Male	Female
0	77.8	75.1	80.5	79.9	76.6	83.3	78.0	75.5	80.6	72.0	68.3	75.8
1	77.2	74.5	80.0	79.3	76.0	82.7	77.4	74.9	79.9	71.8	68.1	75.5
5	73.3	70.6	76.0	75.4	72.1	78.8	73.4	71.0	75.9	67.9	64.2	71.6
10	68.3	65.6	71.0	70.4	67.1	73.8	68.4	66.0	71.0	63.0	59.3	66.7
15	63.4	60.7	66.1	65.4	62.1	68.8	63.5	61.1	66.0	58.1	54.4	61.7
20	58.5	55.9	61.2	60.6	57.3	63.9	58.6	56.3	61.1	53.4	49.8	56.9
25	53.8	51.3	56.3	55.8	52.7	59.1	53.9	51.6	56.3	48.9	45.5	52.1
30	49.2	46.8	51.5	51.1	48.1	54.2	49.2	47.0	51.5	44.4	41.1	47.4
35	44.6	42.3	46.8	46.5	43.5	49.4	44.6	42.6	46.7	39.9	36.8	42.8
40	40.0	37.8	42.1	41.8	39.0	44.6	40.1	38.1	42.1	35.5	32.6	38.3
45	35.5	33.4	37.5	37.3	34.6	39.9	35.6	33.7	37.4	31.3	28.5	33.9
50	31.1	29.2	33.0	32.8	30.2	35.2	31.2	29.4	32.9	27.2	24.6	29.6
55	26.9	25.1	28.6	28.5	26.1	30.7	26.9	25.3	28.5	23.3	20.8	25.5
60	22.9	21.3	24.4	24.4	22.2	26.4	22.9	21.5	24.3	19.7	17.5	21.7
65	19.1	17.8	20.4	20.6	18.7	22.3	19.1	17.9	20.2	16.5	14.5	18.1
70	15.5	14.4	16.5	17.0	15.4	18.3	15.4	14.4	16.3	13.6	11.9	14.8
75	12.2	11.3	12.9	13.7	12.4	14.6	12.0	11.2	12.7	10.8	9.6	11.8
80	9.3	8.6	9.7	10.7	9.8	11.4	9.0	8.4	9.5	8.5	7.5	9.1
85	6.8	6.4	7.0	8.3	7.7	8.8	6.5	6.1	6.7	6.5	5.9	6.8

[1] Life tables by Hispanic origin are based on death rates that have been adjusted for race and ethnicity misclassification on death certificates. Updated classification ratios were applied; see Technical Notes.
NOTES: Estimates are based on provisional data from January 2020 through June 2020. Provisional data are subject to change as additional data are received.
SOURCE: National Center for Health Statistics, National Vital Statistics System, Mortality, 2020.

Figure 2. Life expectancy at birth, by Hispanic origin and race: United States, 2019 and 2020

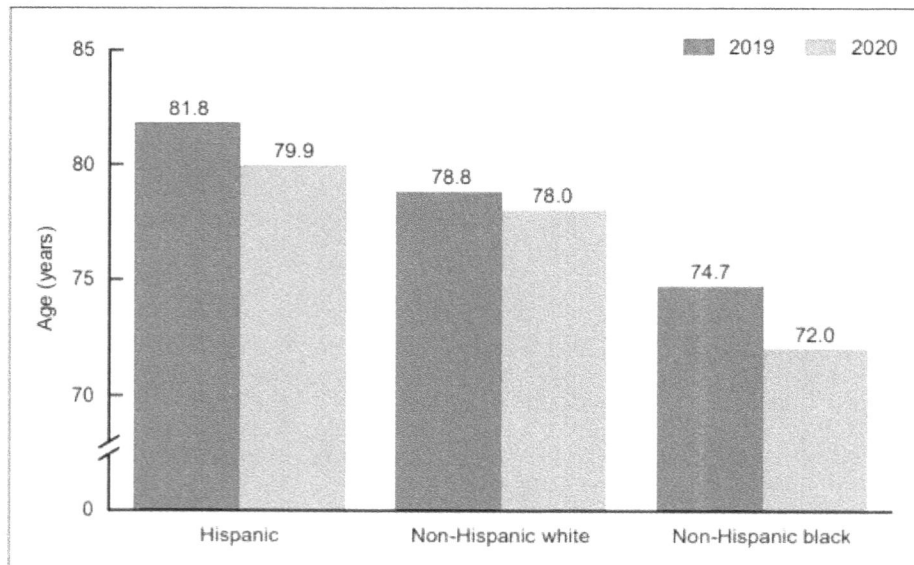

NOTES: Life expectancies for 2019 by Hispanic origin and race are not final estimates; see Technical Notes. Estimates are based on provisional data from January 2020 through June 2020.
SOURCE: National Center for Health Statistics, National Vital Statistics System, Mortality data.

And the following period life table is based on the mortality experience of a population during a relatively short period of time. Here we present the 2017 period life table for the Social Security area population. For this table, the period life expectancy at a given age is the average remaining number of years expected prior to death for a person at that exact age, born on January 1, using the mortality rates for 2017 over the course of his or her remaining life. (https://www.ssa.gov/oact/STATS/table4c6.html)

Period Life Table, 2017

Exact age	Male			Female		
	Death probability [a]	Number of lives [b]	Life expectancy	Death probability [a]	Number of lives [b]	Life expectancy
0	0.006304	100,000	75.97	0.005229	100,000	80.96
1	0.000426	99,370	75.45	0.000342	99,477	80.39
2	0.000290	99,327	74.48	0.000209	99,443	79.42
3	0.000229	99,298	73.50	0.000162	99,422	78.43
4	0.000162	99,276	72.52	0.000143	99,406	77.45
5	0.000146	99,260	71.53	0.000125	99,392	76.46
6	0.000136	99,245	70.54	0.000113	99,379	75.47
7	0.000127	99,232	69.55	0.000104	99,368	74.47
8	0.000115	99,219	68.56	0.000097	99,358	73.48

Use these averages to help you plan.

Risk#2: The increasing cost of health care can have a devastating effect on your retirement income plans.

Costs are rising daily and the following are examples of specific timeframes. Research carefully the health care cost you may incur at retirement.

Many retirees lack adequate health care insurance coverage. Healthcare costs are just plain scary. If I think about it, I really can't tell what I am charged for health care; like doctor visits, physical therapy sessions, etc. because all I pay is my 'co-pay.' However, I do know that when my son Michael went to the emergency room several years ago that the bill for a 4-hour stay was over $2000! Does the public really know why the costs are so high? Have you ever reviewed a medical bill in detail? Maybe we all should start scrutinizing our medical bills. (No wonder our government administrations are making this issue a priority.)

Here are varying perspectives on the rising costs of healthcare in retirement. Review some current statistics, as they change frequently.

Fidelity's® *"How to plan for rising health care costs"* article (5/6/2021) provided this information: (https://www.fidelity.com/viewpoints/personal-finance/plan-for-rising-health-care-costs)

- ○ "It is estimated that the average couple will need $300,000 in 2021 (after-tax) dollars for medical expenses in retirement, excluding long-term care.

- ○ Health care continues to be one of the largest expenses in retirement."

> *"Around 45% of Americans said a major health-related expense could potentially lead to bankruptcy, according to a Gallup poll. Health care expenses can break the bank at any age, but they're especially detrimental to older Americans –– retirees in particular." (104)*

On June 11, 2019, USA TODAY® published an article, *"The expense nearly half of Americans think can bankrupt them"*….

Additionally, the Healthview Services® *"2021 Retirement Health Care Costs Data Report"* (106), projected the amount of out-of-pocket health care costs to be as follows:

- ☒ "Total projected lifetime healthcare costs for a healthy 65-year-old-couple retiring in 2021 are expected to be $662,156."

Kiplinger® (9/2019) reports that a "couple retiring at 65 today will need $ 399,000 in health care costs in retirement." (*"The 5 Biggest Retirement Mistakes to Avoid,"* https://www.kiplinger.com/article/retirement/T047-C032-S014-the-5-biggest-retirement-mistakes-to-avoid.html).

Another source, the Center for Retirement Research® at Boston College, published a working paper, *"How Much Does Out-of-Pocket Medical Spending Eat Away at Retirement Income?"* (10/2017) That report found the following: (107)

- ☒ "…In 2014, the average retiree had only 65.7 percent of his Social Security benefits remaining after OOP (out-of-pocket) spending and only 82.2 percent of total income.

- ☒ Nearly one-fifth (18 percent) of retirees had less than 50 percent of their 2014 Social Security income remaining after OOP spending, with 6 percent of retirees falling below 50 percent of total income."

Therefore,

- ☒ "With less than two-thirds of their Social Security benefits available for non-medical consumption, and limited income outside of Social Security for much of the elderly population, many retirees likely feel that making ends meet is difficult.

- ☒ Medicare spending per beneficiary is expected to resume its decades-long rise by the end of the decade, which will put even more pressure on retirees' budgets." (107)

A Merrill Lynch® source also reported 2014 projected costs for health care: *"Plan now for the cost of health care."* Healthview® updated these expenses in 2018 in the chart below: (105)

(2014) https://www.merrilledge.com/guidance/nearing-retirement/health-care-costs

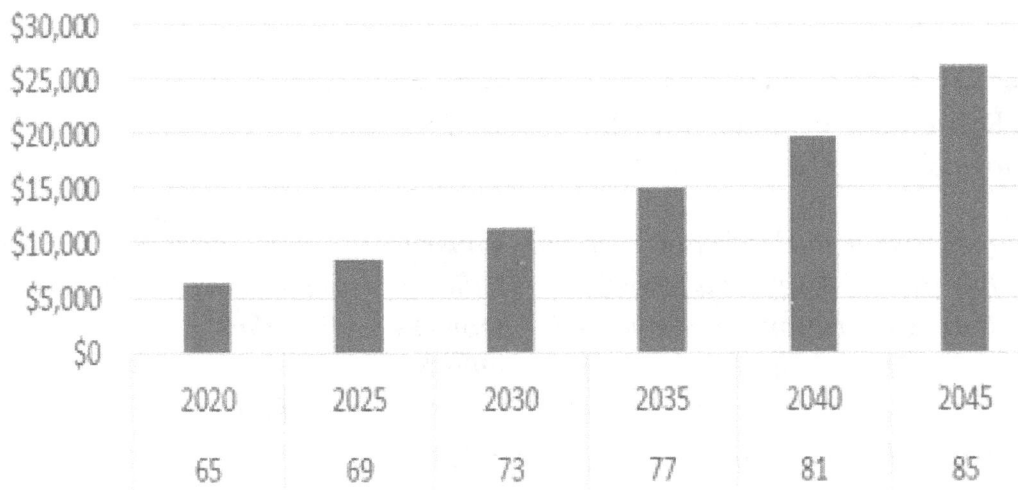

65-year-old Medicare beneficiary projected annual health care expenses

A Harvard University® research report stated that, *"Harvard Study: 60% of Bankruptcies Caused by Health Problems"* (105). And additional reporting by Eurekalert.org (5/2019), further supported this Statement: *"67 percent of bankruptcy filers cite illness and medical bills as contributors to financial ruin."* Fallout from rising health care costs can have a domino effect. Educate yourself, RESEARCH information regarding the rising cost of health insurance. (109)

Life

With rising health care costs, many seniors purchase supplemental Medicare insurance today. I am at an age where I have purchased just such a supplemental Medicare plan.

Research several websites that provide health-care cost information. Note the websites and pertinent data that you find.

_____

Nationwide Retirement Institute(r)'s 9th Annual Consumer Survey (5/7/2020) *"Guiding generations toward healthcare knowledge"*:

"Medicare misjudgments: Medicare remains consistently misunderstood across every generation. Only 1/3 of Americans know how Medicare works to cover retirement medical costs. 8 in 10 of Generation Xers and baby boomers+ wish they understood Medicare coverage better. 66% of Generation Xers and baby boomers+ aren't sure how much they should expect to pay out-of-pocket for Medicare costs. Fewer than 1/3 of Americans know that you do not have to file for Medicare if you work past 65."

Of Course, I Want to Be Cared for Long-Term

Long-term care is very different from health care. A report prepared by the U.S. Senate Special Committee on Aging®, February 2000 (https://www.aging.senate.gov/, 111), described long-term care as follows:

> *"It [long-term care] differs from other types of health care in that the goal of long-term care is not to cure an illness, but to allow an individual to attain and maintain an optimal level of functioning...*
>
> *Long-term care encompasses a wide array of medical, social, personal, and supportive and specialized housing services needed by individuals who have lost some capacity for self-care because of a chronic illness or [a] disabling condition.' (111)*

As with healthcare costs, the following long-term care statistics change rapidly...the following are guidelines for you to consider.

- *"How Much Care Will You Need?,"* (112) reports: *Fact: 70% of people 65 and older will eventually need Long Term Care.*

- LongTermCare.gov (https://acl.gov/ltc/basic-needs/how-much-care-will-you-need), reports that *"One-third of today's (2021) 65 year-olds may never need long-term care support, but 20% will need it for longer than 5 years."* (112)

With so many people potentially utililizing Long-Term Care, we want to take a quick look at some of the cost statistics:

"Long-Term Care Insurance Explained," Barbara Marquand, 7/16/2021, reports:

"1. **To protect savings.** Long-term care costs can deplete a retirement nest egg quickly. The median cost of care in a semiprivate nursing home room is $93,072 a year, according to Genworth's 2020 Cost of Care Survey.

ANNUAL MEDIAN COST OF LONG-TERM CARE IN 2020

Home Health Aide	Homemaker Services	Adult Day Health Care	Assisted Living Facility	Nursing Home Care
$54,912	$53,772	$19,236	$51,600 for a private one-bedroom	$93,072 for a semi-private room $105,852 for a private room"

Source: Genworth 2020 Cost of Care Survey

---

https://www.nerdwallet.com/blog/insurance/long-term-care-insurance/

The National Clearinghouse for Long Term Care suggests, *"40% of people receiving long-term care are working-age adults between the ages of 18-64[1]."* (https://www.acsiapartners.com/consumers/ltc-fast-facts/)

As of this writing, the cost of long-term care is changing so rapidly, there is really NO WAY to report it accurately. RESEARCH COSTS on your own and reach out to Advisors.

An *AgingInPlace®* October 2019, article, *"What Is Long-Term Care Insurance And Who Needs It?"* stated: *"...a survey carried out by the U.S. Department of Health and Human Services, ...there's a 70% likelihood that the average 65-year-old will require some form of lifelong care as they advance in age."* (108)

How individuals pay for their long-term-care needs is also called into question. Lincoln Financial® *"Life Stages Survey"* (2010) of more than 1,000 Americans reported the following to help them fund long-term care: (https://newsroom.lfg.com/press-release/life-insurance/americans-resolve-improve-their-financial-security-lincoln-financial-st):

- ☒ "75 percent said they would use savings.

- ☒ 56 percent said they would be willing to sell their homes.

- ☒ 41 percent said they would be willing to refinance their homes.

- ☒ 21 percent said they would be willing to go into debt.

- ☒ 18 percent said they would be willing to declare bankruptcy to qualify for government aid."

Risk #3: The dramatic effects of rising inflation on the cost of future goods and services erode savings and investment portfolios.

The Fourth Edition of the American Heritage Dictionary® of the English Language provides a technical definition of *inflation:*

,

> *"A persistent increase in the level of consumer prices or a persistent decline in the purchasing power of money, caused by an increase in available currency and credit beyond the proportion of available goods and services."* (116)
>
> *Basically, inflation makes goods and services more expensive and decreases the value of your money in the future.*
>
> *https://www.amazon.com/American-Heritage-Dictionary-Century-Reference/dp/0440237017*

One of the first considerations for planning for retirement is to assess what one's current living costs are, and then to estimate how inflation will affect those costs. Compare these examples: (115)

	In 1979	*In 1999*	*In 2010*	*In 2020*
Average Cost of a Car	$6,848	$20,686	$24,899	$37,851
Average Cost of a Gallon of Gas	$.86	$1.14	$2.79	$1.95
A Movie Ticket	$2.52	$5.08	$7.89	$9.26
A Stamp to Mail a Letter	$.15	$.33	$.44	$.55

In a Wall Street Journal® 2/2019 publication by Glenn Ruffenach, *"When Planning for Retirement, Don't Forget Inflation."* The article reports, *"For instance, inflation averaged 2.46% a year between 1990 and 2018. Sounds fairly "low." Even so, you would need just over $2,000 today to buy what $1,000 would have bought in 1990."* *(https://www.wsj.com/articles/when-planning-for-retirement-dont-forget-inflation-11551387373)* Information regarding how inflation is continuously eroding future purchasing power.

"At a Conservative 2.5% Inflation Rate:………..a $ 1.00 Today (2019) will be worth:

$ .78 in 10 years

$ .61 in 20 years

$ .48 in 30 years" (115a)

To put inflation in further perspective:

- ☒ "If you and your spouse decide to withdraw $40,000 a year from your retirement portfolio (to supplement your Social Security), for instance, you'll need a portfolio value of $1 million when you retire. If you and your spouse want to withdraw $80,000 a year, you'll need $2 million." (116)

- ☒ If you started with $ 100 in 1980 you needed $ 311.36 in 2019 to equal the same purchasing power the $ 100 brought in 1980. (117)

Inflation calculators, like one found on https://www.calcxml.com, can help you project your retirement income needs at different rates of inflation. Additionally, https://finance.zacks.com/inflation-affect-standard-living-9960.html provides an 3/2019 article, *"How Does Inflation Affect the Standard of Living?"* (118), which provides information regarding what effects inflation has on our cost of living. This, and other websites, offer calculators to help you project costs of goods well into the future. https://www.inflationdata.com is another excellent source for inflation data.

Additionally, Bankrate®, https://www.bankrate.com/calculators/retirement/retirement-calculator.aspx, provides a calculator that will illustrate, *"Inflation's Impact on Retirement Income Needs."* Here is one illustration:

- ☒ An annual income of $ 40,000 at retirement would have to grow to over $ 97,000 in 30 years if it were to keep up with a 3% annual rate of inflation.

Obviously, a greater inflation rate drives those numbers up even higher.

Your advisors will assist you with planning for increases in inflation and will 'factor in' an inflation rate. Remember to discuss the hypothetical inflation number your retirement projection program will use. If you are more conservative, you may want to increase the inflation factor that you use in your personalized retirement planning projections. And, who is say that our inflation rates today will not be higher in the years to come?

> *"Inflation is when you pay fifteen dollars for a ten-dollar haircut you used to get for five dollars when you had hair."*
>
> Sam Ewing

As years go by, inflation drives up the costs of products and services, these costs are not static. The statistics and costs provided are for illustrative purposes in an effort to help you begin to understand the gravity of how inflation, and the costs of services, can dramatically affect how you will live when you are retired. Funding health care is a concern for everyone and will be ever-changing as our cultural and political environments ebb and flow.

Risk #4 In an effort to reduce their portfolio risk, retirees can become more 'conservative' in their investing behavior. This behavior further exposes you to inflation risk.

Individuals frequently look to the experts for direction to determine how they should reposition the asset allocations of their investment portfolios when approaching retirement. Retirees' objectives can change from their earlier 'accumulation mode,' to what they perceive to be a less 'risky' allocation. For example, ask a 40 or 45-year-old investor how their retirement assets are allocated, and they might answer that they are invested 60% to 70% in 'equity' products in an effort to 'grow' their assets, if possible. Other investors might even devote a higher percentage to equities. However, when individuals approach retirement, maybe after age 55 or 60, their objectives can start to change… they realize that they have fewer 'earning years' ahead of them and can start thinking that, "I need to keep what I have." This change in objectives can initiate a shift, or modification, in their portfolio allocation. Sometimes there is a call to rebalance their portfolio to reduce equity weightings and increase allocations in bonds and cash. But remember, as we discussed in our last section, merely changing allocations and diversifications to more conservative choices, may not provide enough of a protection strategy. Published on the Society of Actuaries® website, www.soa.org, (also found: https://www.semanticscholar.org/paper/Efficient-Post-Retirement-Asset-Allocation-Fsa/71bee4a557905f6c1280b42336dc49861d0f99b1) Barry Freedman's white paper (July, 2008), *"EFFICIENT POST-RETIREMENT ASSET ALLOCATION,"* suggests the following:

Comparison of Accumulation and Post-Retirement Life Cycle Phases		
Issue	Accumulation Phase	Post-Retirement
Time Horizon	Retirement. Can be regarded as a fixed horizon, or as a source of optionality (e.g., in the event of good investment experience one can choose to retire early). See Bodie (2001).	Death. Should be regarded as a random time horizon. The random variable rep- resenting time of death is highly volatile and has no implicit optionality (see Fig. 1).
Desired wealth at horizon	Enough wealth to retire.	Enough assets at the end of life to pay for medical and long-term-care expenses and to meet bequest desires.
Cash flows (prior to time horizon)	Positive or zero contributions to asset funds.	Systematic withdrawals.
Impact of under-performance	Delay retirement/change projected retirement standard of living.	Inability to meet expenses or unplanned reduction in retirement standard of living.

Table 1

Clearly, any post-retirement asset allocation model needs to address the issue related in Table 1. To accommodate these differences, a few small changes to the classic Markowitz framework might be considered. As discussed, the accumulation phase in the model suggests a portfolio of assets with a random/variable rate of return and a single year time horizon. Here are some steps you may take to adjust the model:

1. Include a constant (real dollar) rate of withdrawal; 2. Replace the one-year time horizon with a variable time horizon set to a projected year of death; 3. Quantify risk and reward as the mean and standard deviation of remaining (real dollar) wealth at time of death, as mentioned in Table 1; this wealth will be used for medical/long-term care expenses and to meet bequest desires (if any). [1]

Note: The probability distribution of age of death is wide and relatively flat, leading to the conclusion that an individual would be imprudent to use life expectancy as the time horizon for retirement planning.

Josh Jenkins, CFA, "*Being Too Conservative Can Be A Risky Strategy,*" (2/24/2020), (https://www.lutz.us/being-too-conservative-risky-strategy/) suggests:

"*While concentrating your assets in "safe" short-term cash and bond investments is a way to prevent red ink from spilling on your portfolio statement, doing so may be simply trading one risk for another. There have been long periods in history where the rate of inflation has exceeded the return on cash and bonds. This less observable risk carries with it the same end result: a loss in the future purchasing power of the portfolio.*"

Risk #5: Withdrawing your portfolio assets at an overly aggressive rate.

When the day comes and you retire, or transition to another line of work, you may begin to draw on your income sources. If your monthly expenses require you to withdraw from your investment accounts, you will want to fully understand how long your money will last, projecting withdrawal streams at varying withdrawal rates. Consider that for every $200,000 in investment assets, at a projected 7% after tax rate of return, and using a 3.5% rate of inflation, your money will generate about $10,000 of annual income (assumes 25 years in retirement). (119) Again, some analysts suggest that taking 4% per year income from savings and investment accounts may provide a reasonable (about 95%) chance for staying on pace with income needs in retirement. But this calculation assumes that you have a sizable retirement account from which you can withdraw. On top of that, poor investment or market performance, overspending, withdrawing too aggressively, or other unforeseen factors, may dramatically increase your odds of outliving your money in retirement.

Fidelity® (102) presents, *"As a rule of thumb, aim to withdraw no more than 4% to 5% of your savings in the first year of retirement, then adjust that amount every year for inflation."* (Past performance is no guarantee of future results.) Remember, again, a 4% withdrawal rate does not necessarily offer security or assure unlimited asset sustainability. Success in retirement regarding continuing your income stream also depends on the performance of your investments, your asset allocation, and your time horizon.

Furthermore. From one of the hypothetical calculations you can run on any withdrawal calculator, it appears that there is a general consensus which suggests that withdrawing more than 5% of your assets may increase the risk of your retirement income plan falling short.

Note: Fidelity's® calculation assumes that you have a sizable retirement account from which to withdraw… *"While conservative investments like bonds or certificates of deposit at banks will help you preserve the funds you currently have left in your retirement portfolio, it doesn't provide the type of growth you need in a portfolio to help sustain a viable long-term retirement income plan to overcome major issues like inflation, spiraling medical costs, and a longer life expectancy."* (102)

There is a myriad of information available that provides 'hypothetical withdrawal' models. These withdrawal models help you plan how much you can spend out of your retirement savings accounts each year. This exercise will help you to address the possibility of running out of money in retirement. The goal is simple, plan on providing yourself with an income stream in retirement --and spend and withdraw as little as possible out of your accounts. Work with an advisor, have them model several allocation and diversification mixes for you. If you conduct this exercise, you will be able to hypothetically determine what asset mix might be the best fit for you, given your goals, retirement income, spending levels, amount of assets, age, and risk tolerance. When the time is right, and you go through this exercise, I believe you and your advisor will find the balance you are looking for. Remember, you can adjust, adjust, and adjust.

Where Will You Get Money To Live On When You Are Retired?

The Social Security Administration, *'Income of the Aged Chartbook,'* 2014 (https://www.ssa.gov/policy/ docs/chartbooks/income_aged/2014/iac14.pdf) reports that on average, 66.8% of retirement income comes from your 'own sources,' (investments, earned income, pension, other) and 33.2% will come from Social Security. See the chart below indicating numbers from the Social Security Administration.

"Social Security provides the largest share of aggregate income for units aged 65 or older."

Income in Retirement

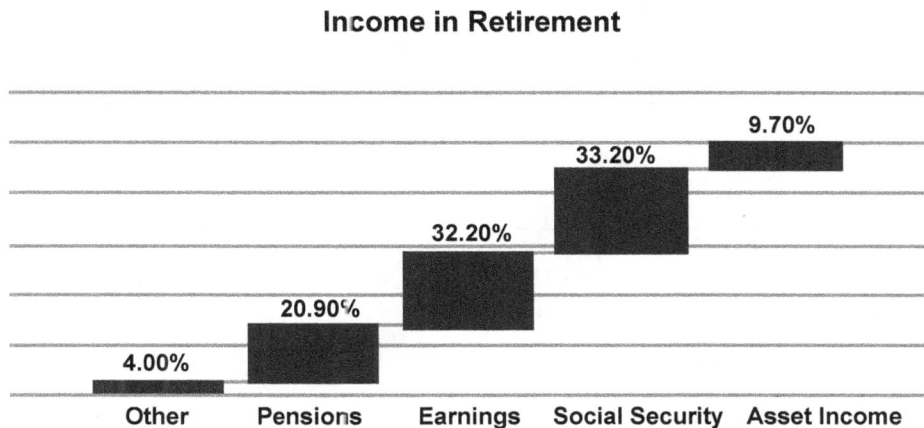

	Other	Pensions	Earnings	Social Security	Asset Income
	4.00%	20.90%	32.20%	33.20%	9.70%

Note: totals do not necessarily equal the sum of the rounded components.

Because each individual has different retirement income needs, it is important to plan and to set goals with your personal financial and tax advisors.

When Is The Right Time For You To Start Drawing Social Security Income?

It [Social Security] assures the elderly that America will always keep the promises make in troubled times a half century ago."

President Ronald Reagan (April 20th, 1983)

Social Security Fact Sheet

"Social Security is the major source of income for most of the elderly.

- o Nearly nine out of ten people age 65 and older receive Social Security benefits.

- o Social Security benefits represent about 33% of the income of the elderly. *

- o Among elderly Social Security beneficiaries, 50% of married couples and 70% of unmarried persons receive 50% or more of their income from Social Security. *

- o Among elderly Social Security beneficiaries, 21% of married couples and about 45% of unmarried persons rely on Social Security for 90% or more of their income. *"

*This information is from 2017. Social Security Fact Sheet, SSA Publication No. 13-11871, (https://www.ssa.gov/news/press/factsheets/basicfact-alt.pdf)

In 1935 President Franklin D. Roosevelt signed the Social Security Act. This Act was designed to help individuals supplement their retirement savings. The program works like a 'forced savings' program. Simply put, as the program is currently set up, the government defers part of your income into a pooled government account which the government manages; and then, when you elect to begin to start taking your benefits, sometime after you turn age 62, you will be sent a portion of your money (as income) to you each month until you die.

One of the questions people seem to ask me over and over is, "When should I start drawing my social security benefits?" "Should I start drawing my benefits at age 62, or wait until 'full benefits' (FRA) kicks in a few years later?"

There are a variety of resources on the internet providing information about Social Security benefits. So research your individual information… once you know your Full Retirement Age (FRA) you may receive:

    a.   "Reduced benefits as early as the first month you reach [age] 62,

    b.   Full benefits at [your] FRA,

    c.   Increased benefits if you wait beyond FRA to collect, up to age 70."

(https://www.justfacts.com/index.asp; https://www.aarp.org/retirement/social-security/info-2018/12-fact-about-ss.html)

Here are a couple of reasons to refrain from taking your social security benefits until you reach your Full Retirement Age (FRA), or older.

    1. If you are still working (presently, there are "earning limits" that may reduce your benefits

        ○ you continue to contribute to social security so you are in a sense increasing what you will receive when you do begin withdrawing;

        ○ "you are required to pay taxes if you have income in addition to Social Security." (ssa.gov) so, adding social security benefits may case you to realize adverse tax consequences; or

    2. If you need as much money as you can get every month to live on in retirement. (119)

https://www.schwab.com/resource-center/insights/content/when-should-you-take-social-security, *"When Should You Take Social Security?"* Rob Williams, 10/2020, has an easy-to-understand article that answers a variety of questions on the *"When Should I Withdraw Social Security?"* topic. Also, Social Security has an on-line calculator to help you determine what your specific retirement benefit estimates are. Visit https://www.socialsecurity.gov/estimator.html to calculate/estimate your "What If" scenarios. Go to https://www.socialsecurity.gov/pubs to access Fact Sheets/Articles to help you make a personal decision to answer the question, *"When should I start taking my Social Security Benefits?"*

One note of diversion: When the first monthly social security benefits were paid out to the elderly population in 1940, they were paid to about 7% of the population. By 2030 our elderly population is projected to be about 20% of our population. (122) In 1945 there were 41.9 workers paying into Social Security for each one beneficiary taking payments out. There are currently 3.3 workers paying into the system for each Social Security beneficiary. Within forty years, there will be only 2 workers paying in per beneficiary. The ratio of funders to beneficiaries is shrinking dramatically.

> *"... the Social Security system is experiencing a declining worker-to-beneficiary ratio, which will fall from 3.3 in 2005 to 2.1 in 2040 (the year in which the Social Security trust fund is projected to be exhausted." (122)*

With such an increase in benefit needs, there has been discussion regarding the long-term solvency of the Social Security program. I present here competing viewpoints on the program's solvency forecast.

☒ The Social Security Office of Retirement and Disability Policy reports that, *"benefits are now expected to be payable in full on a timely basis until 2037, when the trust fund reserves are projected to become exhausted.[1] At the point where the reserves are used up, continuing taxes are expected to be enough to pay 76 percent of scheduled benefits."* (122)

https://www.moneymatters101.com/social-security/social-security-is-not-going-broke/, article: *"Social Security Is Not Going Broke,"* adds to this position... reporting that Michael Astrue (Commissioner of the Social Security Administration):

☒ *"After 2033, even if Congress does nothing, there will still be sufficient assets from payroll taxes to pay about 75 percent of benefits. That's not acceptable, but it's still a fact that there will still be substantial assets there."*

Additionally, Sean Williams reported (1/2018):

☒ *"The latest report from the Social Security Board of Trustees in 2017 forecast that the Trust will begin paying out more in benefits than it generates in revenue by 2022. Just 12 years after that, Social Security's asset reserves are expected to be depleted,"* (123) More data....

https://money.usnews.com/money/retirement/social-security/articles/2018-06-18/what-every-30-year-old-should-know-about-social-security, (6/2018) presents that,

☒ *"The **Social Security** program is projected to have sufficient income to pay out promised benefits until 2034, after which the program will bring in enough revenue to pay out 77 percent of scheduled payments, according to the 2018 Trustees Report." ("What Every 30-Year-Old Should Know About Social Security,"* by Emily Brandon.)

The Social Security program is touted as one of the most successful government programs in our history. However, what is important to recognize here is that the system may not provide nearly enough benefits for you to live on in your retirement. Hopefully this realization will provide a catalyst for you to become an even better saver in the future. I surmise that a change in our system will be forth coming; I don't foresee how the program can continue in its current state, given the economics of the situation. Remember, the objective of the Social Security program was intended to *supplement* retirement savings, not replace savings! (120)

Find someone who is over the age of 70 years old and is already retired. Interview them to determine what they 'fear' most going forward in their retirement years. Elaborate on how they think they will cope or solve that problem.

_____

_____

_____

Taxes In Retirement

While I am NOT a Tax Advisor, the tax treatment of the different investment products impacts how your investments provide you with income in retirement. Consult a tax advisor prior to taking withdrawals from both your investment and your retirement (or tax-advantaged) accounts. I explicitly am not a tax advisor, however, a review of tax treatments of investment products in an investment account, the tax implications of withdrawals from retirement accounts, and tax-deferred investments are important to consider here.

- ☒ **Tax-deferral**. As we have discussed, investments that are held in 'pre-tax' retirement accounts such as Non-Roth 401ks, Traditional Individual Retirement Accounts (IRAs), and annuities, allow for tax-deferred growth. So, taxes are paid at the time you withdraw the money. When the money is withdrawn from a 'tax deferred' account, **taxes are paid at your ordinary income rate the year you withdraw the money** (unless this is changed through legislation). At the time of withdrawal, you will pay both federal and applicable state income taxes.

- ☒ **Capital gains.** This discussion regarding capital gain taxes applies to withdrawing money, or selling investment products, that are held in an after-tax Investment/Brokerage Account (not inside a before-tax or Roth Retirement/Custodian Account). When there is a **sale of an asset** that is held in an after-tax Investment/Brokerage Account, the difference between what you paid for the asset and what the asset was sold for, is either a **gain or a loss.** A gain – or *capital gain* – occurs when the **sale price exceeds what you initially invested**, or initially paid for the asset. Capital gains are recorded as either long-term or short-term. **Long-term capital gains in your investment accounts are calculated for assets held more than one year and a day, and short-term gains are calculated on investments held for less than one year.**

The difference between *long-term* and *short-term* investment gains is that each is taxed at a different rate.*

- **Short-term** capital gain tax rates; currently are taxed at your ordinary income tax rate.

- **Long-term** capital gains are taxed at a rate that is determined by the IRS. The long-term capital gain rates, like ordinary tax rates, can, and do, change.

*Rates can change yearly through legislation.

Losses are also classified as either short-term or long-term. Losses impact your tax consequences; consult a tax advisor for specific details.

Watch your holding dates on your assets, especially if you plan to sell the asset in a short period of time. Understand the tax consequences of your buy and sell investment actions.

⊠ **Tax-free investment products.** Some investment products provide tax benefits. For example, if you purchase an investment product, such as a *state municipal bond*, you may realize both a Federal and State tax benefit. A State Municipal bond **may** exempt you from paying both Federal and State income taxes on the interest (if you live in that state). However, a word of caution: All state municipal bonds *DO NOT* automatically exempt you from paying income taxes. Additional factors, such as a 'private activity bond' and the bond's interaction with your social security benefits may influence or prohibit some of their 'tax-free' status. Be sure that your tax advisor reviews these features with you so you can determine for certain whether or not that specific investment product does provide tax-free income for you. If you are considering a *tax-advantaged* investment product, your advisors will certainly consider your tax bracket to **compare the projected rate of return with projected rates of return on taxable investment products.**

If an investment offers 'tax-advantaged' status, it may produce a lower return, or yield. To compare these tax-advantaged products against 'non-tax-advantaged' products, use this formula:

1. Determine your tax bracket, both federal and state; add the two numbers together

2. Subtract the total from 100

3. Divide the product's yield you are considering by the number you arrived at in step 2

4. Your calculation provides your 'taxable yield equivalent'

Life

Here is an example of the calculation:

You are in a 28% tax bracket (combined state and federal taxes).

If you purchase a municipal bond issued in your state, and *you qualify*, *you may not pay taxes on the interest generated by the bond.*

To determine if this state municipal bond is an appropriate investment for you – compare other 'taxable' investment products by dividing the realized yield of the state municipal bond by the inverse of your tax bracket. This calculation allows you to compare the municipal bond's yield to the *taxable 'equivalent yield'* of other investments.

Municipal bond yield: 4.5 %

Step 1: Tax bracket is 28 % (combined federal and state)

Step 2: Calculate the inverse

      Inverse of your tax bracket: 100 minus 28 % = 72%

Step 3: Divide the yield (4.5%) by .72 (the number you calculated in Step 2)

      Realized yield: 4.5% divided by .72 = 6.25% taxable yield equivalent

Step 4: 6.25% taxable yield equivalent

Clear as mud? Again, ask your advisors for clarification. But try this example yourself:

David's combined tax bracket is 25%. He is considering a State Municipal bond and qualifies for both Federal and State tax-free status. If the investment he is considering is yielding 5% tax-free… how would that compare to a taxable investment yield?

_____

_____

Calculate the tax equivalency of a 3.8% municipal bond if you are in the 25% tax bracket.

_____

Annuities Are Different From Other Investment Products

Annuities Can Be Complicated

Unlike a stock, bond, or mutual fund, an annuity is an insurance product, offered by an insurance company. An annuity is a legal contract between an insurance company and the owner of the annuity. Typically, insurance products are designed, and can be utilized, to help mitigate some of the market risk or to set up an income stream for you in retirement. Two ways an annuity reduces risk is to offer either: a) a 'fixed' rate of return, or b) by the purchase of a 'guarantee income or withdrawal rider' with the contract. Be aware, the *'Rider'* and fixed annuity assets *guarantees* are the sole responsibility of the insurance company and only as good as the financial strength of the insurance company making the guarantee. (124) So, if the insurance company goes out of business, under certain conditions, your money may not be returned to you, and the guarantees and riders, may not be honored.

Some of the reasons an annuity product is utilized: a) an investor wants to purchase an annuity product with a 'guarantee' rider; b) an investor wants to set up an income stream for themselves at a later date (maybe when they retire); c) someone is interested in a Death Benefit feature, i.e. leave money for heirs, or d) a more aggressive investor wants to select an aggressive investment model, but use a 'rider' as a protection aspect.

With the dissolution of company pensions for individuals, and the recent stock market fluctuations, annuity products have had a resurgence in popularity. However, due to the vast amount of moving parts, annuities can be quite difficult to understand. There are many, many different 'flavors' of annuities, meaning you can purchase different types of annuities with different types of riders; and the costs between two annuity product offerings can be quite different. In the past, annuities were sometimes perceived by investors in a negative light because they can be complex and expensive. However, recently I believe the annuity companies have done a good job of countering investor's negative perceptions by developing some new products which offer reduced fees, are more user-friendly, and seem to be less complicated than some of the older annuity products. But, a big word of caution here, the internal costs can be quite daunting… *'research carefully before you purchase.'*

Annuity Terms

Let's start with an outline of some of the very basic annuity terms. To begin with, it is important to understand the parties involved in setting up an annuity.

- ☒ **The Contract Owner:** The person or entity that purchases the contract and is responsible for paying the premiums.

- ☒ **The Annuitant:** The individual on whose life an annuity contract calculates the payout.

- ☒ **The Beneficiary:** The individual(s) or entity (e.g., Trust) that is elected to receive the policy cash distribution.

An important aspect of all annuities are the two phases that they offer.

1. **The Accumulation Phase:** This is the first phase for deferred annuities. During this timeframe the owner is either; a) making contributions to the annuity, b) simply letting the annuity market balance 'fluctuate,' (it grows or declines in market value… the 'guaranteed' income rider is a separate ledger), c) taking regular, planned income withdrawals, or d) considering some type of surrender or periodic withdrawal from the existing balance.

2. **The Annuitization Phase:** During this phase, the owner can opt to 'annuitize' the contract over the life of the named Annuitant. This means that the owner will begin taking pre-determined withdrawals for the benefit of the beneficiary. This Annuitization Phase typically does not need to be initiated. However, having this option is a key trait for this type of investment. The Annuitization Phase sets up an income stream similar to an individual pension. This leads us into a discussion of the various types of annuities.

Types Of Annuities

In general, annuities can be either **immediate** or **deferred**. These two terms refer to the 'initiation time frame for the payouts.'

- ○ The **immediate annuity** has *no accumulation phase* and begins **payouts** shortly after the principal is invested in the contract.

- ○ Alternately, the **deferred annuity** has an *accumulation phase*, and defers the payout phase to a later date.

There are several common types of annuities; *indexed, fixed,* and *variable.* We will focus on the latter two types:

- ○ The **_fixed_ annuity** provides you with a pre-stated interest rate guarantee. The interest rate is applied to the money you invest in the annuity. The stated guaranteed** rate typically lasts for at least for one year, with an interest rate reset for subsequent years. Some fixed annuities will guarantee an initial rate for several years, and then guarantee another rate for an additional number of pre-stated years. So, if your rate is 3%, and you have $10,000 invested, after the end of the first year your fixed annuity has grown to $ 10,300. The fixed annuity will also typically guarantee an *'interest-rate floor.'* This *floor* is the lowest rate that will ever be offered on your contract. For example, if your interest-rate *floor* is 2%, and interest rates decline, your contract interest rate cannot go any lower than 2%.

** These guarantees are subject to the solvency of the annuity company. Your money is NOT held away from the insurance company's assets.

- ○ With a **_variable_ annuity** you select **'separately managed/ or sub accounts' in which to invest your money.** The separately managed accounts are similar to mutual funds and are referred to as sub-accounts/separate accounts. (121) A prospectus will be delivered with your variable annuity purchase. The prospectus will provide details for each separately managed account; including fees, CDSC timeframes, and other important information. Unlike the fixed annuities, your contract does not have a guaranteed interest rate, and your account holdings are held away, 'segregated' (hence the term 'separately managed') from the insurance company's assets. (125) Also, the guarantees stated in the riders are the responsibility of the company, and solvency is important.

Understand how the variable annuity sub accounts are protected (https://finance.zacks.com/variable-annuities-covered-sipc-8511.html):

> *"The SIPC® specifically excludes annuities from its guarantee of coverage. However, the SIPC® may be indirectly covering the sub-accounts you selected for the annuity. If the annuity is invested in a mutual fund, for example, that fund will hold its assets (cash, stock, bonds, certificates of deposit) in custodial accounts managed by affiliated banks." (125)*

Both fixed and variable annuities normally have a **surrender period** schedule, also known as a CDSC, like we discussed earlier in the mutual fund commentary. Be sure you carefully review those schedules to determine which annuity product best suits your *time-horizon.*

Other characteristics that apply to both *fixed* and *variable* annuities are:

1. The gains of the annuity (growth or appreciation of the value of the account) are tax deferred until withdrawal.

2. If an annuity is purchased with after-tax money, the owner cannot take out any of the gains until they reach the age of 59 ½ without incurring an IRS 10% penalty (like with the other types of retirement accounts). In addition, post 8/14/1982, withdrawals are made from gains first (Last In/First Out); i.e. withdrawals are made from earnings first.   (https://www.annuityadvisors.com/reference/detail/annuity-tax-legislation?refid=135)

3. If an annuity is purchased with *before-tax* money, the owner cannot take out money until they reach the age of 59 ½ without incurring an IRS 10% penalty (like with the other types of retirement accounts).

4. When the annuity is liquidated at one time (completely withdrawn), tax implications can be larger due to the 'lump sum' payout.

5. Annuities can be purchased with either 'before-tax' or 'after-tax' money. However, because of their 'tax-deferral' nature, an annuity is often utilized for 'after-tax' money.

6. If an annuity is purchased with *after-tax* money, there is no annual contribution limit restrictions.

7. If an annuity is purchased with *before-tax* money, there is the standard annual contribution limit set by the IRS, similar to the limits that apply to other Retirement-type accounts. (The annuity is also held in a custodian account.)

8. Annuities can provide payouts at the death of the Annuitant (similar to a life insurance policy).

9. Flexible withdrawals, or 'pay-out,' options are offered.

10. The parties that participate (owner, annuitant, and beneficiary) have the same functions for both types of annuities.

11. For a fee, the contract owner can purchase a **'rider(s).'** These *riders* offer you various features which you may add to your annuity contract, doing so adds cost. For example, you may purchase a ***'return of premium' rider,*** or a rider that ***guarantees you a specific income or withdrawal stream,*** or an ***'Enhanced Death Benefit'*** rider.*. (More information on riders follows.)

12. There may be CDSC (surrender time schedule penalties) charges for early withdrawals.

13. Taxes on gains are paid at ordinary income rates when gains are withdrawn. (Check with a Tax Advisor.)

14. Relatively illiquid until CDSC schedule has passed.

Here are a few additional facts about each of the two types of annuities:

The Fixed Annuity

Advantages:

a. Provides a guarantee of your investment, plus a fixed rate of return, similar to a certificate of deposit*;

b. There generally is a minimum interest rate guarantee provided for the annual interest rate reset;

c. Typically contract fees are low.

Disadvantages:

a. The guaranteed rate of return may be low;

b. The *reset rate* and *floor rates* of return may be low;

c. The growth of your money may not keep pace with inflation;

d. No FDIC insurance applies;

e. There is an insurance company risk because the insurance company is responsible for holding the account.

*Unlike a bank deposit, which is, IN MOST CASES, guaranteed by FDIC insurance, when you invest in a fixed annuity it is guaranteed by the insurance company itself, the annuity is not FDIC insured. Therefore, if the insurance company becomes insolvent, your investment may be at risk.

The Variable Annuity

Advantages:

a.   The variable annuity gives you the opportunity to 'grow' your money at a rate that may keep pace, or may out-pace, inflation, based on the performance of the separately managed accounts you select;

b.   The variable annuity provides you with an opportunity to invest in separately managed accounts which you can personally select with your advisor, similar to mutual funds, in an effort to 'grow' your assets at a more aggressive rate than a fixed-rate investment product.

Disadvantages:

a.   A variable annuity DOES NOT provide a guarantee of a fixed rate of return – unless you have purchased a specific rider. A guarantee of return of principal may not be offered;

b.   The fund choices you select, like mutual funds, may lose value if your fund choices decline in value;

c.   Investment management fees are assessed for the separately managed accounts and those fees reduce the performance of the accounts. Administration fees, mortality and expense expenses, distribution charges and the purchase of 'riders' can erode the performance gains as well.

*Remember: Riders and fixed annuity premiums are guaranteed by each insurance company and are subject to the company's solvency. Banks must be FDIC insured for guarantees.

I mentioned that deferred annuities have both an accumulation and an annuitization phase. Few annuities are actually annuitized, but for those contracts that are annuitized by the owner, there are several withdrawal options available:

☒ **Period Certain** – The contract owner chooses a specific period for income to be distributed.

☒ **Life Only** – The income is paid-out over the life of the Annuitant's life span.

☒ **Life with Period Certain** – Income is paid-out over the life of the Annuitant, but a minimum pay-out period is also identified (if the Annuitant's life span does not meet this minimum period the beneficiary receives the income until the pay-out period is satisfied).

⊠ **Joint and Survivor** – The pay-out of income is calculated over the span of two Annuitant's lives and is paid-out until neither of the Annuitants are living.

Should the time arise to select a pay-out, your insurance agent, tax advisor or financial advisor will help you elect the option that is best for you.

Annuity Riders

There are several variations of riders that you can purchase with your annuity; for example: *Long-Term Care, Terminal Illness, Life Expectancy Guarantee*, etc. Three of the most popular riders are: 1) an *Income Rider*, 2) a *Withdrawal Rider*, and 3) the *Enhanced Death Benefit Rider*. Remember not all states offer all varieties of riders; and some riders may initially seem attractive but may not be practical or cost effective for you.

Here is how an *Income Rider* can work: In exchange for a purchase premium or series of premiums, the insurance company guarantees** to pay a stream of income in the future to the *beneficiary*. **This is how Annuities can help individuals convert the annuity money into a stream of income.** If you set up this *'stream of income'* you provide yourself with a *'private pension.'* That is why we are discussing annuities in this retirement section. Annuities are discussed here because they can be an investment product for your retirement years. Like other retirement investment products, annuities also offer a tax-deferral feature, are a longer-term investment option, and annuities uniquely offer income and death benefit guarantees. However, also like other retirement products, annuities have conditions that need to be understood and met in order for you to realize the full benefits of owning an annuity if you choose this investment option.

** These guarantees may cost you money to attach to your contract; and the guarantees are subject to the solvency of the annuity company.

And an additional word of caution. Please understand the implications of purchasing an annuity in *a rising interest-rate environment*. A fixed rate of today (i.e. 4.0%) may be eaten up very quickly by inflation and rising rates... meaning the rate of interest you contract for today will not be worth the same interest rate (have less purchasing power) in the future. However, there may be contracts that offer options to overcome that scenario.... ASK!

Life

For example:

*When you purchase a variable annuity with an **'income or withdrawal rider,'** you elect an option to recover your investment money, even if the market declines. With the new annuity riders, you can typically be 'guaranteed' (by the issuing annuity carrier*) a pre-determined return, or income stream, from your investment if you withdraw the money over a specific, pre-agreed upon time schedule. **It is important to understand that an income rider option does not allow you to access your money in a lump sum. You are paid your money over time – over a pre-stated time period, generally over 20 years, or over your lifetime. There generally is NO LUMP SUM feature on the guaranteed side of the ledger.** We discuss this further later in this chapter.*

Another example of how an income rider can work:

A friend of mine who has a variable annuity experienced a dramatic decline in his 'market value' in 2008. When reviewing his options, he was pleased to learn that he had, in a sense, purchased a type of 'insurance' on his money. The client had purchased an 'income rider'* when he bought the annuity. The rider will provide an income stream for him for the rest of his life – regardless of what the current annuity market value is at the time he initiates withdrawals. Therefore, he should receive a pre-calculated annual or monthly income at some predetermined date in the future; in his case the contract will begin his income payout at age 65.

---

*Insurance company must be solvent. Remember also that riders can be expensive. Over time, the policy holder may be giving up appreciation today for the income stream for tomorrow. The fees paid for the riders are taken out of the gains and will dilute the market-side of the equation. The fees are NOT re-funded if the policy owner decides to withdraw pre-maturely or exchange the contract in the future.

How I Help Clients To Understand Annuities

Again, you probably understand by now, annuities can be very complicated. To help my clients understand annuities better, I use the illustrations that the insurance company provides to each client. The annuity company will calculate a specific, hypothetical scenario for each individual to 'illustrate' the growth, or decline in value, of the money invested over time, based on the criteria selected.

Life

Reading an Annuity Illustration can be difficult... a lot of numbers and legalese. Here are a few areas that will be reviewed with you by the advisor or agent:

1. *The illustration will start with a couple of pieces of information, and assumptions:*

   a. *Your age*

   b. *Amount of money you will invest to start*

   c. *Amount of money you plan to invest over time, or at a later date*

   d. *When you may be thinking of starting to withdraw the money (i.e. when you retire)*

   e. *An investment profile, what asset mix you might use (for a Variable annuity, the underlying separate account choices)*

Life Continued

2. *Most illustrations will provide several pages that identify potential outcomes at different market returns;*

   a. *One scenario may show an outcome using the past 20- or 25-year ACTUAL market performance*

   b. *Another outcome may use a flat average return (i.e. 5% or 6% each year)*

   c. *Typically, one outcome will identify a 0% return to show you what would happen if there was no appreciation*

   d. *Other outcome scenarios may be included*

3. *Expenses will be identified*

   a. *M&E expenses – "mortality and expense" (M&E) charges pay for the insurance guarantee, commissions, selling, and administrative expenses of the contract*

   b. *Fund expenses if you are considering a Variable Annuity*

   c. *Annual account charges if you are considering a Fixed Annuity*

   d. *Costs for Riders*

   e. *Penalties for withdrawing some, or all of your money, before the CDSC timeframe is completed (surrender schedule)*

Life Continued

This is a sample of the general heading for a Hypothetical Annuity Illustration – 1 page out of 11 (not Valid Without All Pages and Legal Disclaimers)

PROJECTED MARKET VALUE (a)   **NON-GUARANTEED**

Age	Premium	Withdrawals $	Annual Net Return	Surrender Value*	Market Value**	Death Benefit	Projected Withdrawal Value***	Annual Income Amount
55	$50,000							
56	0	$0	18.70%					
57	0	$0	-2.60%					
58	0	$0	10.00%					
59	0	$0	10.00%					
60	0	$0	-1.60%					
61	0	$0	14.80%					
62	0	$0	8.10%					
63	0	$0	5.20%					
64	0	$0	4.20%					
65	0	$0	10.00%					
66	0 ****		-3.50%					

*Surrender Value notes the value of the contract MINUS the CDSC charges

**Projected Market Value based on specific market performance; Annual net returns are hypothetical and do not depict actual returns going forward

***Projected Withdrawal Value is dependent on: a) Type of Rider purchased, and b) Market performance

****Hypothetical amount – based on hypothetical market returns indicated in column 4 (a). Values will fluctuate up and down, based on the performance of the investment options you have chosen.

ANNUAL RETURNS AND VALUES ON THIS PAGE ARE HYPOTETICAL, THEY ARE NOT GUARANTEED, they will vary; the average percent gross rate of return used to calculate values are shown in light of the investment options YOU choose. REFER to the Important Information page for a ccmplete description of the annual maintenance charges and other fees associated with this product; such as: M&E expenses, account fees, fund expenses, rider fees and the CDSC period. A prospectus must be provided with all illustrations. No tax information is provided.

Another way I helped people understand annuities is to draw pictures:

STEP 1

- First, I draw a chart that denotes, or point out on the illustration, the percentages you give back (real dollars) if you take money out of the annuity before the 'surrender period' is over. This is my surrender penalty chart. *Surrender charges (CDSC) can occur if you do not keep your money invested until the end of the surrender period.* The length of the surrender period will vary with different annuity products.

* All annuity products differ in features, the above is for illustrative purposes only

Life

The following is an example of a surrender period schedule and illustrates what you would give back for a *$10,000 investment* if you took your money completely out in various years. The example illustrates a 7-year surrender product. So, according to the schedule, if you wanted to take your money out *after* the second year, so you are technically in the 3rd year, (year 3 on the schedule), you would forfeit $ 500 (assuming NO appreciation – for illustrative purposes only). The $ 500 would be subtracted from your market value side.

*Surrender Period	% Penalty	Cost
1st Year	7%	Give back $700
2nd	6%	Give back $600
3rd	**5%**	**Give back $500**
4th	4%	Give back $400
5th	3%	Give back $300
6th	2%	Give back $200
7th	1%	Give back $100
0	Free Surrender	Give back $0

*Also, if you are not 59 ½ years old, you may incur additional withdrawal penalties. (At least 10% more.) Remember the surrender penalty comes out of your account total on the market side (what your annuity value is). So, if you have incurred market losses as well… your account will be less than just the $ 10,000 minus the $ 500 surrender penalty.

STEP 2

- Next, I draw a 'T' on a piece of paper. On the left side I label the column **"Market Value;"** Over the right column is labeled **"Guaranteed."** Be careful about understanding what the *Guaranteed Side* of the illustration is showing you. Your contract will have a minimum appreciation percent noted.

Market Value Side   Guaranteed Side

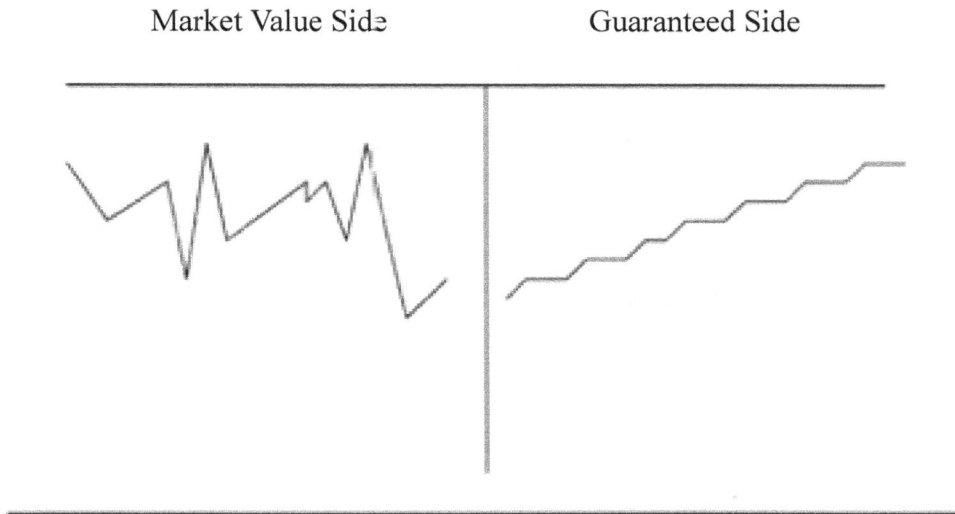

a. **Market Side:** As you see by the picture, the left side of the graph is the **'market side.'** The **market side** illustrates the hypothetical annual value of your account. For example, if you have a variable annuity the market value will fluctuate with the underlying 'separate account' investment choices that you have made. An example of the **market value side** for a ***variable annuity*** is this:

- You invest $ 10,000;

- Your holdings (in the separate account) go up $ 1,000 in 6 months (minus fees);

- Your holdings (in the separate account) go back down $ 500 the next 6 months (minus fees);

- Your 'market value' is $ 10,500 at the end of the first year (minus fees);

The **market value side** will also fluctuate with the interest rate gains according to the *'fixed rate' for a fixed annuity product.* For example, if your annuity has a 5% fixed interest rate:

- ○ You put in $ 10,000;

- ○ Your holdings go up 5% for the year;

- ○ Your 'market value' is $ 10,500 at the end of the first year;

- ○ The $ 10,500 market value will be before annual fees.

The difference… the annual fixed interest rate will always be 5% (if 5% is your rate for your contract).

For the *variable annuity, there is no fixed rate*, so the market value can be more or less each month.

b.   Variable Annuity Guaranteed Side: *If you have purchased an Income/Withdrawal Rider…*

As you see by the chart, the right of the chart is the 'guaranteed side.' The **guaranteed side** is **NOT ALWAYS** the **value** of your account. For example, if you have a variable annuity, the guaranteed value will fluctuate according to the 'rider' you may have purchased. Typically, an **income or withdrawal rider** will be illustrated on the right side of the chart. The illustration will note a schedule that you can access for an income or withdrawal stream **sometime in the future. You SHOULD NOT take your money out in a lump sum (all at once) until your contract is 'out of surrender,' or you may be assessed a penalty. And if you do withdraw the money… you will receive the MARKET SIDE VALUE ONLY (not the guaranteed side value). If you take your money out prior to the stated surrender timeframe (some contracts can have a very long surrender period), your withdrawal amounts will be reduced and 'riders' can be nullified.**

If you have a fixed annuity… the **market side and the guaranteed sides** may be the same.

STEP 3

- **Fees:** A third part of the chart is for the **fees**. Especially for a variable annuity, understanding the fees is quite important. I always review the fees with the client. Do not forget to ask about the fees your contract will charge. The fees are not always transparent to the contract owner, but they will be stated on both the illustration and in the brochures and variable annuity prospectus.

Choose your investment product carefully. As with any investment product, it is imperative that you understand all of the features and fees involved prior to your purchase. The strength and rating of the insurance company offering your annuity product is also important and should be considered. Research the published Insurance Company ratings that are provided by Moody's® and S&P®. Fixed annuity products, and the riders for the variable products, are only guaranteed by the insurance company. Fixed annuities are not FDIC insured and leave the investor at risk of losing their investment. Consult both your tax advisor and your financial advisor; and read the accompanying literature thoroughly before you proceed with the purchase.

What are two features that are common to both fixed and variable annuities?

_____

In what two ways are fixed and variable annuities different?

_____

Annuities may not be **'suitable'** for every investor... your age, liquidity needs, cost of the contract, intended use, investment experience and objectives, risk tolerance and time horizon, tax status, and your current investment and insurance holdings are just a few of the suitability considerations.

One Other Thought

Statistics bring us additional information to consider... in the article from the American Institute of Certified Public Accountants®, *"Less than Half of Non-Retired Americans Confident They'll Reach Financial Goals by Retirement: AICPA® Survey"* (4/2017), "The survey found that only 46 percent of non-retired Americans are confident they will reach their retirement goals, compared with 49 percent who are not confident (29 percent not sure, 20 percent don't think they ever will). Only five percent of non-retired Americans reported that they had already reached their retirement goals."   (https://www. grafwebcuso.com/less-than-half-of-americans-confident-theyll-reach-their-retirement-goals-aicpa/) In what group do you want to be in when you retire? All Americans are facing challenges, and those challenges change frequently... A RealClear® Opinion Research poll summarizes: *"New Poll Shows Health Care is Voters' Top Concern"* 5/2019. (https://www.realclearpolitics.com/real_clear_opinion_ research/new_poll_shows_health_care_is_voters_top_concern.html).

Conclusion:

> *"You can be young without money, but you can't be old without it."*
>
> Tennessee Williams

While no one can plan for every occasion, the process of planning itself is a good place to start. Financial advisors have a myriad of programs that assist them in helping you chart how much money you should be saving for retirement. Once you figure out about how much money you might need for retirement income, determine what investment products you consider appropriate for your risk tolerance, time horizon, and investment profile. It is never too early to begin planning for your future.

Write out a hypothetical retirement plan for someone who wants to retire with $ 1,000,000 in forty years.

_____

_____

In an article, *"Workers More Worried About Retirement,"* published 3/15/2011 (https://www.planadviser.com/workers-even-more-worried-about-retirement/, https://www.accountingtoday.com/news/worker-pessimism-about-retirement-deepens), Matthew Greenwald, of Greenwald and Associates, recounted:

> *"Many people are planning to work longer and retire later because they know they simply can't afford to leave the workplace – both for the paycheck and the benefits."*
>
> Matthew Greenwald

https://www.ebri.org/docs/default-source/ebri-press-release/pr916.pdf?sfvrsn=faf1292f_0

Sources:

(89)   *"Financial Worries Keep Most American's Up At Night,"* Bloomberg®, Luke McGrath, 6/27/2019; January 31, 2011, PLANSPONSOR.com®, *"Boomers Anticipate a Different Retirement than Their Parents,"* Bank of America's® Merrill Lynch® Affluent Insights Quarterly®; https://www.businesswire.com/news/home/20110131005332/en/Merrill-Lynch-Affluent-Insights-Quarterly-Survey-Finds. https://www.plansponsor.com/boomers-tout-benefits-of-using-financial-advisers.

(89a)   https://www.cnbc.com/2019/05/24/25-percent-of-americans-say-they-worry-about-money-all-the-time.html, *"25% of Americans say they worry about money 'all the time,'"* 5/2019m Shawn M. Carter; https://www.wusa9.com/article/news/nation-now/heres-how-many-americans-dont-have-access-to-a-employer-sponsored-401k-plan/465-cf42b20b-24bd-4f77-bec6-607f4e731423, *"Here's how many Americans don't have access to a 401(k) plan,"* Emmie Martin, 3/2018, https://www.cnbc.com/2018/03/12/how-many-americans-dont-have-access-to-a-401k.html.

(90)   https://en.wikipedia.org/wiki/Individual_retirement_account, *"Individual retirement account;"* https://dqydj.com/historical-ira-contribution-limit/, *"Historical IRA Contribution Limit;"* https://investor.vanguard.com/ira/roth-conversion, *"Roth conversions,"* Vanguard®.

(91)   McCourt, Stephen P., *"Defined Benefit and Defined Contribution Plans: A History, Market Overview and Comparative Analysis,"* 'Benefits Compensation Digest,' Vol. 43, No. 2, (2/2006) https://russellinvestments.com/-/media/files/us/insights/institutions/defined-benefit/defined-benefit-plans-a-brief-history.pdf?la=en, *"Defined benefit plans: A brief history,"* Justin Owens, 11/2014; https://www.ifebp.org; https://www.thebalance.com/the-history-of-the-pension-plan-2894374; *"History of Pension Plans in the U.S."*

(92)   https://www.bls.gov/ncs/ncspubs.htm; *"National Compensation Survey,"* Bureau of Labor Statistics.

(93)   https://scholarship.law.georgetown.edu/legal/50/, *"A Timeline of the Evolution of Retirement in the US.;"* https://www.bls.gov/ncs/ncspubs.htm, "Defined-Benefit Pensions, Source: U.S. Bureau of Labor Statistics, National Compensation Survey: Employee Benefits in Private Industry in the United States;" https://www.irs.gov/retirement-plans/choosing-a-retirement-plan-plan-options, *"Choosing a Retirement Plan: Plan Options";* https://www.dol.gov/agencies/ebsa/researchers/statistics/retirement-bulletins/private-pension-plan.

(94)   https://www.ssa.gov/policy/docs/ssb/v69n3/v69n3p1.html, *"The Disappearing Defined Benefit Pension and Its Potential Impact on the Retirement Incomes of Baby Boomers,"* Butrica, Iams, Smith & Toder, SS Bul. Vol. 69 2009; (4/8/2009), Patrick Purcell, Specialist in Income Security, *Retirement Savings and Household Wealth in 2007*, Congressional Research Service (7-5700; https://citeseerx.ist.psu.edu/viewdoc/download?doi=10.1.1.614.8959&rep=rep1&type=pdf); https://www.pewtrusts.org/-/media/assets/2016/09/employersponsoredretirementplanaccessuptakeandsavings.pdf; https://www.researchgate.net/publication/37157188_Retirement_Savings_and_Household_Wealth_in_2007; https://www.barrons.com/articles/the-pension-myth-and-the-financial-realities-1542403959, *"The Pension Myth and the Financial Realities,"* Kapadia, Barron's®, 11/2018.

(95)   https://www.irs.gov/retirement-plans/plan-participant-employee/retirement-topics-vesting, *"Retirement Topics Vesting";* *"Understanding Your 401(k) Vesting Schedule for Retirement Planning."* https://www.thebalance.com/know-the-impact-of-your-401k-vesting-schedule-2894176; Social Security Administration; Transamerica®, *"Unlocking Social Security,"* https://www.SSA.gov. 7:38 p.m. EDT; https://www.transamericaannuities.com/media/PDF/Annuity/Unlocking-Social-Security-Brochure.pdf; https://www.Transamerica.Com/Financial-Professional/What-We-Offer/Education/Field-Guides/Social-Security/; 7:38 p.m. EDT) Robert Powell, *"The Risks and Challenges of Retirement Planning,"* (May/June 2020), file:///C:/Users/Dell/Documents/powell%20 20MayJun-RisksChallengesRetirementPlanning.pdf; https://www.marketwatch.com/story/ten-major-retirement-risks-tips; https://money.usnews.com/money/blogs/on-retirement/articles/2018-02-22/5-financial-risks-in-retirement, *"5 Financial Risks in Retirement,"* Tom Sightings, 2/2018.

(96)   https://www.cbpp.org/research/social-security/policy-basics-top-ten-facts-about-social-security, *"Policy Basics: Top Ten Facts about Social Security,"* Center on Budget and Policy Priorities, 2019.

(97)   https://www.ssa.gov/pubs/EN-05-10024.pdf, *"Securing today and tomorrow, "Understanding the Benefits,"* Social Security Administration | Publication No. 05-10024 ICN 454930 | Unit/Issue 2019.

(98)   *"Take the Guesswork Out of Retirement Savings,"* By Peng Chen, Ph.D., CFA, and Roger Ibbotson, Ph.D. (06-25-07); https://www.morningstar.com/articles/193971/take-the-guesswork-out-of-retirement-savings, Shrestha, Laura B., Specialist in Demography, Domestic Social Policy Division, (8/16/2006).

(99)   https://www.cnbc.com/2018/03/12/how-many-americans-dont-have-access-to-a-401k.html, *"Here's how many Americans don't have access to a 401(k) plan,"* Emmie Martin, (3/12/2018); *"Only half of Americans have access to a 401(k)...,"* Kathleen Elk, 3/18/2019, Stanford Center on Longevity (2018).

(100)   https://www.cnbc.com/2018/09/28/how-much-you-have-to-save-every-month-to-retire-with-1-million.html.

(101)   2011 Society of Actuaries® Key Findings: *"Longevity Report,"* https://www.soa.org/globalassets/assets/files/research/projects/research-key-finding-longevity.pdf.; Fidelity® (2006/2007); American Academy of Actuaries® (2003); https://www.fidelity.com; Robert Powell, May 21, 2008, *"Risk management-The top five risks you face in retirement, and tips on how to handle them,"* MarketWatch, https://www.marketwatch.com/story/the-top-five-retirement-risks-and-tips-on-how-to-handle-them; https://www.marketwatch.com/story/ten-major-retirement-risks-tips, October 2008, SOCIETY OF ACTUARIES®, Schaumburg, Illinois, Copyright© 2008, *"Managing Post Retirement Risks: Guide to Retirement Planning;"* https://www.soa.org/files/pdf/post-retirement-charts.pdf; https://abcnews.go.com/amp/Business/story?id=5537958&page=1; https://institutional.fidelity.com/app/item/RD_13569_41055/five-key-risks-of-retirement.html, *"Five Key Risks of Retirement,"* Fidelity®.

(102)   https://www.fidelity.com/viewpoints/retirement/how-long-will-savings-last, *"How can I make my retirement savings last?"* (8/2018).

(103)   CRS Report for Congress, (received through the CRS Web, Order Code RL32792), *"Life Expectancy In the United States,"* https://www.everycrsreport.com/files/20060816_RL32792_8a7c7fa5bfd3890526d12d42c6df39faa5c67cfc.pdf.

(104)   https://institutional.fidelity.com/app/item/RD_13569_41055/five-key-risks-of-retirement.html, Fidelity®, *"Five Risks for Retirees,"* (2006); https://www.usatoday.com/story/money/2019/05/31/45-american-worried-healthcare-expenses-could-bankrupt-them/1292919001/, *"The expense nearly half of American think can bankrupt them,"* Katie Brockman, 5/2019, USA TODAY®.

(105)   (6/4/2009), Truman Lewis, Harvard Study: *"60% of Bankruptcies Caused by Health Problems,"* https://www.consumeraffairs.com/news04/2009/06/bankruptcy_medical_costs; https://www.merrilledge.com/guidance/nearing-retirement/health-care-costs, *"Plan now for the cost of health care,"* Merrill, A Bank of America Company®; Healthview®.

(106)   https://www.hvsfinancial.com/wp-content/uploads/2020/12/2021-Retirement-Healthcare-Costs-Data-Report.pdf.; https://voyainsights.voya.com/planning-high-cost-healthcare-retirement-nc.

(107)   Center for Retirement Research at Boston College® WP#2017-13, *"How Much Does Out-of-Pocket Medical Spending Eat Away at Retirement Income?"* by Melissa McInerney, Matthew S Rutledge, Sara Ellen King, https://crr.bc.edu/wp-content/uploads/2017/10/wp_2017-13.pdf., https://www.pharmacytimes.com/publications/issue/2016/january2016/the-aging-population-the-increasing-effects-on-health-care, *"The Aging Population: The Increasing Effects on Health Care,"* Anyssa Garza 1/2016); https://www.emaxhealth.com, *"Increased Health Care Costs, Aging Population Pose Concerns;"* https://www.change.org/p/tell-your-story-of-how-high-health-care-costs-are-hurting-you-economically; *"Health care costs to top $8,000 per person; Tell Your Story of How High Health Care Costs Are*

Hurting You Economically;" https://www.daveramsey.com/blog/who-needs-long-term-care-insurance, *"Who Needs, Long-term Care Insurance?"*.

(108)   https://www.aginginplace.org/what-is-long-term-care-insurance-and-who-needs-it/, *"What Is Long-Term Care Insurance And Who Needs It?"* (10/2019).

(109)   (6/4/2009), Truman Lewis, Harvard Study: *"60% of Bankruptcies Caused by Health Problems,"* https://www. consumeraffairs.com/news04/2009/06/bankruptcy_medical_costs.html; *"67 percent of bankruptcy filers cite illness and medical bills as contributors to financial ruin,"* (2/7/2019), https://www.eurekalert.org/pub_releases/2019-02/ pfan-6ob020719.php; 2/2008, https://crr.bc edu/wp-content/uploads/2008/02/ib_8-3_508c.pdf, *"Health Care Costs Drive Up the National Retirement Risk Index;"* www.ltctree.com › long-term-care-statistics, *"Common Long Term Care Misconceptions,"* Long-Term Care Partners, LLC, https://longtermcareinsurancepartner.com/about-long-term-care/myths-facts.

(110)   https://www.tomorrowsmoney.org, https://www.sifma.org/education.html; The SIFMA Foundation® (2009), *"Did you know? Long-Term Care Insurance;"* Henry J. Kaiser Foundation®, MetLife Mature Market Institute® (MMI), https://caregiver.org; https://acl.gov/ltc/basic-needs/how-much-care-will-you-need; (110a) *"Why Long-term Care Insurance Is Important,"* https://www.cbsnews.com/news/why-long-term-care-insuance-is-important/.

(111)   https://www.caregiver.org/selected-long-term-care-statistics, *"Selected Long-Term Care Statistics,"* Robert B. Friedland, PhD, 2015; https://www.prepsmart.com/statistic-long-term-care.html, (1997-2008), *"What Are Your Odds of Needing Long Term Care? Some Thought-Provoking Long-Term Care Statistics."*

(112)   *"How Much Care Will You Need?"*, https://acl.gov/ltc/basic-needs/how-much-care-will-you-need.

(113)   https://www.aaltci.org/long-term-care-insurance/learning-center/fast-facts.php, American Association for Long-Term Care Insurance®, *"Long-Term Care Insurance Facts – Statistics;"* 2019, (2004-2009); *"18 Risks in Retirement,"* (2021), https://www.afmgplanning.com/18-risks-you-face-in-retirement/; https://www.newretirement.com/ Search_Results.aspx?q=top+10+risks&cx=013622316860053227775%3arkuqv4g3sjq&cof=FORID%3a9, *"New Retirement—Secure your future, Retirement 101—Retirement Planning and Risks. Top 10 Risks to Your Retirement Plan: Insufficient Planning, Longevity, Retiring Too Soon, Changes to Social Security, Shortcomings of Social Security, Inflation, Rising Medical Costs, Serious Medical Crisis, Swings in Financial Markets, Debt."*

(114)   https://www.seniorliving.org/nursing-homes/costs/; *"Nursing Home Costs,"* https://www.safeharborterm.com/ services/competitiveness/.

(115)   https://www.usa.gov; https://www.westegg.com/inflation.

(115a)   https://www.wsj.com/articles/when-planning-for-retirement-dont-forget-inflation-11551387373;   https://www. energy.gov/eere/vehicles/fact-915-march-7-2016-average-historical-annual-gasoline-pump-price-1929-2015, *"Fact #915: March 7, 2016 Average Historical Annual Gasoline Pump Price, 1929-2015;"* https://www.statista.com/ statistics/204740/retail-price-of-gasoline-in-the-united-states-since-1990/ *"Retail price of regular gasoline in the United States from 1990 to 2018;"* *"When Planning for Retirement, Don't Forget Inflation,"* The Wall Street Journal, 10/2019; https://blog.chron.com/carsandtrucks/2016/04/cost-of-a-car-in-the-year-you-were-born/, *"Cost of a Car in the Year You Were Born;"* http://www.johnstonsarchive.net/other/postage.html, *"Cost of a first class U.S. postage stamp;"* https://www.msn.com/en-us/money/personalfinance/cost-of-a-movie-ticket-the-year-you-were-born/ ar-AApSYNq, *"Cost of a Movie Ticket the Year You Were Born."*

(116)   https://www.thebalance.com/what-s-your-retirement-number-453995, *"What Is Your Retirement Number?;"* https:// www.ahdictionary.com/word/search.html?q=inflation, The American Heritage dictionary of the English Language.

(117)   https://www.in2013dollars.com/us/inflation/1980?amount=100, Inflation Calculator; Bureau of Labor Statistics (May 23, 2001), *Sources of retirement income, the Editor's Desk;* https://www.bls.gov.

(118)   https://www.history.com/this-day-in-history/fdr-signs-social-security-act, *"On This Day: Roosevelt Signs Social Security Act Into Law"* (Associated Press®), https://www.findingdulcinea.com/news/on-this-day/July-August-08/On-this-Day--Congress-Passes-Social-Security-Act.html; https://finance.zacks.com/inflation-affect-standard-living-9960.html, 3/2019 Ciaran John, article, *"How Does Inflation Affect the Standard of Living?"*

(119)   (July 11, 1997), United States General Accounting Office, Washington, D.C. 20548, B-276326 Jane L. Ross, Director Income Security Issues; GAO Report to the Chairman and Ranking Minority Member, Special Committee on Aging, U.S. Senate, (July 1997) *"RETIREMENT INCOME, Implications of Demographic Trends for Social Security and Pension Reform,"* https://books.google.com/books.

(120)   https://www.govinfo.gov/content/pkg/CRPT-106srpt229/html/CRPT-106srpt229-vol1.htm, *"Selected Long-Term Care Statistics, Special Committee on Aging, Developments in Aging: 1997-1998, Vol.1, Report 106-229. Washington, DC: United States Senate, 2000, United States Senate Special Committee on Aging, Issue: "Social Security and Retirement Savings,"* https:www.aging.senate.gov; https://www.ssa.gov/policy/docs/chartbooks/fast_facts/2004/fast_facts04.html, *"Fast Facts & Figures about Social Security;"* https://www.ssa.gov/OACT/TR.

(121)   https://www.investopedia.com/terms/s/separateaccount.asp (variable annuity link), *"Separate Account",* James Chen, 12/2017.

(122)   https://www.ssa.gov/policy/docs/ssb/v70n3/v70n3p111.html, *"The Future Financial Status of the Social Security Program," "Coping witht the Demographic Challenge: Fewer Children and Living Longer."*

(123)   https://www.thinkadvisor.com/2018/05/07/what-americans-think-about-retirement-income-in-5/, *"What Americans Think About Retirement Income in 5 Charts,"* Emily Zulz, 5/2018); https://www.franklintempleton.com/investor/investments-and-solutions/individual-retirement/retirement-research/, *"Retirement Income Strategies and Expectations (RISE) Survey,"* https://www.fool.com/retirement/2018/01/22/the-taxation-of-social-security-benefits-has-create.aspx, *"The Taxation of Social Security Benefits Has Created Quite the Dilemma,"* Sean Williams, 1/2018.

(124)   https://money.usnews.com/investing/investing-101/articles/things-you-need-to-know-now-about-annuities#guarantees, *"16 Things You Need to Know About Annuities,"* Coryanne Hicks & Philip Moeller, 5/2021.

(125)   https://finance.zacks.com/variable-annuities-covered-sipc-8511.html, *"Are Variable Annuities Covered by SIPC®?"* Tom Streissguth, Zacks Investment Research®.

General Sources: for retirement:

https://www.irs.gov/

https://fidelity.com

https://www.investopedia.com/ask/answers/102714/how-does-simplified-employee-pension-sep-ira-work.asp

https://www.ssa.gov/

Chapter 4
Check For Understanding

For a chapter review, read and complete the following follow-up activities.

- ☒ Evaluate the pros and cons of investing your money in a Non-Roth retirement account.

- ☒ Create a hypothetical retirement savings plan for someone who is making $ 40,000 a year in a 25% tax bracket.

- ☒ Estimate how much you would like to save for retirement, starting from age 25 until age 62. Describe how you calculated that number.

- ☒ Recalling that the article in the Kansas City Star® indicated that a 25 year old needed to put away $ 286 a month, assuming 8% average earnings on that money for 40 years, to accumulate $ 1 million dollars, Do you imagine that: a) this goal is realistic, and b) that you personally could save that much a month? Elaborate on your answer.

- ☒ Describe a 'tax-free' investment.

- ☒ List some of the implications for withdrawing money from a Non- Roth Retirement Account before you are age 59 ½.

- ☒ Name two reasons why annuity products are sometimes perceived as 'complex.' What do you perceive as the primary benefit for each?

- ☒ In your own words, relate the impact of inflation to the cost of goods in 40 years. Choose 2 items, state the current cost, and hypothetically calculate the cost in 40 years.

- ☒ Consider what you believe to be the most important of the five 'Risks for Retirees' that are presented in the text. Elaborate on your reasons.

- ☒ Describe some of the differences between a defined benefit and a defined contribution plan. Which type of plan, on the surface, seems more attractive to you.

- ☒ Explain the implications of a 'vesting schedule' for a company 'match.' With this information in mind, do you imagine you might consider the 'vesting schedule' prior to a job change?

- ☒ Identify what type of retirement plan is typically utilized by a Not-for-Profit organization.

☒ Illustrate how a 'surrender' period might negatively impact a withdrawal from an annuity investment product. Given what you know about 'surrender' periods, what would you do before you considered buying an Annuity?

☒ Calculate the 'capital gain' of a stock that is purchased for $10 a share and is sold @ $14.50 a share after a period of 2 years.

☒ Compare and contrast the characteristics of a 'fixed' and 'variable' annuity.

☒ Contrast the characteristics of an IRA with the characteristics of a Roth IRA.

About Experience Talks...

Everyone has heard someone's 'Retirement' story. Many people have found themselves ill-prepared for retirement or surprised by the cost of living after they retired. One conference I attended several years ago presented that @ 23% of individuals return to some type of work to generate additional income after they 'retire' from their career. I believe Americans today are re-thinking their retirement plans, and in fact, *NewRetirement*®, October 17, 2017, (https://www.newretirement.com/retirement/reverse-retirement-find-out-why-retirees-are-going-back-to-work/) reported in their article, *"Reverse Retirement: Find Out Why So Many Retirees Are Going Back to Work," …"a full 1/3 of those who retire eventually reverse retirement and return to work on either a full or part time basis."* The concept of 'retiring' may be quite different today than in our recent past.

A couple of months ago I was at a luncheon where the speaker noted that," Because the baby boomers had lost so much money in the stock market in 2008, they needed to build up their reserves again before they could consider retirement." Individuals may be working longer and planning more diligently for their new paradigm of 'retirement.'

Everyone's story is, and will, be different. I have recounted some of the experiences that I have recorded through the years here for your review; of course, the names have again been changed to protect the identity of the individuals.

How will your 'retirement' story read?

Experience Talks...

All Your Eggs In One Basket, They Are Liable To Get Broke

G regg, worked for 35+ years for a large company. He loved his company and invested heavily in the company's stock. When it came time to retire Gregg had saved over $3,000,000 in his investment accounts.... The only trouble was the stock price fell from @ $95 per share, to @ $12 per share the year after Gregg retired. Gregg had what is called a concentrated stock position... too much money in just one company. Unless this one stock position appreciates, what once was a $ 3,000,000 account is now worth far less.

Moral of the story: Concentrated positions can be risky; it may be better to consider *diversification*.

Experience Talks...

Early Saving Beats Early Spending

Maggie's retirement strategy was simple... "Go to the front door and find a box of money."

Maggie also commented; "in college I realized I never wanted to have to work, still don't, darn lottery, so elusive."

So, on a more serious note, Maggie began her retirement savings program at the age of 22. She put away $200 to $300 a month but maxed out her Roth account each year. Maggie figured that if her account earns @ 6%, when she turns 65, she should have about $ 707,000 saved. I heartily hope that will be true.

Moral of the story: The early bird gets the worm.... Is *compound interest* the 8th Wonder of the World?

Experience Talks...

Life Is A Highway, Sometimes It Is A Long Trip, Don't Run Out Of Gas

Alice took early retirement from her company when she turned 55 years old. Her passion was to golf, and she wanted to golf about 5 times a week and travel with her husband. Alice and her husband had planned well and had paid off their home and cars. They had no other debt. Although they were not 'wealthy' by some people's standards, if they are careful, they may be able to maintain their current lifestyle. They draw out a certain amount from their retirement accounts each month, and until they are 62 years old and can access their social security benefits, they live on their investment accounts.

However, as you can imagine, there are many expense pitfalls that can throw a wrench into a retiree's financial plans. Retiring at such an early age will certainly cause a drain on their savings and investment accounts, and the market performance of 2008 may have caused them to re-evaluate their strategy.

Moral of the story: Plan for longevity and market downturns. Have a Plan B.

Experience Talks...

Frugal And Thrifty Are Not Four Letter Words

Joshua and June have been frugal most of their married life. Yes, they splurge on vacations, but they scrimp in a variety of other ways. Their 'thriftiness' has not always been appreciated by their children… shopping at the 'Dollar Store,' can be embarrassing for teenagers.

Priority one for Joshua and June is saving money every month. Both partners have shown great restraint in making purchases. Joshua and June report that some of the ways they save are:

○ Staying out of the stores

○ Keeping what they have as long it works or can be repaired

○ Teaching their children how to 'bargain hunt'

○ Eating at home as much as they can… coming home for lunch, or taking a brown bag

○ Minimizing dry-cleaning bills

○ Staying at one job a long time to build equity

○ Paying cash for their cars

The plan is that when Joshua is around 62 years old, they hope to have a nice nest egg saved, and they will use the "spousal Social Security options" to maximize their Social Security benefits. By the time Joshua is 62, their house will long be paid-off… they won't have any car payments… their fixed expenses should be minimal. Joshua and June also have not only one, but two Long-Term Care insurance policies each; and the policies were purchased at a young enough age that the monthly payments are very small.

Moral of the story: In fact, June doesn't plan to retire until she is 70 (and even then, she'll probably do something part time after 'retirement'). June and Joshua realize that the longer you work, the less money you draw out of your retirement savings, and the more opportunity you have to put a little extra away.

Experience Talks...

You Need More Than Just Social Security

Christopher was speaking with a Mutual Fund representative who quoted this statistic: "53% of those who collect Social Security have only that money to live on with nothing put away for retirement." When Christopher relayed this statistic to me, I went online to see what I could find…

"Tips for Retiring on Social Security Alone," Eileen Ambrose, AARP®, provides guidance for individuals who find themselves living solely on Social Security. (https://www.aarp.org/retirement/social-security/info-2016/ways-to-retire-on-social-security-alone.html). Also,

The *"Social Security Fact Sheet,"* https://www.ssa.gov/news/press/factsheets/basicfact-alt.pdf, provides up-to-date data on Social Security benefits:

"In 2019, about 64 million Americans will receive over one trillion dollars in Social Security benefits:

☒ Social Security is the major source of income for most of the elderly.

☒ Nearly nine out of ten individuals age 65 and older receive Social Security benefits.

☒ Social Security benefits represent about 33% of the income of the elderly.

☒ Among elderly Social Security beneficiaries, 50% of married couples and 70% of unmarried persons receive 50% or more of their income from Social Security.

☒ Among elderly Social Security beneficiaries, 21% of married couples and about 45% of unmarried persons rely on Social Security for 90% or more of their income."

Moral of the story: Social Security benefits alone might not be enough. What is your plan B?

Experience Talks...

The More Plans The Merrier

Cathy was a teacher for over 25 years. Unfortunately, she became unable to work, due to a severe case of diabetes and other health complications. So, several years ago Cathy retired with a reduced pension (she hadn't taught quite enough years to receive a full pension) and some disability income. Cathy had also managed to put some money aside each month for her retirement. Although he hadn't saved a lot of money, with her small pension and disability income she was financially solvent.

Cathy had also owned a home, which she sold and invested the proceeds. Today, Cathy lives in a retirement home setting and is managing her affairs well.

Moral of the story: A solid plan, well executed!

Experience Talks...

If It Sounds Too Good To Be True – It Just Might Be!

n 2007 Greg and Diane were 75 and 73 years old respectively. They owned their own home, which was worth about $250,000, and had no other outstanding debts. Greg and Diane asked their financial planner to run a hypothetical retirement projection for them. The financial advisor did so and reported to the couple that they may be in trouble. If they continued to withdraw their assets at their current spending rate-- forecasting a 7% projected average annual growth rate of return on their investment account, their investment account funds would only last about 10 more years.

Looking for ways to generate some additional money, Greg and Diane had visited a seminar on the topic of reverse-mortgages and were thinking about cashing out the equity on their home. They said they wanted to give the money to their financial planner to invest and "make even more money." This additional money could be used to fund their retirement.

The financial planner was adamantly against this strategy. He suggested that if they followed this approach, they potentially could lose the money they invested in the market, and they also would not own their largest asset anymore – their home. Greg and Diane, at that time, decided NOT to go ahead with the reverse-mortgage… Good idea, since in 2008 the market took a steep downturn. (I wonder if they reduced their monthly spending?)

Moral of the story: Before you make an important financial decision, seek out the counsel of your trusted advisors. Don't risk more than you can afford to lose.

Experience Talks...

Resist Upsizing, Your Wallet and Your Waistline Will Thank You

Mike worked at a manufacturing plant, and Deena was a teacher. They had one 14-year-old son. Mike and Deena were just six years from paying off their mortgage on their smaller, three-bedroom home. This was a great feat. Except that Deena wanted to sell their smaller home and get a larger house. Deena said they could afford to do so, and she was worried about not having a tax deduction when the home was paid for. She wasn't looking forward to paying more taxes.

Mike was happy where he was. He reasoned that in a few short years it would be just the two of them when their son went to college and they really wouldn't need a larger house; and as for paying more taxes, when the mortgage was paid off, they would have more money to 'defer' into their retirement plans at work. Deferring the money would reduce their gross income, and they may pay lower taxes.

It took some convincing, but Deena compromised by remodeling their kitchen.

The moral of the story: Bigger is not always better.

CHAPTER 5

An Introduction To Protection Strategies

LEARNING OBJECTIVES:

After reading Chapter 5, you should be able to:

a. Articulate your understanding of the advantages of protecting your assets.

b. Describe the safeguards put in place by our government to protect your assets; Securities Investor Protection Corporation and the Federal Deposit Insurance Corporation.

- Illustrate how these agencies work; identify what the agencies oversee and protect.

c. Explain the general differences between Term and Permanent life insurance.

- Identify the general advantages and disadvantages for Term and Permanent life insurance;

- List and demonstrate an understanding of the key terms associated with life insurance policies.

d. Describe what long-term care is; how it is different from health care.

- Exhibit familiarity with the terms related with long-term care insurance.

e. Identify the differences between a Will and a Trust; identify the advantages and disadvantages of each type of document.

f. Provide a list of activities that help individuals to safeguard themselves against *Identity Theft*.

Experience Talks...

Estate Planning Is Not Something You Put Off

Estate Planning took on a whole new meaning when my grandmother passed away in 1999… it became personal. Not because I was directly affected in a financial sense by her passing, but that was the event that immersed me in my mother's financial life for the first time. And the financial planning accelerated when my father passed away the following year.

Working with my mother to help her define her estate, and to help her protect her inherited assets, involved first introducing her to the concept of estate planning.

Like many clients, my Mom really had no idea about what estate planning involved. I walked her through the various steps and introduced her to new terms. She decided on her own what she wanted to leave to the grandchildren and how she wanted her possessions to be distributed. She also articulated her wishes for her healthcare, should she become unable to care for herself.

With six boys, you might understand that it is important that John and I have our affairs in order. John has seen too many incidences of families not being prepared for a loved-one's passing, and family members wanting to be able to remember their loved-one by keeping a particular possession. But what can happen when several children or family members want the same keepsake?

Navigating How to Protect What You Gather

Estate Planning also encompasses wealth protection. As you review the following section, topics will be introduced that will encourage you to look well into the future, when you may be more established with your financial life.

Chapter 5
An Introduction To Protection Strategies

Protection

The concept of 'protection' is generally linked with the idea of 'reducing loss.' Protecting against loss of a loved one, loss of a specific asset, like a car or home, or protection against loss of income. Purchasing insurance can help us to mitigate, or reduce, loss. In theory, insurance is:

> *The act of protection, or the state of being protected; preservation from loss, injury, or annoyance; defense; shelter; ....*
>
> *...That which protects or preserves from injury; a defense, a shield; a refuge." (126)*

You're probably not thinking about insurance much, except maybe about your car insurance and how expensive it is? But no discussion about assets would be complete without touching on the subject of '*asset protection.*' To protect your assets, you will probably purchase insurance.

'Insurance' might also be thought of as the transfer of risk from one person or entity to another.

> SafetyInsurance.com offers this simple definition of 'insurance:
>
> *"Insurance is a social device where many share the losses of a few by transferring a portion of the risk of loss to the insurance company in exchange for a certain cost."*
>
> https:www.safetyinsurance.com/custsupport/definitions.html (127)

By and large insurance is purchased to help you safeguard your assets so that if loss or damage occurs you may be reimbursed, either in the entirety, or for a partial loss. You work hard to accumulate assets, so it is vitally important to consider buying insurance to help defray costs if 'disaster' strikes. There are many forms of insurance, the subject can get complicated. For our purpose we will concentrate on some of these areas of asset protection; life, disability, long term care insurance; 'wealth protection and transfer;' and protection from identity theft. However, there certainly are many other types of insurance areas, like: property and casualty, professional malpractice, Errors & Omissions, dental, vision, etc. But all types of insurance have one thing in common.... They all involve pre-PLANNING.

I'm sure you have some experience with insurance because you drive a car. Wikipedia® suggests that car insurance is required in 48 U.S. States, and two additional states require that you purchase either car insurance or post a financial bond. I'll assume you understand that the premiums you pay monthly are for protection for you and others if you have an accident. When you pay your premium (money you owe each month to keep the insurance active) you are honoring your contract with the insurance company. That contract states, in some fashion, that if you pay the insurance company so much money a month the insurance company will reimburse you in some regard for damages.

When you purchase car insurance there will be a variety of 'coverage' choices. One choice is 'liability' coverage. ***Bodily liability* insurance covers any bodily injuries or death for which you are responsible.** Whereas, ***property damage liability*** insurance covers another type of damage in a car accident: damage to property. Property damage liability includes coverage for the damage to other cars, buildings, and anything else that may be injured in an accident. Car *liability insurance* is different than *comprehensive* car insurance. ***Comprehensive car insurance* (other than collision) can include covering the cost of the car if it is stolen or damaged by hail, vandalism, fire, flood, an animal, or by anything other than a car collision. *Collision car insurance* covers damage to your car when your car hits, or is hit by, another vehicle, or another object.**

When you look at your policy the first page of your insurance policy is called the 'Declaration Page.' The Declaration Page lists the names of the drivers and the Vehicle Identification Numbers (VINs) for each vehicle insured; also noted is the corresponding coverage for each. When you look at a Declaration Page the liability limits are commonly listed as:

☒ **Bodily Injury per person/Bodily Injury per occurrence/ Property damage: 100/300/50**

These numbers represent hundreds of thousands of dollars and are the limits that the insurance company will pay in the event you are at fault in an accident. Put another way, in the example above, if you are involved in an accident with another car your auto policy will pay up to $100k in medical or legal bills per person (in the other car) not to exceed $300k total for the accident, and up to $50k to replace or repair the other vehicle or any property damage that was caused. Liability coverage pays the other party involved. Here's some additional general explanation of types of CAR insurance reviewed from valuepenguin.com… (128, chart below)

What Insurance Covers	Required Car Insurance Types	Range of Limits
Your passenger's and your injuries	Personal Injury	$1,000 to $50,000
	Protection/Medicare Benefits	$15,000 - $50,000 per person/double per accident
Other Driver's injury	Bodily Injury Liability	
Other Driver's car or house damage	Property Damage Liability	$5,000-$25,000 per accident
Your injuries, when the Other Driver is Uninsured	Uninsured/Underinsured Motorist Bodily Injury	$20,000-$50,000 per person/double per accident
Your vehicle damage when the Other Driver is Uninsured	Uninsured/Underinsured Motorist Property Damage	$5,000-$25,000 per accident

Life

Here is one friend's story:

*I have a friend, James, who is now in his 50s. James still remembers his painful **insurance lesson**.*

*James worked in a restaurant, starting at age 14 and saved his money diligently... so at age 17 he bought the car of his dreams... a **suped-up Camaro**. At the time, James spent $ 7,000 and paid cash for his car.*

*James' didn't know too much about car insurance at the time. He was ready to sign up for **full comprehensive and collision coverage** when he was advised by a friend to, "just buy liability... it'll be fine."*

About a month later James was sitting waiting to make a left turn when another car lost control and hit him hard from behind. Luckily no one was hurt, but James' car was 'totaled.'

*And, because James did not have 'full coverage,' remember, he only had **liability insurance,** he didn't get any of his hard-earned money back... The driver that hit his car had no insurance at all. Basically, James was out of luck without a car.*

Because James had spent all of his savings on that first car, he only could afford an old, 'beater' car for transportation. James drove that 'beater' the rest of his High School years. It was a very painful, and, as he tells it, embarrassing lesson

Research how much full car insurance protection is, vs. liability only, coverage. Report your findings here: Find a Declarations page and review it.

_____

_____

Note: Some states have 'underinsured' motorist coverage that can step in and pay your medical/ legal bills if the other party is at fault, and either doesn't have insurance, or doesn't have as much insurance as you do. Check with a licensed Insurance Agent

Big Government Protection For Your Money

Before mid-September 2008 I would have thought that a commentary about insurance on investment accounts and cash deposits would be perceived as dull and boring. However, in light of recent occurrences, the subject of 'protection' has become more popular. Once we own something of value, we want to keep it from harm.

When The Unthinkable Happens!

As we already have noted, the American financial markets periodically have declines, sometimes they feel like drastic, unprecedented events. For example, in 2008, we had the largest bankruptcy in history with the demise of Lehman Bros®.; investment banks were restructured; and the credit industry was turned upside down. In this same time period, there emerged a myriad of insurance questions, many of which were centered around the safety of cash and investment accounts. When the financial industry was imploding, people wanted to understand how their assets were protected. One of my financial advisor associates sent out an e-mail that he had read. The e-mail noted that the Securities Investor Protection Corporation (SIPC®) had received more in-bound calls in a period of 9 days in mid-September 2008 as they had received in the previous 25 years all together. (128) To put it mildly, Americans were worried about the safety of their cash and investments.

So let's clarify what the safeguards are:

- ☒ **The Securities Investor Protection Corporation (SIPC®)** was formed in 1970 by federal law to protect clients of U.S. securities firms from loss of their security investments in the event the securities firm itself failed. The protection is provided for each client up to $500,000 for each aggregate account, to include a maximum for $250,000 in cash. (129) *

    > ○ **For example:** This means that if you put in up to $ 400,000 in stocks and investment products, and $ 100,000 in a money market, in your investment or custodian/retirement account with JKL Securities Firm you are covered by the SIPC® to get your $500,000 returned to you.

    ***Please Note:** Money you place in a non-deposit 'Money Market' account is technically not cash; the Money Market is a **security. AND**… It is important to note that many firms carry excess-SIPC® insurance to protect clients against losses greater than the amounts that the SIPC® covers. (Must be a SIPC® member- See the chart- next page.)

- ☒ **The Federal Deposit Insurance Corporation, or FDIC**, provides protection for a different group of your assets. **Bank deposits** or **'cash'** are NOT securities, so they are not covered by SIPC®.

What does the SIPC® insurance cover, (among other securities)? (130, direct quote)

- note,

- stock,

- treasury stock,

- bond,

- debenture,

- evidence of indebtedness,

- any collateral trust certificate, preorganization certificate or subscription,

- transferable share,

- voting trust certificate,

- certificate of deposit,

- certificate of deposit for a security, or

- any security future as that term is defined in section 78c(a)(55)(A) ⊠ of this title

- any investment contract or certificate of interest or participation in any profit-sharing agreement or in any oil, gas, or mineral royalty or lease (if such investment contract or interest is the subject of a registration statement with the Commission pursuant to the provisions of the Securities Act of 1933 [15 U.S.C. 77a et seq.]),

- any put, call, straddle, option, or privilege on any security, or group or index of securities (including any interest therein or based on the value thereof), or

- any put, call, straddle, option, or privilege entered into on a national securities exchange relating to foreign currency,

- any certificate of interest or participation in, temporary or interim certificate for, receipt for, guarantee of, or warrant or right to subscribe to or purchase or sell any of the foregoing, and

- any other instrument commonly known as a security.

- (Certain investment products are ineligible for SIPC® coverage, and does not cover currency, commodities or related futures contracts, warrants/rights.)

Instead, cash in an FDIC INSURED bank and/or financial institution deposit balances are insured by the FDIC. To protect people who lost money in the wake of the 1929 stock market crash, the FDIC was created by President Franklin D. Roosevelt in 1933 to insure *thrift* and *bank deposits* (NOT stocks, bonds, investment products, purchased through a bank, financial institution, or broker/dealer, etc.). Similarly, the **National Credit Union Administration (NCUA.gov)** was also created to insure the deposits of credit unions.

As part of the 2010 Frank Dodd Wall Street Reform and Consumer Protection Act, the FDIC insures cash (see list on next page) in either a FDIC insured bank/retirement account or an 'Investment/Brokerage Account' up to $ 250,000 per individual, per depositor account. *

☒   So, for example, when you purchase certificates of deposits from an FDIC insured financial institution, which are cash products, be careful not to exceed $ 250,000 for the total amount of your cash AND certificate of deposits, at any ONE bank or financial institution, in any SINGLE NAME Account. If the financial institution has a problem and is unable to return your cash to you, the FDIC is required to pay you the principal, plus any accrued interest, prorated to the date of the closing of the relevant depository institution. Of course, the current applicable FDIC payment limitations would apply. (131)

---

* Limits change periodically so be sure to check the websites regularly. Single name accounts with a POD, joint accounts, and Trust accounts may allow you to hold additional cash in a FDIC covered account. Check: https://www.fdic.gov and https://edie.fdic.gov/ for the latest rules and regulations.

Note: A financial institution MUST present an SIPC® membership disclosure and/or FDIC membership number in order for accounts to be governed/insured by the SIPC® and FDIC.

Here are the general cash instruments that are insured by the FDIC: (direct quote, 130)

- Savings deposits

- Checking deposits

- Deposits in NOW accounts

- Christmas club accounts

- Certificates of deposit

- Cashiers' checks

- Officers' checks

- Expense checks

- Loan disbursement checks

- Interest checks

- Outstanding drafts

- Negotiable instruments are money orders drawn on the institution

- Certified checks, letters of credit and travelers' checks, for which an insured depository institution is primarily liable, also are insured when issued in exchange for money or its equivalent, or for a charge against a deposit account (130)

On September 25, 2008 President George Bush addressed the American public regarding the state of the economy. In his speech President Bush stated that in the last 75 years no investor had lost a penny on a FDIC insured deposit.

⊠ The **Security Exchange Commission (SEC)** was formed in 1934. Prior to the *Great Crash of 1929*, there was little support for federal regulation of the securities markets. However, 'widespread abuse of margin financing and unreliable information about the securities in which they [the investors] were investing… [coupled with] the stock market crash in October 1929, [caused] public confidence in the markets [to] plummet'…This event spurred 'a consensus that for the economy to recover, the public's faith in the capital markets needed to be restored. Congress [then] held hearings to identify the problems and search for solutions.' (132)

The outcome of the hearings was that Congress passed of the Securities Act of 1933 and the Securities Exchange Act of 1934. The Securities Exchange Act created the SEC. Both of these laws were designed to not only upgrade the level of oversight for investment practices, but to restore investor confidence in our capital markets. These goals were to be accomplished by furnishing more reliable information and "clear rules of honest dealing." (13)

The SEC was charged with monitoring the following activities to ensure compliance:

1. "Companies publicly offering securities for investment dollars must tell the public the truth about their businesses, the securities they are selling, and the risks involved in investing.

2. People who sell and trade securities – brokers, dealers, and exchanges must treat investors fairly and honestly, putting investors' interests first." (132)

Further clarification: "SIPC® coverage provides …

☒ Up to $500,000 in total coverage per customer for lost or missing assets of cash and/or securities from a customer's accounts held at the institution.

☒ Up to $250,000 of that total can be applied to protect cash within a customer's account that is not yet invested in securities.

☒ Protection in case of unauthorized trading or theft from an account.

SIPC® insurance doesn't cover …

☒ Investment losses or worthless stocks or other securities.

☒ Losses due to account hacking, unless the firm was forced into liquidation due to the hack.

☒ Claims against bad or inappropriate investment advice. Complaints about firms are handled by the Financial Industry Regulatory Authority (FINRA®), the Securities and Exchange Commission (SEC) and state securities regulators." (130)

Another vital oversight responsibility of the SEC is to supervise the disclosure of the security world's participants (the securities exchanges, investment advisors, mutual fund companies and managers, and the securities brokers and dealers). In short, the SEC regulates the securities markets. The SEC is also responsible for ensuring that your investment assets are **'segregated'. In other words, your investment accounts, and the investment holdings, cannot be commingled with the assets of the investment corporation who holds your accounts. A Depository Trust Company (DTC) holds your fully paid securities in a separate account.** Again, the SEC is monitoring this process.

Life

An illustration of this point:

1. Your investment advisor works at ABC Investment Firm and you have an investment account there.

2. ABC Investment Firm is purchased by XZY Firm.

3. More-than-likely your financial advisor now works with you under the XZY umbrella, and your statements have XZY Firm on the letterhead instead of ABC Investment Firm.

4. Your funds are not, were not, co-mingled with the assets of the ABC Investment Firm.

5. So, it is business as usual for you and your assets are still in your segregated account. All of the holdings are the same in your new XZY Firm account, in your name.

Complete this chart, Circle Yes or No

	Covered by FDIC		Covered by SIPC®	
Savings Deposits	Yes	No	Yes	No
Money Markets	Yes	No	Yes	No
Mutual Funds	Yes	No	Yes	No
Annuities	Yes	No	Yes	No
Cashier's Checks	Yes	No	Yes	No
Stocks and Bonds	Yes	No	Yes	No

Using 'Margin' – What is that?

We cannot move away from this subject without the mention of another important outcome of the creation of the SEC and Federal Reserve oversight. In the 1920s, ***investors could borrow money to purchase more securities or other assets, using their investment account holdings as collateral.*** This collateral feature was called buying on ***margin.*** Investment/Brokerage account holdings were offered as collateral against which the investor could borrow money. (Reportedly NOT allowed in IRA/Retirement Accounts, etc.)

Many historians have noted that in the 1920s margin account requirements were very lax, and investors were not required to put very much of their own money up as collateral in these investment margin accounts. In fact, leverage, or margin, rates of up to 90 percent debt in these investment margin accounts was not uncommon in the late 1920s. Today, the Federal Reserve's margin requirement limits debt to 50 percent of the purchase price of securities that can be purchased on margin. And, once you use your margin, you will have a 'maintenance requirement:' you will be required to keep a minimum of 25% of the total market value of the securities in your account. Clear as mud… Here's an example of how maintenance requirements work, taken from the SEC government website -https://www.sec.gov/investor/pubs/margin.html:

- "Let's say you purchase $16,000 worth of securities by borrowing $8,000 from your firm [financial institution] and adding $8,000 in cash or securities. If the market value of the securities drops to $12,000, the equity in your account will fall to $4,000 ($12,000 - $8,000 = $4,000). If your firm [financial institution] has a 25 percent maintenance requirement, you must have $3,000 in equity in your account (25 percent of $12,000 = $3,000). In this case, you do have enough equity because the $4,000 in equity in your account is greater than the $3,000 maintenance requirement.

- But, if your firm [financial institution] has a maintenance requirement of 40 percent, you will not have enough equity. The firm would require you to have $4,800 in equity (40 percent of $12,000 = $4,800). Your $4,000 in equity is less than the firm's $4,800 maintenance requirement. As a result, the firm [financial institution] may issue you a "margin call," since the equity in your account has fallen $800 below the firm's maintenance requirement."

https://www.sec.gov/reportspubs/investor-publications/investorpubsmarginhtm.html

If the value of your investments in your margin account begins to decline, you may experience a 'margin call.' The margin call will initiate a requirement for you to regain the 'margin maintenance percentage' back to the required minimum account value; you can do this by either adding money to the account or selling securities to reduce the margin percentage. In addition, there are a few more points for you to consider regarding margin accounts: a) minimum account balances may apply, b) not all investors qualify for these types of accounts, c) not all products are eligible for margin, and d) different investment products can have different 'marginable percentages.' I strongly suggest that you avoid using your investment accounts as collateral for loans. Focus on keeping your debt… loans… as low as possible.

Investopedia.com/terms/m/margin.asp, *"Borrowing Money to Pay for Stocks,"* presents KEY POINTS…

☒ "Margin refers to money borrowed from a brokerage to trade securities.

☒ Margin trading therefore refers to the practice of using borrowed funds from a broker to trade a financial asset, which forms the collateral for the loan from the broker.

☒ A margin account is a standard brokerage account in which an investor is allowed to use the current cash or securities in their account as collateral for a loan.

☒ The collateralized loan comes with a periodic interest rate that the investor must repay to the broker.

☒ Leverage conferred by margin will tend to amplify both gains and losses. In the event of a loss, a margin call may require your broker to liquidate securities without prior consent."

Life Insurance Anyone?

Insuring assets are one thing, insuring your life, or the life of a loved one, is altogether different. Let's talk life insurance. You may be unsure, like many others, when you should purchase life insurance, or if you really need to ever purchase life insurance. And. if you do make the decision to purchase life insurance sometime down the road, the question remains, *'What You Should Know About Buying Life Insurance?'* The answer to that question is somewhat subjective. Here is one answer that is provided by American Council of Life Insurers® (ACLI®):

> *"Everyone's needs are different. A life insurance agent or financial advisor can help you determine what level of protection is right for you and your family based on your financial responsibilities and sources of income. There are online calculators that also can help you; however, sitting down with an insurance professional to review your financial needs can give you a more personalized view of your needs… In general, deciding how much life insurance you need means deducting the total income that would be lost upon your death from the total sum of your family's ongoing financial needs. Consider ongoing expenses (day care, tuition, mortgage, or retirement) and immediate expenses (medical bills, burial costs, and estate taxes). Your family also may need money to pay for a move or to cover daily expenses during a job search.*
>
> *While there is no substitute for evaluating needs based on your own financial information, some experts suggest that if you own a life insurance policy it should pay a benefit equal to seven to 10 times your annual income. Your need could be higher or lower depending on your situation." (133)*

Another suggestion for calculating how much life insurance you might need is offered by Tamarind Financial Planning® (https://tamarindfinancial.com/buying-life-insurance-how-much-what-kind/):

> *"A popular approach to buying insurance is based on income replacement. In this approach, a formula of between five and ten times your annual salary is often used to calculate how much coverage you need. Another approach is to purchase insurance based on your individual needs and preferences." (134)*

☒ How much life insurance you buy generally is guided by how much money you need to leave to your loved ones to cover their financial needs if something should happen to you. Life insurance is commonly purchased to leave money to your dependents to:

- cover bills;

- pay estate taxes;

- provide an income stream for loved ones;

- guard against the loss of retirement income; and

- protect against losing a business in the event a key employee dies.

There is an AXA® article that does an excellent job of defining the various types of life insurance, to include the advantages and disadvantages, (website, https://us.axa.com/axa-products/life-insurance/articles/buying-life-insurance-what-kind-how-much.html), *"Buying Life Insurance: What Kind and How Much."* Here is a snippet of what the article suggests,

> *"If there are individuals who depend on you for financial support, or if you work at home providing your family with such services as childcare, cooking, and cleaning, you need life insurance. Older couples also may need life insurance to protect a surviving spouse against the possibility of the couple's retirement savings being depleted by unexpected medical expenses. And individuals with substantial assets may need life insurance to help reduce the effects of estate taxes or to transfer wealth to future generations."* (135)

When you begin to consider insurance, consider these points:

- ☒ Your goal for the insurance… identifying your goal(s) will help you determine the correct type and amount of insurance to purchase;

- ☒ Understand that life insurance illustrations are offered in a 'hypothetical manner,' … the illustrations presented are built on assumptions you and your advisors make;

- ☒ <u>Be 100% truthful on the application … failure to disclose information will only cost you time and money;</u>

- ☒ If you want to purchase life insurance, do not put off applying for it … don't take a chance that a 'disqualifying event' may change everything.

Visit 2 websites that offer information regarding reasons to purchase life insurance; record the websites and list 4 reasons that you find here:

_____

_____

Term or Permanent?

Another fundamental consideration for the purchase of life insurance is whether you should purchase term life insurance or permanent life insurance. In simple terms:

- *Term* life insurance pays your beneficiary a benefit if you die during a specific, **pre-stated time period**, assuming your policy is still 'in-force.' The pre-stated period is generally based on a 10, 20- or 30-year schedule that is elected at the time of purchase. **Term life insurance** is pretty straight forward, and the options are generally concentrated in three areas: price, the length of coverage, and the strength of the insurance company you select.

- *Permanent* life insurance also pays your beneficiary a benefit when you die but is **generally** calculated to remain in-force over the length of your **life span, or for a long period of time.** Like with term insurance, your policy must also be 'in-force' for the policy to 'pay-out.' **Permanent life insurance c**an be somewhat complex because permanent life insurance offers a few different varieties which have assorted characteristics, for example: Whole Life, Variable Life, and Variable Universal Life. There are pros and cons for each type of policy.

The following presents a *very* brief overview of both Term and Permanent life insurance policy 'advantages' and 'disadvantages.' When you are ready to purchase life insurance, identify your goals and then consider which option best meets your needs. Consult a licensed life insurance agent to research the details of each policy carefully before you buy. Research your options before purchasing (https://www.usnews.com/life-insurance/articles/which-is-better-for-you-term-or-permanent-life-insurance). (136)

Term Life Insurance

Here's a short list to provide you with a quick reference for the general advantages and disadvantages for both term and permanent life insurance. Let's begin by reviewing pros and cons for Term Life Insurance:

Advantages

a.   Generally, a less expensive option when compared to permanent life insurance

b.   Some policies can be converted to permanent life insurance if needs change

c.   Simple to understand (usually)

d.   May be used to fund financial obligations for a specific timeframe- to cover a mortgage, college expenses, etc.

e.   Can provide coverage timing flexibility, i.e..: choose 10/20/30 year term.

Disadvantages

a.   Typically, policies do not build cash value

b.   The policy is only in-force for a limited period of time, (usually) not for life

c.   If your health changes, you may not be able to increase or change your coverage later

d.   Policies do not offer loan options

e.   No cash is available for distributions

f.   Premium costs are usually level for an initial period, but premiums may increase as you grow older, making planning more difficult.

As an aside…. I had one of my 63-year-old clients call me recently and he asked why his TERM insurance company was asking him to convert to PERMANENT insurance…. "My TERM insurance is PERMANENT, right?"

Not exactly correct… Term insurance has an *expiration date* for the 'locked-in' premium he is now paying; the policy either lapses or he will more-than-likely see his premiums increase dramatically if he wants to continue with the same Term insurance policy in the future. KNOW YOUR INSURANCE TERMS.

Permanent Life Insurance

Here's a short list to provide you with a quick reference for the advantages and disadvantages for Permanent Life Insurance.

Advantages

a. Can build cash value

b. Assuming premiums are paid, typically coverage is for life, or for a long time

c. Premiums can be designed to meet your financial needs; either flexible or fixed

d. May offer the opportunity to take out 'loans' against your cash / surrender value

e. If you have built up a cash value, you may surrender your policy for cash, or convert the policy to an annuity

f. It is not necessary to re-new the policy, so declining health is not an issue

g. Typically, the premiums are level so it is easier to plan your cash flow (however interest rate risk can cause premiums to rise)

h. The accumulated cash value can also be used to pay premiums or to buy more coverage under certain conditions

Disadvantages

a. Typically, coverage is more expensive than term life insurance

b. Higher fees may be assessed than term policies; both up-front fees and administrative fees

c. You may experience interest rate sensitivity; you may also find your premiums increasing when interest rates decline

d. If your health changes, you may not be able to increase or change coverage later (133, 135, 136)

Life

If you get married, you may consider purchasing some life insurance on yourself or spouse. Early on in your life you may only be able to afford term life insurance; however, as time goes by you may want to consider buying permanent life insurance. What you may want to do is protect yourself so that if you die, your family will have some additional resources.

My husband and I both have term and permanent life insurance. So, if either of us die the other one, and our boys, will have some extra money for living. By having permanent life insurance, I am relatively confident that our life insurance coverage will not run out (like the term probably will).

Key Life Insurance Terms:

- **Death Benefit** – "The death benefit is a tax-free payout to a beneficiary named by the insured." (6/2019) (134)

- **Face Value** – The original death benefit amount stated on the contract.

- **Convertibility** – The opportunity to convert your life insurance policy from one type of life insurance policy (term) to another (permanent), usually without a physical examination.

- **Cash Value** – The accrued money or savings component of a policy that can be borrowed against or withdrawn.

- **In Force** – In effect; active.

- **Premiums** – Monthly, quarterly, or yearly payments you submit to assure your coverage/policy remains 'in-force.'

- **Beneficiary** – The individual(s) or entity (e.g., trust) that is elected to receive the policy cash distribution.

- **Paid Up** – A policy that does not require further premium payments due to prepayment or earnings, a policy that has been paid-in-full. (135

Choose one type of insurance you might consider and explain why.

_____

_____

Ready To Apply For Life Insurance?

Once you have sorted through the tough questions, you are far from done with your homework. Next, if you decide that you need life insurance, you will 'apply' for coverage. This decision sets off a sequence of events. Here is a synopsis:

1. First, your agent will run an initial *'insurance quote illustration'* for you, based on information that you provide. The **illustration** shows you a schedule of payments and coverage for you and will project the cost of the insurance before you fill out the application, so you have some idea of the cost.

2. Next, you will complete the application…. Answer *ALL* of the questions. Along with the application you will also sign a Release and Health Information Privacy Act of 1999 (HIPAA) form. The form provides your consent for the Life Insurance Company to obtain your medical records.

3. Then, while the insurance company is waiting for your medical records to be supplied to them, an attendant will come to your home, or place of business, to draw blood and ask you a few more questions.

4. Next, your medical records and the additional information you provided to the attendant will be evaluated by the Life Insurance Company underwriters. The underwriters determine, with an actuarial, if the company will make you an insurance **offer.** Just because you received an insurance *illustration*, you are not guaranteed that the insurance company will *offer* to insure you.

5. After this process has been completed, your agent will present you the *offer*, or final coverage details… the amount of insurance the insurance company will give you, along with the exact premium amount (cost of the insurance).

6. At this time you can either *accept the offer or decide to decline the offer*. You typically have 30 days to review the contract/offer. You can take your time to consider the offer, especially if the cost of the policy, or the insurance *face amount (how much coverage you are being offered)*, is considerably different from your original 'quote.'

In an effort to protect against a large disparity between your original quote, and the final quote, you should disclose all of your medical information during your initial conversation with your agent. The more data you provide at the onset, the closer your final offer is likely to be to your original insurance quote.

Life

Sometimes the agent will ask you for a check at the time you submit the application. Or, you may be asked to write a check for the premium (cost of insurance) at the time the policy is delivered to you. This is an important fact to note because providing a 'check' may begin your coverage or put the policy 'in-force.' Be sure to ask when the policy is 'in force.'

Never cancel any current insurance coverage you may have in place until you are sure, and have confirmation, the new insurance is 'in force.'

The purchase of life insurance can be a complicated decision. Talk with your trusted advisors to become comfortable with the terminology, and to understand the different options.

What If Disaster Strikes?

The word 'disaster' can conger up a variety of images. These topics are typically not comfortable to discuss or dwell on; therefore, we put them quickly out of our mind. But *loss, loss of property, life, or loss of income due to a physical **disability** can be devastating.* The possibility of a physical disability should be addressed in a most serious manner.

Let's start with the *'probability facts'* surrounding disability. Insurance companies provide many statistics on the instances of disability. (Again, statistics change quickly, these are recorded here for reference only.)

For example:

Disability statistics, provided by the Social Security Administration, SSA Publication No. 13-11700, released February 2021, https://www.ssa.gov/pubs, states that:

"It happens more often than you'd imagine:

- Over 37 million Americans are classified as disabled; about 12% of the total population. More than 50% of those disabled Americans are in their working years, from 18-64. SSA Publication No. 13-11700, released February 2021, https://www.ssa.gov/pubs.

- 9.8 million disabled wage earners, over 5% of U.S. workers, were receiving Social Security Disability (SSDI) benefits at the conclusion of 2020, SSA Publication No. 13-11700.

- "In December of 2012, there were over 2.5 million disabled workers in their 20s, 30s, and 40s receiving SSDI benefits." U.S. Social Security Administration, Disabled Worker Beneficiary Data, December 2012. (https://www.brookslawgroup.com/blog/where-to-start-when-applying-for-social-security-disability, 6/13/2017); Annual Statistical Report on the Social Security Disability Insurance Program®, 2016, https://www.ssa.gov/policy/ docs/ statcomps/di_asr/2016/di_asr16.pdf).

- The Social Security Administration Disability Benefits Publication: 'Disability Benefits,' (2019) presented that, *"Studies show that a 20-year-old worker has a 1-in-4 chance of becoming disabled before reaching full retirement age."*

- *"Disability Statistics 2015"*, *"Just over 1 in 4 of today's (2013) 20 year olds will become disabled before they retire."* US Social Security Administration, Fact Sheet, February 7, 2013.(133).

- The '2017 Disability Statistics Compendium' reported that *"likelihood of experiencing a disability for adults +65 was 35.2%..."* (137)

- The U.S. Census Bureau, (July 2006) reported that, *"51.2 million Americans have some level of disability."* In 2016 those numbers rose to 61 million Americans, as reported by CDC (https://www.cdc.gov/mmwr/volumes/67/wr/mm6732a3.htm?s_cid=mm6732a3_w).

- According to the National Safety Council®, the possibility of becoming disabled transpires all too frequently:

> *"Based on new injury statistics, an American is accidently injured every second and killed every three minutes by a preventable event."* (2016)
>
> https://www.nsc.org/membership/member-resources/injury-facts

The Council for Disability Awareness® reports the following regarding who and how Americans are accessing disability insurance:

- "69.1 million working Americans receive disability insurance as part of their employee benefit plan, and their employer pays some or all of the cost of coverage

- 7 million have chosen to purchase disability insurance through their employer, but are paying the entire cost out of their own pockets

- As many as 7.8 million working Americans belong to some kind of group like a professional organization or alumni society that provides access to disability insurance, and that's how they purchase coverage

- 6 million have worked with their financial advisors to obtain their own individual disability insurance policy (which may or may not be the only one that provides them coverage)"

(Fred Schott, April 26, 2018, *"How Many Working Americans Have Adequate Disability Coverage?"*
https://blog.disabilitycanhappen.org)

As the term implies, **disability insurance provides for income replacement in the event you experience either a short-or-long-term-period when you may not be able to work because you are disabled in some way and cannot perform your on-the-job duties.** In the current economy, the need for income replacement has been polarized.

Disability income replacement will not cost the same for all individuals; costs vary by age and career. For example, some careers (like firefighters, oil rig workers, and policemen) offer a higher risk of injury; *logically the disability insurance costs may be more for people in those jobs*. Other professions require more skill and education (like medical professions, lawyers, air traffic controllers). Individuals in these careers may also *require a higher level of income replacement*. Do not overlook this insurance option. You may be your own most important asset, consider protecting your income stream against loss due to disability.

Back To Long-Term Care

According to a variety of sources: 'Someone turning 65 today has almost a *70% chance of needing long-term care services.'* So now we move to a discussion regarding the potential need for Long-term Care insurance. Below are varying statistics, from several sources. I believe you will see the trend:

> ☒ *https://www.prepsmart.com/statistic-long-term-care.html reported:*
>
> o   *"As the Baby boomers age, the number keeps rising. Now experts say that 65% of people over 75 need long term care. The average facility stay for older folks is about 3 years." Business Week® (This is a nursing home only stay estimate and does not include home care or assisted living, which usually come first.)*
>
> ☒ *"63% of those 85 and older [use assistance] devices and [get] personal assistance." (139)*
>
> ☒   *"Over 50% of all people entering a care situation are penniless within one year." Harvard University. (138)*
>
> ☒ *The Wall Street Journal® reported, "According to the administration, about seven in 10 people (69%) turning age 65 today will need, at some point, some type of long-term-care services." (139)*
>
> ☒ *The "How Much Care Will You Need," article suggests, "One-third of today's 65-year-olds may never need long-term care support, but 20 percent will need it for longer than 5 years." (139)*
>
> ☒ *Below:"75 Must-Know Statistics About Long-Term Care: 2018 Edition" provides several important Nursing Home Care statistics (Morningstar®, 8/2018, Christine Benz, https://www.morningstar.com/articles/879494/75-mustknow-statistics-about-longterm-care-2018-ed): (139)*

Duration Probability of UsingNursing Home Care

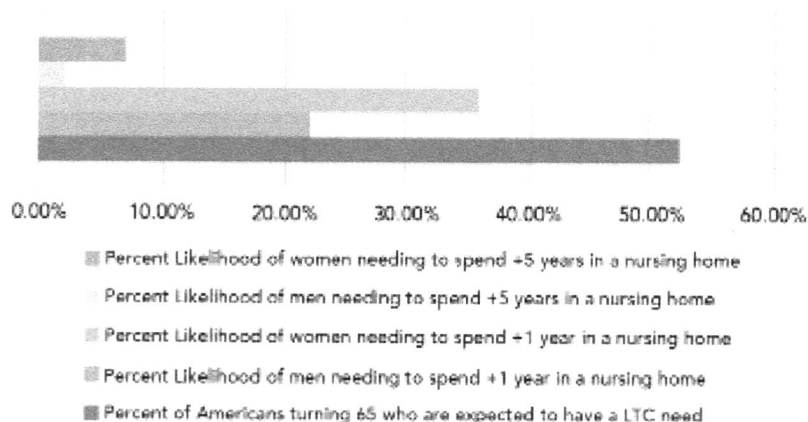

0.00%   10.00%   20.00%   30.00%   40.00%   50.00%   60.00%

▨ Percent Likelihood of women needing to spend +5 years in a nursing home

 Percent Likelihood of men needing to spend +5 years in a nursing home

▨ Percent Likelihood of women needing to spend +1 year in a nursing home

▨ Percent Likelihood of men needing to spend +1 year in a nursing home

▨ Percent of Americans turning 65 who are expected to have a LTC need

The long-term care options are too numerous to discuss here. However, as an overview…here are the four major decisions you will make when you purchase long-term care insurance:

1. The length of coverage you want to purchase (number of years: 1 year to lifetime);

2. How much benefit (dollars you will receive) you want to buy on a daily basis (typically $100 a day and up);

3. The length of the 'elimination period' you will select (how long you will wait until your benefits start: 30/60/90 or 180 days);

4. What company should you purchase your policy from? (Determine the company's financial strength before selecting.)

Multiple sources recommend that a person research long-term care options carefully. In the future, if you are interested in long-term care, speak with your financial advisor BEFORE you, or a loved one, has a precluding medical condition arise. What this means is, that before you experience an event that labels you 'uninsurable,' ask about Long-Term Care insurance. I also ask my clients about long-term care insurance for their parents because many times the children will bear the expense for parent care later on.

Life

Accordingly, at age 80, I personally had my mother purchase Long-Term Care Insurance. At the time, I expected that my Mom would live to be at least 100 years old; and like my grandmother, she may have needed some type of care services.

By purchasing long-term care at an earlier age, we had taken measures to help ensure that we were prepared to defray some of the costs, should they be incurred, later.

Terms For Long-Term Care

All long-term care policies are not alike. First, be sure you research your long-term care insurance company. Insurance companies are rated by independent agencies like A.M. Best®, Moody's®, Weiss®, Fitch®, and Standard & Poor's®. Second, it is imperative that you understand the terms associated with the purchase of a Long-Term Care insurance policy. Many sources are available (such as: https://www.hhs.gov/about/agencies/omha/filing-an-appeal/glossary/index.html, https://longtermcare.acl.gov/the-basics/glossary.html) that present the **long-term care terms** that you should be familiar with before you purchase long-term care insurance.

Here are a few of those terms for your review:

- A **'cost-of-living rider'** is a way that you can increase your original daily benefit amount over time, meaning that as inflation increases, so does your benefit.

- The **'daily benefit'** specifies how much money you will receive for care per day.

- The **'elimination period'** is the time before your coverage begins, the time after the diagnosis and confirmation that you need to start your care benefits, and the time the benefits begin to be paid.

- The **'exclusions'** specify what conditions are not covered by your policy; what care will not be paid for by your policy.

- **'Guaranteed renewability'** provides you with the opportunity to renew or lengthen your coverage without having to provide new 'evidence of insurability.'

- The **'grace period'** is the time the policy will remain in effect if you are late with your premium payment.

- **'Home health-care benefits'** are the benefits your policy will pay for care if you stay home. The criteria for receiving care at home may also vary from the care benefits you may enjoy in a care facility.

- **'Increase in premiums'** will take effect if your policy premiums DO NOT remain 'level.' In other words, your premiums can increase over time under certain conditions.

- The **'length of benefits'** statement explains how long your benefits will pay-out.

- **'Nursing home benefits'** state what your policy will pay for care if you are receiving care in a nursing home.

- **'Pre-existing conditions'** are conditions that you have prior to obtaining your long-term care policy. These conditions are explicitly eliminated from your benefit coverage; those conditions will not be covered by your policy.

- The **'waiver of premium'** rider permits you to stop paying premiums while you are receiving benefits.

- The **'restoration of benefits'** re-establishes your long-term care policy, back to the original full maximum value, if your health is restored.

- The **'return of premium'** pays your premium back to you if you cancel your policy. (140)

You should also note that, unless you have purchased a specific product or a 'return of premium' rider, if you don't use your long-term care insurance, then your premiums may NOT be returned. That means that you will not get money back for not using your benefit. Like buying car insurance, if you never need to file a claim, you do not get a refund.

If you are interested in purchasing long-term care insurance, also explore other options, two of which are: 1) Purchase life insurance with a long-term care rider, meaning some of the policy might convert to covering long-term care expenses if you should need the long-term care later. 2) Purchase a long-term care policy that is designed to be 'shared' between a husband and a wife. For example, if you purchase a shared 6 year long-term care policy, then one of you could use one to six years of the benefits, and the other spouse could use the balance… it doesn't matter who uses the policy, but the care would be limited to a total of six years. Research these and other options.

One word of wisdom… I have presented Long-Term Care Insurance information to many people in the last several years. Only a few people have been interested. Unfortunately, a couple of those people called me some time after our discussion to ask if they could still explore buying a Long-Term Care contract. Upon further investigation, it was discovered that the individual had an 'illness event' after our talk. An 'illness event' is a health issue that precludes the person from purchasing the long-term care coverage. Don't wait until it's too late. While you might not be thinking about Long-Term Care for yourself just yet, maybe you should mention this type of insurance to your parents and loved ones.

Life

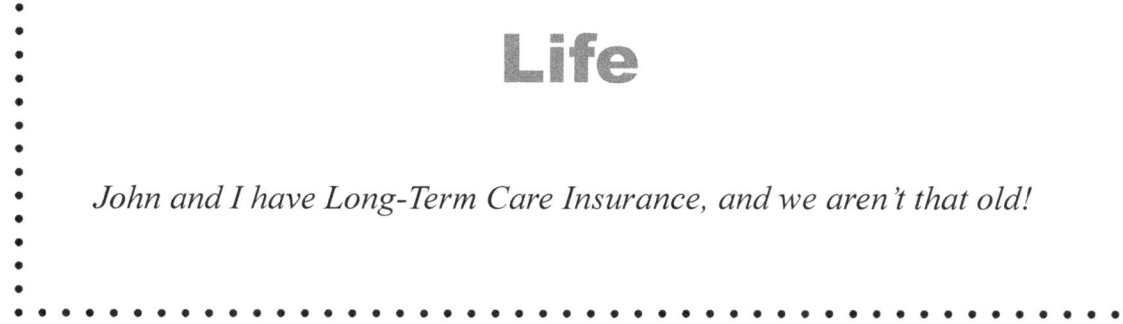

John and I have Long-Term Care Insurance, and we aren't that old!

Find someone who has long-term care insurance and ask them to describe their policy to you.

Company Name? _____

Daily Benefit? _____

Length of Benefit? _____

Does the benefit amount go up every year? _____

When You Have Assets, Responsibilities Follow: Estate Planning

Another aspect of protection is **Estate Planning**. Setting up your Will or Trust; Buy/Sell agreements; or other provisional documents for transfer of assets, early in your lifetime will be important as you accumulate those assets. It is imperative that you do not over-look this important planning and protection step.

If you intend to pass your assets on to your family, friends, and charities, you either have a plan for the distribution of your assets in the event of your death or incapacity, or you do not. In the first case you direct your assets according to where you want them to go. In the latter case, you allow others to direct the distribution for you. As you accumulate assets, you should invest the time to properly distribute your assets through estate planning and save your loved ones the chore of trying to secure the assets you intended them to have in the first place. A comprehensive wealth protection and transfer plan can either be quite complex, or you can comprise a simple plan, depending on the assets you have and how you want them to be distributed.

> "**Estate planning** is the preparation of tasks that serve to manage an individual's asset base in the event of their incapacitation or death. The **planning** includes the bequest of assets to heirs and the settlement of **estate** taxes.
>
> Most **estate** plans are set up with the help of an attorney experienced in **estate** law." Jun 25, 2019
>
> https://www.investopedia.com/terms/e/estateplanning.asp

Estate planning can contain of a variety of documents. However, for our purposes here we will briefly review **Wills, Trusts, and Buy-Sell Agreements**. At a minimum, Estate planning documents are designed to: a) safeguard your assets, b) identify and direct the distribution of your assets in the event you die or become incapacitated, c) name your beneficiaries, d) provide your health care directives, e) appoint a guardian for your children if they need one, and e) direct payment of expenses and taxes of your estate. Other estate planning areas of concern: Appointing a Power of Attorney to help manage your estate; life insurance planning; asset titling; caring for special need children; or protecting a non-US spouse; etc.

An estate attorney will work with you to draw up the estate planning documents. The attorney will ask you many questions to ensure that your directives are captured correctly in the legal estate planning documents. The goal is to ensure that you protect your estate from distribution and taxes that you hadn't planned for… in other words, your estate plan helps identify what assets you want to give to whom, and to plan accordingly.

The estate planning documents provide instructions for direction of the distribution of your assets, including not only the tangible assets you have titled in your Trust, but your 'rights to future income' assets as well. So, in order to ensure that your assets are managed through your Trust, you need to first re-title your assets *into your Trust.* For example: The Jane B. Mickey Revocable Living Trust, dated 2/14/1974 will own your car, your house, your Investment/Brokerage account assets, your boat, any asset that has a 'title.' Your estate attorney will review this re-titling process with you in detail. Be sure you carry out the attorney's instructions carefully. If your assets are not titled properly your Trust will not be effective.

Let's look at some of the characteristics of each of the estate planning documents:

Wills:

A Will Is A Legal Document, Signed By The Maker Of The Document

⊠ *Advantages of distributing assets through a Will*

- ○ Preparing a Will is usually less expensive than preparing a Trust.

- ○ As with a Trust, a Will provides flexibility for income tax purposes because when you value the estate you can use either a fiscal year or a calendar year calculation for income tax purposes.

- ○ Distribution can be settled through the probate court.

- ○ The probate process can lessen the time allowed for creditors to make claims against your estate.

- ○ Unlike a Trust, which becomes effective at the time of execution, a Will is not effective until the Maker's death, when the Will is presented to probate.

⊠ *Disadvantages of distributing assets through a Will*

- ○ When assets are distributed through a Will the distribution process goes through a legal procedure called probate. The probate process does not provide you with any privacy because it is a public hearing. The Will is a public document. Also, if the assets named in the Will are in more than one state, the Will has to be probated in each affected state.

- ○ Fees charged by the estate fiduciary to disperse the estate may be a percentage of the gross estate and can be high if it is a large estate.

- ○ Processing a Will through probate is typically long and drawn out.

- ○ Wills do not make provisions for you if you should become incapacitated. In case of disability you would need a separate document called a Durable Power Of Attorney to allow your fiduciary to manage your affairs.

Trusts:

A Trust Is A Contract That Identifies A Three-Party Arrangement Involving A Grantor, A Trustee And A Beneficiary

a. **Grantor: A Grantor is the creator of a trust document.**

b. **Trustee: A holder of trust property on behalf of a trust beneficiary.**

c. **Beneficiary: An individual or entity named to receive assets at the time of an owner's/ grantor's death.**

⊠ *Advantages of distributing assets through a Trust*

- ○ A Trust is a private document that is not available for public review.

- ○ A Trust provides direction in cases of incapacity.

- ○ Consideration is given to estate shrinkage and taxes.

- ○ Property titled into a Trust typically passes to beneficiaries without oversight by a judge (avoids a legal process known as "probate").

☒ *Disadvantages of distributing assets through a Trust*

- ○ Setting up a Trust can be more expensive than creating a Will.

- ○ If the assets are not titled in the Trust, then the Trust is not as effective, so work needs to be done on your part… YOU STILL NEED A WILL and an ESTATE PLAN. (141)

When an estate grows to a certain dollar amount, the Federal Government can impose a substantial tax on the estate. The estate tax must be paid before any property can be distributed to heirs. The estate taxes can change with new legislation. This is the same for assets named in a Will. So, it is important to understand that part of the estate plan should provide for *liquidity of some of the assets.* Some part of the estate should be liquid and available to pay estate taxes, attorney fees, and funeral expenses when needed. It is vital to set up liquidity options when creating your estate plan.

Kyle E. Krull, an estate planning attorney, reminds us that:

> *"Every American age 18 and older must make their own personal, health care, and financial decisions."* (142)

Life

When my two boys were over the age of 18, and not married, I was worried that if they had some kind of health 'issue,' or were unable to speak for themselves, then without the proper legal documents I could NOT help them out. So, I consulted my Estate Attorney and he drew up the Durable Power of Attorney Health Care and Financial Directive paperwork for my boys and I to sign. These documents allowed me to act as their legal guardian and supervise their affairs if something were to happen to them.

For example, if one of them were to get hit by a bus, then I could now work with the doctors to get the information that I needed to get them proper care. If I didn't have those legal documents, then the doctors could not talk to me about the situation (HIPAA); I would not be able to direct my son's care; or move him; or manage his financial affairs, etc.

Planning is extremely important. A few dollars spent, up-front, to prepare for the potential 'disasters' in life, may be worth their weight in gold if something does happen. If nothing happens, then, just like your car insurance, I am out the money.

As an aside: Three of John's boys were in the military and the military prepared these, and other documents, for them.

As you accumulate assets, please ensure that you properly plan for your future. Consider setting up a Will or Trust. Setting up your Will or Trust early in your lifetime will be important as you accumulate assets. Tax forecasting will also be a very important part of your financial planning. When you find yourself in a position of having enough assets to pass down to your heirs, you will need to consult the advice of both an accountant and an estate attorney. Note that, moving money out of your 'estate' into someone else's estate, or gifting to charity (check with your tax advisor because certain assets 'gifted' during a year may have AGI limits, and the rules can certainly change), may have tax implications that you will first want to consider.

Transfer on Death (TOD) is another estate planning tactic. Like in our earlier discussion about titling Investment/Brokerage Accounts, if you want to name a beneficiary, and you do not have a Will, you add a TOD. The TOD will pass the asset directly to the named individual or entity when you die. Simply stated, upon your death (only), your asset will become the property of whomever you have named as your TOD. This avenue virtually costs you nothing to put in place; you can add a TOD to your checking account (typically referred to as Payable on Death, POD), car title, Investment/Brokerage accounts, or other titled property, at no cost.

Mark E. Lindstrom, an Estate Attorney in Kansas recommended that, "you review your Will and basic estate plan every three to five years to be sure that it continues to meet your needs. Such a review should be made if there are any changes in your family situation or if there are any events that might affect the suitability or availability of executors or trustees, etc. A review is also indicated if there are any significant changes in the size or composition of your estate."

Take Mr. Lindstrom's suggestion; review your estate planning documents every few years. You may need to update beneficiaries, increase protection, change language due to changes in the law, or reevaluate your asset structure. Estate planning can help provide you with peace of mind. It is critical that you do not overlook this important planning and protection step.

Do you know someone who has a Trust? Ask them to describe the benefits.

_____

_____

How Far Can You Stretch?

While we are on the subject of Estate Planning AND Tax Planning, let's spend a quick minute speaking about beneficiary planning for your retirement accounts. *Stretching an IRA* is typically employed for estate planning purposes. The rules for stretching an IRA changed January 1, 2020, however, some provisions remain the same for spouses, chronically ill or the disabled.   **Currently, For Example:**

<u>You inherit</u>:

- ☒ <u>f you inherit an IRA/401k/Roth account from a **NON-spouse**</u>, you are now required to *Stretch the payouts/withdrawals over 10 years*. The *Stretch IRA* is created by the non-spouse beneficiary of the inherited IRA and allows for the continuation of the tax-deferral status of the investment assets for 10 years ONLY. THERE IS A 50% PENALTY IMPOSED FOR VIOLATING THE 10 YEAR RULE. THE PENALTY WILL BE ASSESSED ON THE ASSETS <u>NOT DISTRIBUTED</u> UNDER THE 10 YEAR RULE.

- ☒ <u>If you inherit a spousal IRA</u>, you can roll it over to your name and take Non-Roth RMDs at age 72.*

<u>You leave</u>: If you have a *Traditional/Roth IRA/401k* to leave when you die, the assets can transfer to:

- ☒ A non-Spousal beneficiary:

  - ○ the non-spouse beneficiary can keep the tax-deferral status of the (non-Roth) account and take distributions for 10 years by keeping the 'beneficiary status' and rolling the inherited assets into an 'Inherited IRA.' Withdrawals from the Inherited IRA taken before age 59 ½ by the beneficiary are 'early-withdrawal penalty free.' The assets must be withdrawn by the non-spouse beneficiary within a 10-year period.

- ☒ A spousal beneficiary*:

  - ○ the spouse beneficiary can roll the inherited spousal IRA into his or her name IRA, relinquishing the 'beneficiary' status… or keep the account as is and be the "designated beneficiary.". For example: If the account is in the spouse's name, the **Non-Roth** RMDs would be initiated after age 72, and the beneficiary would still be penalized for early withdrawals before age 59 ½. The spouse can *stretch/maintain* the account's tax-deferral status and take non-Roth RMDs over the course of their lifetime, but only if they follow the specific rules for doing so.

    *Rules that apply for the spousal beneficiary also apply for chronically ill or disabled beneficiaries, and beneficiaries not more than 10 years younger than the owner. (143)

Be careful, if you inherit an IRA as a beneficiary, **please consult your tax advisor and estate attorney, along with your financial advisor, to determine what type of distribution you might elect that will best suit your needs. Please do so right away**, as specific dates become an important factor in selecting your options, and failure to act within a certain timeframe can dramatically change the outcome of the transaction. Please Note: Laws/rules change, so research your options cautiously with your advisors.

Buy-Sell Agreements:

When business owners prepare to sell their business, or pass their business on to other partners, they may enter into a *Buy-Sell Agreement*. Having a *Buy-Sell Agreement* in place and funding a buy-sell agreement plan can have several advantages. Here are a couple to consider:

- Makes liquid assets available for the business owner's family (if the buy-sell plan is funded) when the business is transferred;

- Reduces the possibility of dispute among the partners of the business when it comes time to transfer the business;

- Allows for the transfer of the business to the intended parties only;

- Creates a vehicle for a pre-arranged transition of the business in the event of the death, disability or departure of the business owner;

- Because a pre-agreed-upon price has been determined for the market value of the business, (assuming the price meets IRS guidelines) tax issues may be streamlined. (144)

There are several types of Buy-Sell Agreements. If you become a business owner, or are a key employee, check with an attorney to determine which type of agreement might best fit your purposes.

Go On, Give A Gift

Some individuals want to give back to their community and possess the resources to do so. These individuals find themselves in a position to be able to, or they want to, make a contribution of some of their assets to a charity or to another individual or group. The individual offering the donation is called the **donor**. If the *contribution, or gift, or donation*, is made while the donor is still alive, the donor ***typically donates, or gives, voluntarily.***

> *"Before you speak, listen. Before you write, think. Before you spend, earn. Before you invest, investigate. Before you criticize, wait. Before you pray, forgive. Before you quit, try. Before you retire, save. Before you die, give. "*
>
> William A. Ward

The IRS sets guidelines for how much can be 'gifted' to others each year without causing a taxable event. Meaning that there is a limit on how much money you can gift each year before you, or the donee *(the person or entity that receives the gift)*, **incurs tax consequences**. There are also tax 'exclusions' available for gifting considerations. The tax exclusions allow a portion of your estate to pass on to others without causing a taxable event. Remember that the IRS limits regarding how much you can *gift* without a tax consequence each year can change. On-the-other-hand, donating money or assets to a non-profit organization does not trigger a tax consequence (you might even be eligible for a tax savings), unless you do not follow the rules/guidelines. Also, <u>when you give to a charity there are annual IRS limits</u>. Check with a tax advisor to get the up-to-the-minute tax rules and regulations. (*"The IRS Donation Limit: What is the Maximum you can Deduct?"* G.E. Miller, 1/4/2020, https://20somethingfinance.com/irs-maximum-charitable-donation-limit/; https://turbotax.intuit.com/tax-tips/estates/the-gift-tax-made-simple/L5tGWVC8N)

The transfer of wealth is extremely complex. However, depending on your objectives, there are several avenues available to you for making an asset transfer. Those options include, but are not limited to, establishing or contributing to: Irrevocable Life Insurance Trusts, Qualified Personal Residence Trusts, Grantor-Retained Annuity Trusts, Donor-Advised Funds, a Private Family Foundation, a Charitable Lead Trust, or a Charitable Remainder Trust. Please check with your estate attorney and accountant to review the intricacies and the benefits of each of these avenues. Also, meet with your attorney and financial advisor to review your beneficiary designations for your accounts, policies, Trusts and Wills regularly.

Identity Theft

Information about protection would not be complete without a comment about a 20th century crime - *Identity Theft*. **Identity theft is the act of stealing important information from another individual with the purpose in mind to assume that person's identity; with the intention of exploiting that individual's credit in an effort to realize personal gain.**

Many of our financial institutions publish information that outlines avenues you can take to help you protect your identity from being stolen. Thieves are gaining access to names; addresses; driver's licenses; social security numbers; birth dates; and other personal information (such as your PIN number; credit card and bank and investment account numbers); for the explicit purpose of using the information to out-right steal assets. You have a responsibility to be aware of this practice, and to know what specific steps you can take to guard against being a victim of Identity Theft. Some ideas for safeguarding your identity are presented here:

☒ Do not put any sensitive information in the trash can. Be sure any materials that have important information regarding your identity, accounts, etc. are shredded in a cross shredder.

☒ Be sure you are not carrying vital identity information in your purse or wallet, which if misplaced or stolen, will provide identity information to the thief (i.e. Social Security card).

☒ Be sure to keep a copy of your credit cards and the emergency 800 numbers for each in a safe place at home.

☒ Be careful when you are purchasing an item on-line. Using your credit card on a 'non-secure' website is not recommended. If you are not sure you are in a secure site, attempt to call the merchandiser to purchase your item directly. Remember, the Fair Credit Billing Act guards you from billing errors and fraud.

Life

One of my colleagues told me that he has a client who has a credit card designated for 'on-line purchases' only. This is one way to limit exposure and safeguard you against on-line theft.

☒ If you will be traveling overseas you may consider calling your credit card company and letting them know ahead of time where you will be.

Life

I had a client who enrolled in an educational program in England for 9 months. She spoke with her credit card company to make them aware of potential 'unusual' charges.

☒ Be cognizant of any visitors that come to your home. Workmen, babysitters, housekeepers and other individuals who might work for you are generally trust-worthy. However, by being sure your valuable information is located in a safe place and not easily assessable, you help protect yourself. Place important items and documents in a safety deposit box to guard against prying guests.

☒ When you make purchases in stores and restaurants guard against credit card/identity theft. Avoid letting your credit card out of your sight. Watch the transaction process whenever possible.

Life

Sometimes in a restaurant the server asks if he or she should run a tab... only if your credit card stays with you. As a general rule, pay-as-you-go is the better option.

☒ One of the best safeguards for Identity Theft is to monitor your bank and other account statements carefully.

Life

I have had clients tell me that they just "file their statements away" and look at them later. One such client discovered an erroneous charge 6 months after the initial purchase. So, for 6 months the service company had been charging her for a service that she thought she paid for once a year. If she had checked her statements each month, the confusion could have been avoided.

☒ The absolute best way to receive bank account and investment account statements is on-line. Avoid paper-trails whenever possible. (Some financial institutions will provide you with a compact disk at the end of the year that captures all of your monthly statements.)

☒ Along the same lines, employing a credit-report service to alert you to when new credit applications are made in your name is in-valuable. On the rare occasion when I have opened a new credit card, I have been notified by e-mail of the event.

☒ Check your credit report at least once a year. You are entitled to one free credit report from each of the three major credit agencies. (See https://www.annualcreditreport.com/index.action. See the Finance Section.)

☒ Carry only credit cards that you need, leave any additional cards at home.

☒ Safeguard any PIN numbers. Never write them down or carry the numbers with you. (145)

If you are a victim of Identity Theft contact your local police and file a report immediately; notify all financial institutions you work with; contact the credit bureaus (Equifax® (888-548-7878), Trans Union® (800-916-8800), Experian® (888- 397-3742); call each of your creditors to notify them as well. Be sure you keep notes of all pertinent conversations* and follow-up to ensure any requested documentation has been received. You can also file a report with the Federal Trade Commission. *The Federal Trade Commission is a government agency charged with protecting you, the consumer.* (132) While the agency does not prosecute, they investigate companies who may not be diligent in protecting their clients. *Ask for the name of the representative you speak with, note the time and date as well.

We cannot leave this section without the mention of a couple of the avenues available to you to help you manage the process of navigating through the process of repairing your identity if it is stolen. There are several companies that offer a type of 'identity theft insurance.' While the contracts may not wholly insure you against having your identity stolen, they set up alert systems to help you monitor your credit and other triggers that signal you may be a victim of identity theft. Many companies also offer services to help you navigate the process of reestablishing your identity if you have been a victim of identity theft. It is worthwhile looking into these programs.

Life

My home and car insurance company offers an 'identity theft' program for a nominal monthly fee. I take advantage of the service and 'alerts' are e-mailed to me when my credit has been changed. For example, if I open a new credit card account, I will get such information sent to me in an e-mail.

What are some of the safeguards you have put in place to help ensure that you do not become a victim of Identity Theft?

_____

_____

Conclusion:

As you obtain assets throughout your life you will want to ensure that you carefully plan for a loss, 'exit strategy,' disability, or 'hardship.' Using insurance properly can assist you in averting or minimizing disaster if it should strike. Seek out an insurance professional to advise you and help you plan for your insurance needs. Protect yourself and your family against potential loss.

> *"I have no use for bodyguards, but I have a very special use for two highly trained certified public accountants."*
>
> Elvis Presley

Maybe this was Elvis' way of saying you should, of course, carefully plan for your financial future.

Barry Zimmer's article, *"Key Reasons why Asset Protection Planning is Important,"*, found on https://zimmerlawfirm.com/blog/asset-protection-2/key-reasons-asset-protection-planning-important/, states:

> *"Asset protection planning is very important if you have any money, investments, or property that you want to protect. If you own a business or are starting one, you also need to make sure you have a solid plan in place to protect your personal assets.*
>
> *There are many different risks to your financial security, and your plan for asset protection needs to focus on the things that are most likely to impact your nest egg."*
>
> Barry Zimmer (6/2016)

Sources:

(126) https://www.brainyquote.com/words/pr/protection207637.html.

(127) https://www.safetyinsurance.com/custsupport/definitions.html; https://content.naic.org/consumer_glossary.

(128) https://www.autoinsurance.org/what-do-the-three-numbers-on-car-insurance-mean/, *"What do the three numbers on auto insurance mean?"* e-mail, Financial Advisor @ Merrill Lynch® (9/24/2008). *"What is the Minimum Car Insurance Required in Your State?"* https://www.valuepenguin.com/minimum-car-insurance-required-your-state.

(129) https://www.sipc.org/about-sipc/statute-and-rules/statute, *"Securities Investor Protection Act of 1970,"* 15 U.S.C. §78aaa-lll, as amended through July 22, 2010 *1.

(130) https://www.sipc.org/for-investors/what-sipc-protects, *"What SIPC® Protects.;"* https://www.nerdwallet.com/blog/investing/sipc-insurance-what-it-does-and-does-not-protect/.

(131) https://smartasset.com/checking-account/are-certificates-of-deposit-cd-fdic-insured. *"Are Certificates of Deposit (DCs) FDIC Insured?"* Lauren Perez, CEPF, 12/2018.

(132) https://www.SIPC.org; https://www.sec.gov; https://www.sec.gov/about/whatwedo.shtml.

(133) https://www.acli.com;   https://advisorinsuranceresource.com/disability-statistics-2015/,   ACLI®;   https://www.fidelity.com/viewpoints/wealth-management/things-to-know-about-life; *"What You Should Know About Buying Life Insurance."*

(134) https://www.investopedia.com/ask/answers/050615/what-difference-between-death-benefit-and-cash-value-insurance-policy.asp, *"Insurance Policy Death Benefits and Cash Values,"* Melissa Horton 11/2019.

(135) https://equitable.com/life-insurance/articles/buying-life-insurance-what-kind-how-much; *"Buying life insurance: what kind and how much?"* *"What You Should Know About Buying Life Insurance,"* https://www.acli.com/-/media/ACLI/Files/Consumer-Brochures-Public/What_You_Should_Know_About_Buying_Life_Insurance.ashx?la=en.

(136) https://finance.yahoo.com/news/better-term-permanent-life-insurance-190358510.html, *"Which is Better for You: Term or Permanent Life Insurance?"* Daniel Solin, 2/26/2014.

(137) https://disabilitycompendium.org/sites/default/files/user-uploads/2017_AnnualReport_2017_FINAL.pdf *"2017 Disability Statistics Annual Report;"* OneAmerica®, Survey: https://www.prnewswire.com/news-releases/survey-most-americans-not-protecting-their-paychecks-300456182.html, *"Most American Not Protecting Their Paychecks,"* (5/2017), https://oneamerica.com/newsroom/news-releases/harris-oneamerica-disability-insurance-survey.

(138) https://www.schaferinsurancesolutions.com/ltc/,   *"Long-Term   Care;"*   https://www.prepsmart.com/statistic-long-term-care.html.

(139) https://www.morningstar.com/articles/879494/75-mustknow-statistics-about-longterm-care-2018-ed *"75 Must Know Statistics About Long Term Care 2018 Edition;"* https://www.prepsmart.com/statistic-long-term-care.html, *"Some Thought Provoking Long Term Care Statistics;"* https://www.wsj.com/articles/the-odds-on-needing-long-term-care-11559836590, *"The Odds on Needing Long-Term Care,"* *"How Much Care Will You Need?"* https://acl.gov/ltc/basic-needs/how-much-care-will-you-need.

(140) https://www.hhs.gov/about/agencies/omha/filing-an-appeal/glossary/index.html, *"U.S. Department of Health and Human Services – Glossary of Terms;"* https://www.longtermcareliving.com/glossary, Glossary of Terms; American Health Care Association- National Center for Assisted Living®, *"Consumer Information About Long Term Care;"* https://ltcconsumer.com/; https://www.mrltc.com/long-term-care-glossary.html, *"Ask Mr. Long Term Care - Long Term Care (LTC) Glossary of Terms."*

(141) https://www.thebalance.com/pros-and-cons-of-revocable-living-trusts-3505384, *"The Pros and Cons of Revocable Living Trusts."* Julie Garber, 9/2019; https://palmcitylawyer.com/blog/estate-planning-101-the-advantages-and-disadvantages-of-an-irrevocable-trust/, *"Estate Planning 101: The Advantages and Disadvantages of an Irrevocable Trust, John Mangan, P.A.;"* https://www.estateplanning.com/Estate-Planning-Glossary/; https://www.crosslawgroup.com/blog/10-benefits-estate-planning/, *"10 Benefits of Estate Planning,"* 1/2017; https://www.thebalance.com/benefits-advanced-estate-planning-3505076, *"Benefits of Advanced Estate Planning,"* Julie Garber, 6/2019.

(142) Kyle E. Krull, J.D. CFP (2009), *"Life & Estate Planning."*

(143) https://www.investmentnews.com/the-stretch-ira-is-dead-175775, "*The stretch IRA is dead;"* Ed Slott; 12/27/2019, *Investment News*; "*The Secure Act changes the way people will inherit money - are you hit by the new rules?*" (1/9/2020), Alessandra Malio, https://www.marketwatch.com/story/the-secure-act-changes-the-way-people-will-inherit-money-are-you-affected-by-the-new-rules-2019-12-27.

(144) https://www.modernwoodmen.org/financial-planning/business-planning/benefits-of-a-buy-sell-agreement/, *"Benefits of a Buy-Sell Agreement,"* © 2019 Modern Woodmen of America; https://www.epgdlaw.com/buy-sell-agreement/, *"The Benefits of Having a Buy-Sell Agreement,"* EPGD Law, 12/2017; (144a) https://www.apa.org/news/press/releases/stress/2017/state-nation.pdf; *"November 2017 Stress in America The State of our Nation,"* American Psychological Association®.

(145) https://www.capitalone.com/learn-grow/money-management/use-credit-wisely, *"6 Habits to Help You Use Your Credit Wisely;"* https://www.fidelity.com/viewpoints/personal-finance/credit-cards, *"7 Credit card tips,"* Fidelity Viewpoints®, 3/2019; https://www.consumercredit.com/debt-resources-tools/credit/credit-education/how-to-use-credit-wisely/, *"How to Use Credit Wisely;"* Experian® (2019), https://www.experian.com/blogs/ask-experian/credit-education/preventing-fraud/fraud-prevention/ *"Fraud & Identity Theft Fraud Prevention;"* https://www.experian.com/consumer-products/credit-monitoring.html, *"Credit monitoring;"* https://www.ct.gov, Department of Consumer Protection, https://portal.ct.gov/DCP/Common-Elements/Common-Elements/How-You-Can-Safeguard-Your-Identity, *"How You Can Safeguard Your Identity;"* https://www.usa.gov/identity-theft, *"Identity Theft, How to protect yourself against identity theft and respond if it happens;"* https://www.experian.com/blogs/ask-experian/how-to-protect-yourself-from-identity-theft/, *"How to Protect Yourself from Identity Theft,"* Brian O'Connell, 3/2018.

Chapter 5 Check For Understanding

For a chapter review, read and complete the following follow-up activities::

- ☒ List some of the things you might do to protect your identity.

- ☒ Discuss why the FDIC and SEC were established. Relate your statement to how the two organizations are important in today's economic environment.

- ☒ Describe, in your own words, why you might buy life and disability insurance in the future. (If you haven't already.)

- ☒ Explain the term 'face value' as it relates to a life insurance policy.

- ☒ Ask someone you know well, if they will share how much insurance they have on themselves… and how they decided upon that amount.

- ☒ Report on the criteria an individual might consider when they choose the amount of life insurance to purchase.

- ☒ Interpret the difference between health insurance and long-term care insurance.

- ☒ Compare and contrast a few of the characteristics of Term verses Permanent Life Insurance.

- ☒ Identify the benefits of establishing a Will.

- ☒ Who assists the maker in the creation of a Trust?

- ☒ Evaluate the importance of naming a beneficiary for your assets.

About Experience Talks...

The topic of protection and insurance can be really boring. Paying for anything that you may not ever need seems silly to some of us. Of course, we are required to carry Homeowners (if you own a home) and Car Insurance (if you own a car), but we sometimes put off purchasing other types of insurance, even if it might be prudent to do so.

Following are some stories that describe experiences with using insurance, as reported by friends, family, or clients. The information is provided to you to help you understand real-life situations; to help you better prepare for your future.

Experience Talks...

No Future Is Certain, Prepare And Protect As Well As You Can

Shirley inherited about $ 2,000,000 from her mom when her mother passed away.

Shirley worked as a waitress in a restaurant and was a single mother. Introducing her to the concept of a TRUST was not easy. A Trust is a legal contract to help individual's direct the disbursement of their property in the future. Shirley didn't understand that she would need to provide some definitive guidelines and directions for her money, property, her pets, and the care of her daughter if something happened to her. I introduced Shirley to the concept, 'With money, comes responsibility.'

Unfortunately, Shirley passed away about 5 years after I met her. She did leave a daughter, who was only about 13 years old at the time. By having her Trust in place Shirley was assured that her wishes were carried out for her daughter's care.

Moral of the Story: Preparation has its just rewards.

Experience Talks...

Long-Term Care, Because You Are In It For The Long Haul

nsurance is an anomaly. No one wants to pay for insurance year after year, and not use it… but no one wants to get into a situation where they need to use their insurance, and not have it in place. I sometimes observe this dilemma when I talk to people about life insurance, but I most certainly hear about this perspective when I discuss Disability and Long-Term Care insurance.

Nancy's mother, Marcia, had purchased long-term care insurance in 1994. About two or three years after purchasing the policy, Marcia was diagnosed with a degenerate disease. Marcia's disease was not fatal, but over time Maria would need around-the-clock-care.

Nancy brought Marcia's policy to me in 2003 when the doctors determined that Marcia could no longer care for herself independently. As we read though the details of the policy, Nancy was relieved to learn that Marcia's policy benefits would cover most of Marcia's daily expenses. What a blessing to learn that Marcia had financially prepared for this possibility, and that her family's assets would not be diverted from her husband's much-needed resources.

Marcia's care was about $5,000 a month in the long-term care facility where she resided. Without the policy her husband would not have been able to continue in his current lifestyle, other arrangements would have had to be made.

Moral of the story: Make an unpleasant situation easier, be informed and aware.

Experience Talks...

Disability Insurance

My friend Gayle sold Disability Insurance to business owners. She had recounted to me several times how she would be so concerned for her clients when they were not protected. Gayle told me about a client who was a Dentist. He had purchased disability insurance after Gayle insisted.... And not too long after the policy was in-force, he had an incidence that caused him to lose the ability for one of his hands to function. The event meant that he couldn't practice dentistry any longer.

Gayle was so happy that the event didn't cause her client to make a life-style change. I remember Gayle saying to me, "My client kept his house and his children were still were able to go to college."

The moral of the story: Sometimes we need to be 'nudged.'

Experience Talks...

Trust Funds Are Not Just For 'Rich Kids'

Jenny was in her 70s when her 50-year-old son passed away, leaving his three children.

Jenny's son was not married. He had named Jenny as his beneficiary on his 401k account at work. Jenny wanted to give her son's money equally to her three grandchildren. Jenny's grandchildren were in their early 20s at the time of their father's death. Jenny was afraid if she gave the money to each of the grandchildren in a lump sum that they would spend it all at once. So, what she did was take out a small amount, about $ 3,000 each year, and gave it to each of the grandchildren. As she suspected, the money was gone within a couple of months after each distribution.

However, because Jenny was managing the money without a Trust, she had to be careful about the tax implications, the 'gifting' limits, etc. In retrospect, Jenny thought it might have been better to have named a Trust as the beneficiary and have her named as the Executor of the Trust. If the money had been put in a Trust, then Jenny's son could have specified how he wanted his money to be distributed to his children.

The moral of the story: Trusts can relieve stress!

Experience Talks...

When You Are Older, Talking To Your Parents About Money Is Not The Same AS Asking For Your Allowance

For Larry, who is only 27, the idea of a 'Trust' was brought up at some point during his early childhood; he remembers that the 'seed' was planted early on.

Now that his parents are around 60 years old, Larry is more interested in the topic. Larry is concerned about his parents' well-being and financial situation. He understands that if his parents do not plan properly, he may end up being their sole financial caregiver in the future.

Asking those tough financial questions is sometimes difficult for a child because many times adult parents are hesitant to share their personal 'financial standing.' On-the-other-hand, if those important questions are not posed, and planning has not been completed, and time passes without safeguards in place …. It may be too late. The topics of wealth protection and estate planning should be addressed earlier, rather than later.

The moral of the story: The early bird may protect the worm.

Experience Talks...

Where There Is A Will, There Is A Way To Make Sure Things Are Done According To Your Wishes

One of my Estate Attorney friends told this story in a workshop:

Frank was a widower. Frank had lost not only one, but two wives to cancer. Therefore, he was very superstitious and vowed not to marry again. So, when he met his girlfriend Sadie, they decided they would not get married.

Frank wanted to leave Sadie his house when he died, along with some money he had saved, so Sadie would be taken care of. To accomplish this, Frank went onto the internet and found a 'form for a Will.' Frank filled out the Will form and put it in his safety deposit box.

About 12 years later Frank passed away. Sadie took out the Will and went down to the courthouse and bank to present the Will to move the house deed and savings account into her name. But there was a problem. The Will hadn't been filled out or filed properly.

Unfortunately, Frank's belongings were distributed through the courts to Frank's four children. Sadie received none of Frank's belongings as Frank had evidently thought he had directed.

The moral of the story: Consider professional help.

Experience Talks...

Read The Fine Print,
And Get A Second Opinion If Needed

Mary and Sam are a married couple in their 60s. They had owned a successful business and had recently sold it to XYZ Company just a few months before they met their Financial Advisor, Jeremy. As a normal part of Jeremy's practice, Jeremy reviewed not only Mary and Sam's investments, but their life insurance policies as well.

In the case of Mary and Sam's policy, the policy premiums were being paid by the XYZ Company; the payments were part of the 'business sale settlement.' XYZ Company was paying the premiums for a stated period of time, to be reimbursed at a later date.

Upon close scrutiny of their life insurance policy Jeremy discovered, what he thought to be, a problem. The life insurance policy was a 'survivorship' policy, meaning that the policy paid out after the second spouse passed away. That, in of itself wasn't the problem, the problem was this:

- **When the first spouse died, the surviving spouse owed all of the previously paid premiums back to XYZ Company.**

- The implication of this: If one spouse died, the second spouse had to come up with XXX amount of money to reimburse XYZ Company for the premiums that the company had paid in to-date…. And then, the surviving spouse was to take over and start paying for the subsequent premiums as well. The premiums were very expensive (@ $6,250 a month/$75,000 a year)… that was a lot of money to repay!

What Jeremy did was to work with the insurance company and the XYZ Company, and Mary and Sam to separate the one current policy that covered two lives into two separate policies, one policy on each of the lives of the spouses. The premium payment structure was also revised so Mary and Sam now took over responsibility for paying the premium payments themselves. With this new arrangement, if one spouse died, the benefit payout would be free and clear to the surviving beneficiary.

To say the least, Jeremy's clients were very appreciative… especially since one of the spouses did pass away about 5 years after these re-configurations. Thank goodness Jeremy reviewed those policies!

Moral of the story: A second opinion never hurts.

Experience Talks...

You Don't Want To Die And Leave Your Family With Bills

My guess is that most life insurance salespeople have at least one story like the following: These two life stories that were told to me by a Farmers Insurance Agent.

Grayson has had to deliver two insurance checks in his short career as a Life Insurance Agent, here are the two life scenarios. Grayson delivered both checks personally.

1) Grayson delivered the first check for around $ 10,000 to the deceased client's wife. The wife was waiting intently for the check, as she had to pay for the funeral and was in need of the money to do so.

2) The second check was for $1,000,000 and was delivered by Grayson to the two children of their deceased father (their father was divorced). Although the children appeared to Grayson to be relatively 'well off,' they were grateful that their father had done some financial preparation for them. The children certainly felt more financially secure after they received their tax-free check.

Moral of the story: Consider life insurance when you start a family… you might want to leave a legacy.

Experience Talks...

Remember... You Are Never Too Old To Learn

When Lizzy was about 62 years old she inherited enough money to live a comfortable life. She was convinced that the money she had would be enough to take care of her if she became ill and needed extended care. Therefore, Lizzy was not interested in purchasing long-term care insurance; she thought she was 'self-insured.'

Everything was going well until 2008 when Lizzy's investments lost about 50% of their value. In 2008 Lizzy was nearing 70 years old. Her change in wealth prompted Lizzy to re-think her 'self-insured' approach. Now the prospect of spending most, if not all of her wealth for assisted living care was daunting. Lizzy began to investigate the purchase of long-term care insurance.

The moral of the story: Flexibility may have its merits.

Experience Talks...

Don't Let Fraud Catch You

A couple of months ago my friend told me that her husband came home and said that he had been e-mailed at work by an attorney in London, England that he might be heir to a 'long-lost-cousin's' dowry. The person who had passed away (the supposed relative) had the same last name as her husband. While they were both skeptical, the first thing they did was google the Law Firm from which the letter was generated.

When they googled the Law Firm, a very reputable webpage appeared, and it looked like the Law Firm was a very prestigious one. In a word, it looked legitimate.

Their next call was to their son, who as a local lawyer. They asked him to research the Law Firm further, and he did. Only about 10 minutes went by before they received a text message from their son... "Total Scam."

Great, one minute they were potentially rich, and the next minute they were no worse off... And that was a good thing.

As an Advisor, I have had a couple of incidences where my clients had been contacted with a somewhat similar story – usually by telephone. Typically, the person on the other end (the generator of the correspondence) asks the client to send "money to process" the transaction, or transfer of the 'inherited' money back to the client. The catch is that 'inherited' money is typically never received by the client. Also, my husband (who was a detective) has worked too many cases where money goes out of the victim's account and no trace can be made to where they sent the money; therefore, the client is just out the money.

Moral of the story: "Too good to be true"— just might be... error on the side of caution.

Thoughts...

Identity Theft

No one is too old to be worried about Identity Theft. Nathan is 89 years old and owns a shredder. Nathan is careful not to put any sensitive information in the trash… he shreds any correspondence concerning an account number, DOB, social security information, etc.

> *"An ounce of prevention is worth a pound of cure."*
>
> Benjamin Franklin

Today, *Cyber Fraud* is a growing concern. You have heard time, and time, again to guard your passwords and private information diligently. There are various companies that offer 'protection programs/software' to help you do that (i.e.: Webroot/McAfee/Last Pass/Norton, etc.). I am NOT endorsing any one company… research and ask your trusted advisors for suggestions. But, do not ignore this important security aspect!

Health Insurance, etc.

Your car insurance may be the only piece of wealth protection that you can relate to at the present time. But I bet you are also aware that you may or may not have health insurance? Health insurance may currently be provided by your parents, or you may be covered at work if you are employed by a company that offers that benefit.

So, as you enter the workforce you may be faced with choices regarding Health Insurance and other types of insurance, for example: Disability or Life Insurance may be offered. Don't gloss over those choices… do your research.

Conclusion

You may avoid problems if you arm yourself with knowledge. Financial worries can invoke stress and are known to cause health problems. As we move hurriedly through our multi-tasking lives, we are juggling work, family, leisure, and responsibility, only to find ourselves worn-out and stressed at the end of the day. Bailey, Woodiel, Turner & Young, in a research study titled, *"The Relationship of Financial Stress or Overall Stress and Satisfaction"* (152) report,

> *"...as much as 50% of overall stress could be reduced by improved financial management, thus contributing significantly to their [your] personal and work satisfaction, which counter-balances stress with lower productivity."*

☒ FURTHERMORE, according to the American Psychological Association® 2017 study, "money is the second leading source of stress in the United States." (144a)

☒ Additionally, Joo & Grable (2004) present in their work, *"An Exploratory Framework of the Determinants of Financial Satisfaction:"*

> *"It was determined that financial satisfaction is related, both directly and indirectly, with diverse factors including financial behaviors, financial stress levels, income, financial knowledge, financial solvency, risk tolerance, and education."* (153)

In other words, as reported by Martha Menard, PhD (2/1/2018) in her presentation, *"The Surprising Scope of Financial Stress"* (153) (https://medium.com/@martha.menard/the-surprising-scope-of-financial-stress-and-why-it-matters-ad8ad06610f6), ***"Financial stress is affecting almost everyone. A lot.*** *Several recent surveys conducted by different organizations have consistently documented that American workers across all demographic groups are experiencing increased levels of financial stress. In spite of an overall economic recovery following the Great Recession of 2008, workers at all income levels are struggling."*

Obviously, the more you know about financial matters, the more likely it is that you can reduce the stress related to financial topics and be more satisfied with your financial outlook.

> *"Always bear in mind that your own resolution to succeed is more important than any other one thing."*
>
> Abraham Lincoln

It is a fact of life that, we need money to survive in our current society. We just can't get along without using money to buy the necessities of life… food, clothing, shelter, etc. However, what might be a good course of action is for each of us to reassess our *'Needs vs. Wants'* lists in an effort to begin to reduce the 'spending' column and to increase the 'saving' side of the ledger. This behavior may help to lower our stress regarding money management for today, and for our 'tomorrows' in our retirement years. Give yourself an opportunity to increase your sense of well-being and to enjoy life to the fullest!

We started with *How Money And I Were Introduced*… and if we fast forward to the present, I can certainly attest to the fact that those early financial habits instilled in me by my father, coupled with the financial tools I gathered along the way, have allowed me to succeed in my financial life.

It took a lot of hard work and careful planning. Your personal financial journey will be fraught with trials and tribulations that you will face in life: making a career choice; educating yourself so you can get a job in the profession you choose; deciding if, and when, to start a family, taking care of your family; demonstrating discipline in managing your financial matters; and developing a wealth protection plan; will all be activities that will test your reserve. Managing your money will be one of the most important, and most difficult, aspects of your life.

As with most matters in life, being prepared can go a long way, and preparation can certainly contribute to the success of any project. The same is true with financial management. I believe that with our willingness to persevere, we will have a better chance to succeed. As Abe Lincoln suggested, your *'resolution to succeed'* will be huge! *Resolution* was certainly key for me…. *'Failure was NOT an option!'* I hope the use of this handbook will evoke a desire in you to begin to re-evaluate the manner in which you approach money management in your life. I cannot stress enough how important it is for you to pay attention to your financial matters. Start early and take this subject seriously. You, and only you, will be responsible for your own financial quality of life.

Here's to wishing you a ***resounding financial triumph***.

Sources:

(152)   Bailey, Woodiel, Turner & Young, in a research study titled, *"The Relationship of Financial Stress or Overall Stress and Satisfaction"* (1998, p. 198) https.//citeseerx.ist.psu.edu, https://clutejournals.com; *"2018 Survey of the States Reveals Slow to No growth in K-12 Personal Finance and Economic Education"* (2/2018). https://www.councilforeconed. org/2018/02/08/2018-survey-states-reveals-slow-no-growth-k-12-personal-finance-economic-education/.

(153)   https://medium.com/@martha.menard/the-surprising-scope-of-financial-stress-and-why-it-matters-ad8ad06610f6; *"The Surprising Scope of Financial Stress,"* Martha Menard, Phd, 2/1/2018; *'Journal of Family and Economic Issues,'* (Vol. 25/No. 1), Joo, So-hyun & Grable, John E., (March, 2004, pages 25-50), *"An Exploratory Framework of the Determinants of Financial Satisfaction,"* https://link.springer.com/article/10.1023/B:JEEI.0000016722.37994.9f, *"What is Stress?,"* The American Institute of Stress.

Glossary

401(k): An (non-Roth) employer-sponsored retirement plan that allows employees to make pre-tax contributions; contributions reduce the employee's taxable income.

403(b): A public school or non-profit employer-sponsored retirement plan that allows employees to make pre-tax contributions; contributions reduce the employee's taxable income; also, sometimes known as a Tax-Sheltered Annuity.

Accidental Death and Dismemberment (AD&D): If a death occurs due to an accident; or if a limb above the wrist or ankle joints are severed due to an accident, insurance payments are made.

Accrued Interest: The accumulation of interest added to a bond's contract price; calculated from the last interest payment to the settlement date; does not include settlement date.

Addendum: A legal document added to a contract.

Adjusted Gross Income (AGI): Net income; all earned, passive, portfolio income and capital gains, minus allowable deductions.

Affidavit: A written statement that is sworn to an/or notarized.

Alpha: A measurement of investment product gain that is not credited to the market.

American Depositary Receipt (ADR): Bought and sold in the U.S. Securities Markets, a negotiable certificate representing a specific number of shares of stock in a foreign corporation.

American Stock Exchange® (AMEX): A non-profit, private New York corporation that executes securities trades.

Amortization: Principal and interest payments collected as per a stated schedule to repay a mortgage obligation in full at the completion of the term of the contract.

Annual Expense Ratio: Percentage of a mutual fund's assets that are subtracted annually to pay for fund expenses like sales/operating costs, 12b-1 fees, management fees, administrative fees, etc. Costs incurred by the mutual fund to manage the fund.

Annual Percentage Rate: (APR) The annualized rate for the total finance charge on a loan; includes the interest rate, points, mortgage insurance, and fees.

Annual Percentage Yield: Annual rate of return paid out if held for the full year period.

Annual Return: Total gains for an investment; includes any interest or dividends and capital gains or losses calculated for a year period.

Annual Yield: The total amount of interest to be distributed based on the interest rate (coupon) and frequency of compounding for a yearly period.

Annualized Return: The average gain of an investment, measured over a specific period of time.

Annuitant: The individual on whose life an annuity contract calculates the payout

Annuitize: To decide to take an income stream from an annuity policy; to move from the accumulation phase (growth of assets) to distribution (payout) phase of the contract.

Annuity: An insurance contract that can provide an income stream and has distributions options for the annuitant or owner.

Any Occupation: A disability term that describes when an individual is diagnosed with a qualifying disability that causes them not to be able to work in any occupation which they are 'reasonably' trained.

Appraisal: A statement of property value provided by a qualified professional.

Appreciation: The gains that investments enjoy; an increase in asset value.

Asset: Any item that has value; Anything tangible or intangible that value can be attached to..." (61)

Asset Allocation: The proportion of asset classes in an investor's portfolio. For example: 60% equities, 40% Bonds and Cash.

Asset Class: Specific kind of investment; i.e. Cash, Bonds, Equities, etc.

Average: A mathematical calculation to determine the midpoint of a number of prices.

Back-end Load: A sales fee or commission that is levied when mutual fund shares or annuity contracts are redeemed before a pre-determined time.

Balance Sheet: A report identifying an entity's assets and liabilities for a specific time period.

Bankruptcy: A legal announcement of inability to repay debts.

Basis: The cost of a security or asset.

Bear Market: A length of time when either equity stock prices or bond coupons decline.

Beneficiary: An individual or entity named to receive assets at the time of an owner's death.

Benefit Period: The duration of time that an individual receives benefits as described in an insurance policy.

Beta: A measure of a specific mutual fund's comparative volatility verses a specific market index. If the Beta is more than 1, then the fund is more volatile than the market.

Blackout Period: A time period when trading is frozen.

Blue-Chip-Stock: Common stock of U.S. companies with historical earnings growth and dependable profits.

Bond: An instrument to allow entities to raise capital. The bond is a pledge to return principal at maturity, as well as pay a specific coupon (interest) for a specific period of time. Bonds are issued by a variety of entities such as cities, corporation, and the Federal Government.

Bond Equivalent Yield: The taxable yield an investor should achieve when compared to a tax-free bond.

Borrower: One who receives money and in return is obligated to repay the debt over a specific time period at a stated rate; the borrower's name is acknowledged on the promissory note and mortgage contract.

Break Points: An aggregate dollar amount an investor invests with one Mutual Fund Company to qualify the investor for reduced mutual fund fees.

Budget: A spending plan by category.

Bull Market: A length of time when stock price or bond coupons rise.

Business Cycle: A long-term pattern of stages of economic growth and decline; the four phases are: expansion, peak, reaction and trough.

Buy-sell Agreement: A contract to purchase a business owner's interest in a business at a preset price or formula.

Call Date/Provision: The ability of an issuer to repay fixed-income product at an earlier time than the stated maturity; a date on which the issuer of a bond or fixed-income instrument may redeem the instrument at par; similar to an early maturity date.

Call Option: A contract that provides an investor with a 'right' to buy a stock, bond, commodity, or other investment instrument at a pre-determined price within a predetermined and specified time period. The investor-buyer is not obligated to 'exercise' that right and can let the option expire. This is the opposite of a put option (which provides the contract holder of the option contract the 'right' to sell shares.)

Call Risk: More likely to occur in a falling-interest rate environment, the potential for a bond to be called prior to maturity so the investor doesn't receive the bond's current income.

Capacity: A calculation of an individual's ability to repay a loan, given their income stream.

Capital: Money or goods on hand for use in achieving appreciation and growth.

Capital Appreciation: An increase in the investment's market price.

Capital Gain: Realized net gain achieved when an investment is sold for a higher price than the purchase price.

Capital Loss: Realized net loss achieved when an investment is sold for a lower price.

Capital Risk: Unrelated to the financial issues, the investor has a possibility to lose the invested principal.

Cash Advance: Use of a bank teller, automated tell machine, or instant loan from a credit card to access a cash withdrawal.

Cash Dividend: A portion of a corporation's current earning or profits paid to stockholders.

Cash Flow: Money in and out.

Cash Surrender Value: The amount of money that an owner can withdraw from an insurance policy at the surrender of the policy.

Certificate of Deposit: An interest-bearing account deposit that offers the investor a specific rate of return for the deposit, if left in the account until the maturity date.

Certified Public Accountant: (CPA) A trained person who assists in tax matters.

Closing: A meeting to complete a real estate transaction.

Collateral: Assets that are pledged for a guarantee of a loan.

Commission: A third party fee assessed for a business transaction.

Compound Interest: Money paid on both principal and interest according to a stated schedule.

Consumer Price Index (CPI): Measures the change of consumer goods and services.

Contract: A signed legal agreement to document a transaction between two parties.

Contingent Beneficiary: The person(s), or entity (i.e. trust), to whom proceeds are paid if the primary beneficiary has died.

Conversion Price: A convertible security's par value when exchange for one share of common stock.

Convey: Transfer of title of property from one party to another.

Corporate Bond: A private or public debt obligation.

Corporation: A type of business organization whereas the total worth of the corporation is divided into shares of stock; each share represents a unit of ownership.

Correlation: When two assets' performance move in the same direction in the market.

Correlation Risk: Risk that the correlation between two investment products does not equal the anticipated performance by the fund management.

Cost Basis: The price paid by an investor for an investment.

Cost of Living Rider: To offset the effects of inflation, this rider offers annual benefit increases; often tied to the Consumer Price Index.

Coupon: Percent interest rate the debt issuer pays investor for an explicit time period; paid on a specific pre-determined schedule to investor.

Credit: Right to use resources in return for a 'promise to pay.'

Credit Report: Confidential report documenting a consumer's credit use history: payment history, total debt, length of credit history, credit requests, and types of credit in use.

Credit Risk: Risk that the issuer of an investment product, or a participant in an investment transaction, will not honor the terms of the transaction, or fails to meet commitments to the investor or to the fund. For example, Credit Risk occurs when the company with which you may hold a bond cannot make interest or principal payments, causing you to lose interest payments.

Currency Risk: When the exchange rate of the U.S. currency adversely affects the value or an investment product.

CUSIP Number: The nine-digit number assigned by the Committee on Uniform Security Identification Procedures that identifies stocks and registered bonds.

Custodian: An entity chosen a fiduciary to manage another's assets.

Cyclical Industry: An analyst term for an industry that is responsive to the business cycle.

Debenture: Debt obligation backed by the issuer.

Debit: A charge against assets.

Debit Card: A card that directly draws funds from a bank deposit account.

Debt Security: A security identifying an investor's loan to an issuer.

Debt-to-income Ratio: A calculation of a person's outstanding debt obligations to income.

Debt-to-security Ratio: Long term debt divided by equity.

Declaration Date: The date that an announced dividend amount, pay date, and record date is announced.

Deduction: A reduction taken against income to reduce taxes.

Deed: A written document that is recorded at the courthouse; the document records the transfer of property from one party to another.

Default: The failure to pay interest or principal when due.

Defensive Industry: An analyst's description for an industry that is impervious to business cycles.

Deferred Compensation Plan: A retirement plan funded with before-tax or Roth after-tax money; expected to be withdrawn after age 59 1/2; money set aside for individual's retirement, for non-working years.

Defined Benefit Plan: A retirement plan funded with before-tax contributions that identifies payouts to the employee at retirement.

Defined Contribution Plan: A retirement plan funded with before-tax or Roth after-tax money, expected to be withdrawn after age59 ½; money set aside for an individual's retirement, or non-working, years.

Deflation: A steady and quantifiable fall in the general level of prices.

Delinquent: An account that is past due.

Depreciation: A calculation of diminishing value for tangible assets relative to the assets' income contribution or value. A reduction of taxes calculated by deducting certain businesses expenses from income.

Depression: A time of falling economic weakening.

Dilution: When additional shares of common stock and conversion of convertible securities are issued, there is a reduction in earnings per share.

Direct Deposit: Funds are sent directly to an account per a previously signed agreement.

Disability: An injury or illness that prohibits an individual from earning an income.

Disclosure: Information is provided to parties of a transaction, as required by law.

Discount: The variance between the lower price paid for a security, and the security's face value at issue.

Discount Points: Additional fees assessed up-front to enable a borrower to reduce the interest rate of a principal loan.

Discount Rate: The 12 Federal Reserve Banks set this interest rate for short-term loans made to member banks.

Dispute: The credit card holder calls or writes to advise the credit card issuer of a charge believed to be incorrect. The credit card issuer must respond within 30 days. The credit card holder is not required to pay for the disputed charge during investigation.

Diversification: A risk management practice to reduce the overall impact of any one investment vehicle within a portfolio; to lessen risk by acquiring non-correlated investments in a portfolio.

Dividend: The distribution of either stock earning (cash or stock) or mutual fund's net investment income (cash, typically reinvested in fund) paid to shareholders.

Dollar Cost Averaging: Investing a pre-set amount of money in mutual funds or stocks on a pre-determined schedule.

Donor: A person or entity that makes a gift of securities or money to another; the donor gives up all rights to the gift upon transfer.

Dow Jones Composite Average® (DJCA): A widely utilized market indicator; an index of 65 stocks from the Dow Jones Industrial®, Dow Jones Transportation®, and Dow Jones Utilities® Averages.

Dow Jones Industrial Average® (DJIA): A widely utilized market indicator; an index of 30 industrial U.S. companies.

Dow Jones Utilities Average® (DJUS): A widely utilized market indicator; an index of 15 utility U.S. companies.

Due Diligence: A term utilized to describe a thorough examination of reported information for verification.

Durable Power of Attorney: A legal document granting authority to an entity or individual, on another's behalf.

Earned Income: Money resulting from working; includes wages, salaries, tips, commissions and bonuses.

Earnest Money: Money provided to 'bind' a real estate contract.

Earnings Per Share: Divide the company profit for specific period of time by the number of outstanding shares of common stock.

Education IRA: An account that allows contributions of a stated amount per year, per child, to fund qualified higher-education expenses tax-free (inclucing gains).

Effective Tax Rate: Add together both federal and state taxes and divide by gross income to determine percentage.

Efficient Market Theory: A theory presenting that information is processed by the stock market and is immediately reflected in the 'fair price' of stock.

Elimination Period: The time period an individual 'waits' before they receive benefits.

Emerging Markets: Newly developing markets in nations without mature stock markets.

Employee Retirement Income Security Act of 1974 (ERISA): Law that oversees corporate pensions and benefit plans; plans meeting ERISA standards qualify for beneficial tax treatment.

Endowment: Insurance that pays the face value either at a pre-determined date or age; or at the insured's death.

Equity/Equity Security: Common and preferred stockholders' ownership shares in a company; or the value an owner has established in real estate – the value minus the debt owed.

Escrow: A deposit made by a buyer to be held in a third-party account and is delivered upon completion of a provision of a contract.

Evidence of Insurability: Individuals who apply for insurance must supply documentation to satisfy requirements for medical, occupational, and financial insurability.

Ex-Dividend: When a stock is purchased 'ex-dividend' the seller keeps the scheduled dividend (not paid yet) because the buyer will not own the stock on the 'record date.'

Exercise (an Option): The Stock Option has a specific price at which the owner/holder of the option may purchase the stock. The owner exercises the Option, thereby purchasing the stock at the pre-determined Option price.

Expense: The charge for a good or service.

Expense Ratio: Operating expenses of a fund is divided by the net assets in the fund.

Expiration Date: Expiration of the Option. This is the date on which the holder forfeits the rights to exercise the Option.

Face Amount: The death benefit of an in-force life insurance policy.

Fair Market Value: Without duress, an agreed-upon price by both the seller and buyer of real property to transfer property from one party to another.

Federal Deposit Insurance Corporation (FDIC): Government agency that insures deposits for member banks to prevent bank and thrift collapses.

Federal National Mortgage Association (FNMA): A public corporation that buys conventional and government agency mortgages.

Federal Reserve Board (FRB): A Presidential appointed, and Congress ratified, seven-member board that is responsible for the operation of the Federal Reserve System.

Fiduciary: A legally named person who manages assets for another's benefit; one who acts on another's behalf.

Finance Charge: Charges to be paid as a result of extending a loan.

Fiscal Policy: Set by the United States President or Congress, the policies affect government spending, interest rates, and tax rates; ultimately to manage the U.S. economy.

Fixed Asset: Physical property, i.e. computers, buildings, land.

Fixed Rate: An unchanging annual percentage rate. Coupon (or interest rate) fixed to maturity.

Flat Yield Curve: An illustration depicting short-maturity bond yields are equal to long-maturity bond yields.

Flow-through: Business income, deductions and credits are reflected directly on an individual business owner's personal tax return.

Floating Rate: Coupon (or interest rate) is adjusted to another financial instrument; changes over time.

Foreclosure: The lender takes possession of the mortgaged property.

Foreign Exchange Rate: The value of one country's currency in relationship to another country's currency.

Fractional Share: Less than a whole share.

Fraud: Intentional deception of a material fact.

Front-end Load: An up-front sales fee or commission that is levied when mutual fund shares or annuity contracts are purchased.

Funds (Mutual Funds): general guidelines:

- Global: +/- 25% of portfolio holds securities traded outside the U.S.

- Global Income: Debt securities with exposure in countries outside the U.S.

- Growth: Objective of the fund is appreciation. Growth funds typically invest in companies with longer-term earnings that demonstrate potential to appreciate faster than the appropriate index.

- High Yield: Objective is high yields from fixed income investments. No quality or maturity restrictions; invests in lower grade debt issues.

- Income: Objective of the fund is current income through income generating stocks, bonds, and money market holdings.

- Intermediate U.S. Bond: +/- 65% of assets are in U.S. government or government agency debt instruments with dollar-weighted average maturities of 5 to 10 years.

- Intermediate U.S. Treasury Bond: +/- 65% of assets are in U.S. Treasury bills/notes debt instruments with dollar-weighted average maturities of 5 to 10 years.

- International: Most securities held in fund are non-U.S. companies.

- Value: Objective of the fund is to hold companies that are considered 'undervalued' verses the index.

Fundamental Analysis: Analysts investigate a company's financial strength, overall economy and industry conditions to assess a specific stock's value.

Futures and Options: Exchange-traded contracts that require either the seller to deliver, or the buyer to receive certain assets at a specific, pre-stated time:

- Futures have 'leverage' and 'correlation risk;' and potential also to have currency and political risk.

- Options may involve currency and political risk.

Gain: Sale price of the investment minus the investment cost which equals a surplus.

General Partnership: Whereby each partner is liable for the total partnership's liability; does not require legal formation.

Good Faith Estimate: A itemization of expected costs of a mortgage transaction provided to a borrower prior to closing.

Government National Mortgage Association (GNMA): A government-owned corporation that issues pass-through mortgages.

Grace Period: The number of days stated in the policies which notes how many days after the payment due date that the individual has until coverage lapses or the contract terms are voided. Typically, the individual can remit payment without penalty during this timeframe.

Gross Domestic Product (GDP): The production of goods and services for one year; includes: consumption, government, purchases, investments and exports, minus imports.

Gross Income: All sources of taxpayer income.

Growth Stock: Company whose earnings are growing faster than the industry average.

Guardian: A fiduciary responsible for the supervision of assets for the benefit of a minor or an incompetent person.

Hazard Insurance: Insurance purchased to reimburse the insured in case of loss or damage.

Homeowners Insurance Policy: A contract protecting a private dwelling and the contents against loss and damage.

Household income: Money attained from all household sources such as: salary, bonuses, commissions, alimony, child support, Social Security, wages, retirement benefits, disability, compensation, investment product income (dividends and interest), and unemployment benefits.

HUD-1: A standardized form to note all transaction costs at closing.

Income: Interest or dividends paid to an investor.

Index: Performance of a number of similar investment vehicles with similar objectives is calculated for a particular period of time.

Individual Retirement Account (IRA): Individual Retirement Account is an account that holds pre-taxed contributions; gains are tax-deferred and the individual pays taxes (current tax law) at an ordinary income tax rate upon distribution. Certain eligibility, contribution limits, and withdrawal rules apply. (Non-Roth)

Inflation: The measurable increase in the level of goods, usually calculated on an annual basis.

Initial Public Offering (IPO): First offer of sale of company stock; not previously offered.

Insurance: A protection contract against the loss of assets, life, health, and disability.

Insured: The individual on whose life is insured by a life insurance policy.

Intangible Asset: A non-physical property, such as copyright, goodwill.

Interest: Money paid by the borrower for use of loaned money.

Interest Rate Risk: The potential loss of a security's value due to the change in interest rates.

Inverted Yield Curve: An illustration depicting lower yields for longer-term bond maturities, compared to the higher yields of shorter-term bond maturities.

Investing: Placing money aside for the purpose of growing it to meet longer-term financial goals.

Investment Grade: Based on Moody's® BAA3 or higher; S&P BBB- or higher ratings; credit quality ratings given for bonds.

Irrevocable Trust: A Trust that may not be revoked or removed.

Issuer: The entity, i.e. corporation, company, government, agency that issues the security or bond.

Joint Account: The ownership of assets by two or more individuals. There are various kinds of joint account arrangements:

1   Joint Tenants with Rights of Survivorship (JTWOS): Upon the death of one of the account owners, the assets pass to the other account owners.

2   Tenants in Common (TIC): The assets are held in 'shares'/separate interest for each of the account owners; at death the shares pass to the heirs of the owners.

3   Community Property (COMM): Assets acquired after marriage are considered joint property.

Joint Life With Last Survivor: A payout option that concerns more than one person; the benefit does not payout until the last person on the contract dies.

Joint Life Policy: A payout option that concerns more than one person; the benefit pays out at the death of the first person, and then the policy terminates.

Keogh Plan: A tax-deferred retirement plan for self-employed and unincorporated individuals funded with either pre-tax or after-tax dollars.

Key-Employee (Person) Insurance: Insurance for a person who is important to the well-being of a company.

Lagging Indicator: An economic market marker that confirms a market trend after the economy has demonstrated a change.

Lapsed policy: A terminated period (at the end of the grace period) due to non-payment.

Leading Indicator: An economic market marker that predicts a market trend prior to the economy demonstrating a change.

Legal Description: A narrative depiction of property utilized for legal purposes.

Legislative Risk: The possibility that changes in investment or tax laws can negatively affect an investor's investment value.

Level Premium: A premium that does not change for a stated period of time.

Leverage: A method of increasing investment return by using borrowed capital.

Liability: A debt or financial obligation.

Lien: A legal claim to property to recover payment of a loan.

Life Insurance: A contract that pays benefits to a beneficiary upon the loss of the insured's life.

Limited Liability: Limiting the amount of financial loss to the sum invested.

Line of Credit: An established loan amount available as ready money.

Liquid Assets: Assets that are quickly converted to cash.

Liquidate: To exchange an asset into cash.

Liquidity Risk: When a specific investment product cannot be sold at a time when it would be beneficial to do so. The possibility that when an investor wants to sell an investment, he or she may not be able to; real estate property is an example of liquidity risk.

Load: The front- or back-end sales charge assessed for a mutual fund. 'No-load' funds do not charge a front- or back-end fee.

Long-term Gain: The realized gain after holding a capital investment for at least 12 months.

Long-term Loss: The realized loss after holding a capital investment for at least 12 months.

Loss Carry-over: A realized loss that is carried over for use to reduce tax liability from one year to the next.

Lump Sum: A one-time payout of the total proceeds or benefits.

Market Risk: The possibility of investment loss due to everyday market volatility.

Market Value: The price at which an investor pays or sells an investment.

Maturity: When a fixed investment's guarantee period ends, and the principal is returned.

Medicare: Managed by the Social Security Administration, a program to cover specific health-care expenses for U.S. citizens who are ages 65 or older.

Money Market: A short-term security that is generally liquid.

Moody's® Investors Service: Credit quality of issuers is rated by this organization.

Mortgage: To borrow from a lender and give partial interest in a property as collateral for the payment of the obligation.

Mortgage Insurance: Insurance to protect the mortgage lender against loss due to default.

Municipal Bond: States, cities, countries and various government agencies raise money by offering municipal bonds to finance public projects.

Mutual Fund: A professionally managed basket of stocks, bonds, and/or cash investments; managed to a pre-determined fund objective.

NASDAQ® Composite: The National Association of Securities Dealers Automated Quotations® (NASDAQ®) system that embodies the largest domestic, over the counter, electronic screen-based equities trading market.

Negotiability: The ability of an owner to assign, give, transfer or sell a security to another person.

Net: The gross amount, minus fees and charges.

Net Asset Value (NAV): The assets of an open-ended fund, minus the liabilities, divided by the number of outstanding shares.

Net Investment Income: The difference between a company's operating expenses and the total realized dividends and interest.

Net Worth: What an individual owns, minus what is owed.

New Issue: Initial public offering or re-financing of existing corporation; the Securities and Exchange rules and regulations oversee all new issues.

New York Stock Exchange®: A Board of Directors of the exchange corporation sets policy, oversees the operation of the Exchange and member activities, lists securities, and conducts all necessary tasks in operating the exchange.

No-load Fund: No commission or sales charge is received when a mutual fund is purchased.

Nominal Yield: The interest rate paid on a debt instrument; bond yield.

Non-investment Grade Securities: Debt securities generally known as "junk bonds," rated below investment grade.

Non-Qualified Retirement Plan: Contributions into the plan are not tax-deductible; the plan does not meet the ERISA guidelines.

Non-recourse Financing: A pledge for a loan that utilizes the purchased asset to secure the loan but does not hold the borrower personally liable.

Non-taxable Income: Money that is not taxed by one or more agencies: the federal, state, or local government.

Normal Yield Curve: An illustration depicting the maturity of longer-term debt instruments producing higher yields than shorter-term debt instruments.

Note: Short-term debt investment that typically has a 5 year or less maturity date.

Odd Lot: Generally, less than a unit of 100 shares of stock.

Open-end Investment Company: Same as Mutual Fund.

Operating Expenses: Costs sustained in running a business.

Operating Income: An annual profit for a business.

Opportunity Cost: The gain that is forfeited by selecting an investment product that does not perform as well as another product choice.

Option: A contract to purchase or sell a specific number of shares of stock at a pre-set price on/before a particular date.

Ordinary Income: Revenue that is from other than capital gains.

Origination Fee: Payment for the processing of the application and coordination of a loan.

Overdraft: Funds are not available to cover a submitted check.

Own Occupation: A disability insurance term stating that an insured will receive benefits if they become disabled and cannot work in the in their trained occupation.

Paid-up Policy: A life insurance policy that is in effect and does not require any additional premium payments to keep it in force.

Par: The dollar amount designated when the investment is issued, for a bond, also the value assigned at maturity.

Partnership: A type of business where all owners are liable for expenses and debt.

Partial Disability: When an insured cannot carry out all of his/her own occupation responsibilities.

Passive Income: Revenue realized from non-active business participation, like rental property.

Passive Loss: Losses realized from non-active business participation, like rental property.

Past Due: When payment has not been received within the stated billing period.

Pension: A retirement benefit paid at regular intervals to a retiree.

Periodic Rate: A description of an interest rate in relation to a specific stated time period.

Per Stirpes: If a named beneficiary is deceased, the proceeds pass down to their heirs.

Political Risk: Risk of investment losses due to government or legal events.

Posting Date: The recorded date on the credit card or (any) statement that identifies a purchase, fee, cash advance, or charge.

Power of Attorney: A document assigning legal rights to a fiduciary to act on another's behalf.

P/E Ratio – Price Earnings Ratio: Divide the current stock price by dollar earnings.

Preferred Stock: Ownership in a corporation; issued with a stated dividend that is paid prior to dividend payment to common stockholders; general characteristics are: offered in increments of $25, $50, $100, and $1000 par values, pay quarterly dividends, trade on the exchanges (i.e. New York Stock Exchange® and others), and typically are callable.

Premium: Payments for insurance contracts (annuity, life insurance, disability, etc.); the variance between a higher price paid for a security and the face value of the security at issue.

Price-to-Earnings Ratio: (P/E) The current stock price divided by the stock earnings. If a high P/E is calculated (over 20) then the stock is predicted to have growth potential.

Primary Beneficiary: The first named beneficiary to receive proceeds.

Prime Rate: The interest rate the banks offer their best corporate customers.

Principal: The money that is initially invested; a beginning amount to buy an investment.

Principal Transaction: A broker-dealer buys or sells securities from its own inventory.

Proceeds: The money paid to beneficiaries from an insurance policy at the death of the insured.

Profit: The difference between revenue and expense which nets a positive result.

Profitability: The generation of income and gain that exceeds expenses.

Profit-sharing Plan: A retirement plan where the employer shares a portion of the company profits with the employees.

Progressive Tax: A tax that increases as income increases.

Prospectus: Documentation that presents all relative financial and legal information for an investment (for a stock, bond, mutual fund, etc.).

Proxy: A stockholder authorizes another person to vote on stockholder issues on a specific issue; a limited power of attorney.

Public Offering: When an issue of common stock is offered; new shares or additional company shares.

Purchasing Power Risk: The possibility that inflation will erode the value of money and investments.

Put Option: A contract that gives the owner of the underlying investment position the 'right' to sell a pre-determined amount of the underlying security at a pre-determined price within a named time period. The owner of the contract is not obligated to sell the contract, the investor can simply let the contract expire. This is the opposite of a call option (which provides the holder of the option contract the 'right' to buy shares.)

Qualified Retirement Plan: A retirement plan that allows a) employees to make pre-tax salary deferrals, and b) employers to contribute to employee accounts also on a pre-tax basis. (Non-Roth)

Rate of Return: Expressed as a percentage, the return earned on an investment or deposit.

Rating: An assignment given to a corporate or municipal bond based on the issuer's capacity to repay principal and make interest payments.

Real Estate Investment Trust (REIT): A trust or corporation that collects investor capital to purchase income property or mortgage loans.

Realized Gains/Losses: The amount the investor has after the sale of an asset; the sale value minus the initial purchase price; either an increase or decrease in value verses the cost basis of the asset.

Rebalancing: Reallocation of assets to bring in line with pre-stated allocation.

Receipt: Documentation of payment.

Recession: An economic turn down continuing from 6 to 18 months.

Record Date: The date that a corporation's Board of Directors determine that identifies which stockholders are entitled to receive dividends or rights distributions.

Redemption: The return of principal to the investor.

Refinancing: To pay off an existing loan and enter into a new debt contract.

Repossession: Collateral is seized by lender when a borrower falls significantly behind in reimbursement payments.

Retained Earnings: An accounting of a corporation's net income, after the payment of dividends to stockholders.

Return: A calculation of the increase, gain minus cost, of a portfolio's performance; to include capital appreciation, yield and dividends.

Return on Investment (ROI): The gain or loss from a sale of an investment; expressed as a percentage.

Reverse Split: A decrease in the total number of outstanding shares; increases the per-share price.

Rider: To add something to a policy for a cost.

Risk: Possibility for an investor to lose invested assets due to conditions other than an issuer's financial strength.

Risk Tolerance: An assessment of an investor's attitude towards risk and return.

Rollover: Moving money within a 60-day period from a qualified (pre-tax) account to another qualified plan to maintain the tax-deferred status of the assets.

Roth IRA: A non-deductible retirement account available to individual within certain income levels; gains are tax-free; no required withdrawals at age 72.

Revocable Trust: A trust that provides for amendment options.

Sales Charge: A load or sales commission charged when a Mutual Fund is bought or sold.

Savings: Placing money aside for short-term goals or emergencies.

Savings Bond: A government issued debt security; not negotiable or transferable.

Savings Incentive Matching Plan for Employees (SIMPLE): A qualified, or pre-tax, retirement account that provides small businesses an opportunity to offer a generally low-cost, simple way for employees to defer part of their salary until retirement. Like an IRA, gains are tax-deferred until withdrawal; if a withdrawal is made before the owner is 59 ½ years old, the IRS levies a 10% tax penalty. Taxes are paid at withdrawal. (Certain other rules apply to setting up the plan and for contribution limits, rollovers, withdrawals, etc.)

Second Mortgage: A loan obtained on a property that has an existing loan; the added loan is subordinate to the first loan.

Secondary Market: Various investment vehicles are offered for sale and re-purchase on the secondary market; vehicles bought and sold on the secondary market are not primary offerings.

Sector: Securities are grouped by same economic segments, such as; Health Care, Natural Resources, Technology, etc.

Securities and Exchange Commission (SEC): Congress established this commission to oversee the securities markets and to safeguard investors.

Security: Investment vehicle deployed by a government, corporation, or any entity that tenders equity or debt vehicles.

Sell: To transfer ownership of an investment or asset for money or value.

Settlement: The repayment of a debt in full.

Share: A unit representing a part ownership of a company.

Share: A division of capital stock of a corporation or company into equal parts.

Short-term Capital Gain: The net profit from the sale of an asset that has been owned for 12 months or less.

Short-term Capital Loss: The net loss from the sale of an asset that has been owned for 12 months or less.

Simple Interest: Rate credited on the principal amount only.

Simplified Employee Pension Plan (SEP): A type of qualified retirement account where the employer ONLY contributes to a retirement account for the employee. (Certain other rules apply to setting up the plan and for contribution limits, etc.)

Size and Style: Securities are grouped by like size and style, such as; Large-cap Growth, Mid-cap Value, Small-cap Growth, etc.

Social Security: FICA deductions fund this federal government program that provides funds for retirement, disability, or loss of income to qualifying U.S. individuals at age 62 or beyond.

Sole Proprietorship: A simple business structure for a one-person business.

Split-Dollar Life Insurance: A contract where two beneficiaries share the responsibility of premium payments on a single policy. However, one beneficiary receives the net death benefit (death benefit less cash value) and the second beneficiary receives the cash value of the policy.

Spousal IRA: A retirement account set up for a non-working spouse by the working spouse who is eligible themselves for an IRA.

Standard and Poor's Composite Index® of 500 Stocks (S&P 500®): A basket of 500 funds that are tracked as an equity market index.

Standard Deviation: A measure of the investment's historical volatility; a measure of the divergence of returns from their average.

Stock: Part ownership of a company; an entitlement on the company's assets and profits.

Stock Bonus Plan: Company bonuses are awarded to employees in shares of stock.

Stock Certificate: Written proof of ownership of shares in a corporation.

Stock Split: Proportionate holdings of the stockholder remains the same, however the number of outstanding shares increases.

Supply: Availability of goods and services for purchase by consumers.

Supply-side Economics: A theory that advocates stimulation of an economy can be initiated by an increased supply of goods to consumers.

Surrender Charge: A penalty cost imposed to withdraw funds before the termination of the surrender charge period.

Symbol: Letters assigned to identify a security.

Tax Credit: A dollar for dollar reduction in taxes derived from IRS approved programs.

Tax Deduction: Certain expense that reduce a taxpayer's gross income; affects (lowers) the amount of income upon which taxes must be paid.

Taxable Income: Money attained from all household sources: salary, bonuses, commissions, alimony, child support, Social Security, wages, retirement benefits, disability compensation, investment product income (dividends and interest), and unemployment benefits that will be taxed by either the federal, state, or local government.

Tax-Deferred: Gains are not taxed until they are distributed.

Tax-Equivalent Yield: A comparison of the rate of return that a taxable bond must provide to be equivalent to the tax-exempt earnings on a municipal bond; rates change depending on individual investor's tax bracket.

Tax-Exempt Fund: The primary purpose is to generate tax-free income.

Tax-Sheltered Annuity (TSA): A retirement plan for non-profit organizations that is similar in structure to a for-profit company 401k; individuals may make salary deferral elections to their qualified (pre-tax) retirement account; gains are tax-deferred until withdrawals are made; withdrawals are taxed at ordinary income rates; premature withdrawals are penalized with an additional IRS 10% tax. (Other rules may apply.)

Term: The stated period of time that is identified in a contract to complete a transaction or service.

Term Insurance: A type of insurance policy that is in-force for a specific term; typically, 10, 20 or 30 years; no cash value is accrued.

Time Value of Money: The purchasing power of money, compared at different intervals, considering the effects of inflation.

Title: A legal document denoting ownership.

Trade Date: The date when a security transaction is completed.

Transaction Fee: A charge assessed for service or administration of a credit or investment account.

Treasury Bill: A U.S. Treasury debt obligation with a maturity of less than one year.

Treasury Bond: U.S. Treasury debt obligations with a maturity of less than thirty years.

Treasury Note: U.S. Treasury debt obligations with a maturity between one and ten years.

Trust: A legal contract to describe the distribution of property according to the directions given by the grantor/owner.

Trustee: A legal appointment to perform on behalf of a beneficiary.

Truth-in-lending Statement: A standardized format for the full disclosure of credit terms.

12b-1 Fee: The fee that a mutual fund company may assess for sale, promotion, or expenses incurred for distribution of its shares.

Underwriting Process: For the purpose of determining the applicant's eligibility: Review of the application, documentation, property, or other records, prior to the issuance of a contract or loan.

Unearned Income: Income realized from sources other than employment services.

Uniform Gifts to Minors Act (UGMA): A custodial account that is held for a minor's benefit; income and capital gains are taxed at the minor's tax rate; the minor has legal right to the account.

Unit Cost: Cost of purchase price of an investment; includes commissions and fees.

Unit Investment Trust (UIT): A professionally managed portfolio of securities that offers shares by an investment company; organized under a trust agreement, not a corporate contract.

Unrealized Gains/Losses: The gain or loss of an investment recorded on a specific date for an investment that has NOT been sold yet.

U.S. Savings Bond: A U.S. Treasury fixed-income investment instrument that appreciates 100% of premium at maturity.

Variable Annuity: An insurance contract that guarantees a minimum total payout to the annuitant in the annuitization stage; principal and gains are held in insurance separate accounts and performance of these accounts determines the total payout, minus contract expenses; gains grow tax-deferred until they are withdrawn; IRS penalties incur for withdrawals prior to age 59 1/2; withdrawals on gains and pre-tax money are taxed at ordinary income rates. (Other factors/rules apply.)

Variable Rate: An interest rate that is not fixed, but changes over time.

Variable Universal Life Insurance Policy: An insurance contract that offers flexible terms and investment options. Death of the insured triggers a tax-free payout to the beneficiary; principal and gains are held   in insurance separate accounts and performance of these accounts determines the cash surrender amount (minus the policy expenses).

Vesting: A schedule for a retirement plan that determines the length a time that an employee must be employed to take ownership of certain types of employer contributions; deferrals made by the employees into their own accounts are immediately vested.

Volatility: The standard deviation of the return of the investment; a measure of the variation in an investment's price.

Wash Sale: Buying a security within 30 days before or after selling a characteristically duplicate security for the purposes of generating a tax loss.

Working Capital: The liquid assets that a corporation has available to meet short-term cash needs.

Yield: Rate of return on an investment; rate of interest paid on a bond or note.

Yield Curve: A pictorial depiction of the fixed-income yields, relative to their maturity dates.

Yield to Call: Performance of a callable investment, measured from the time of purchase to the call date.

Yield to Maturity: Performance of an investment, measured from the time of purchase to the maturity date.

Zero Coupon Bond: A debt instrument that does not pay interest until maturity; at maturity both principal and total interest (compounded semi-annually) is paid.

Glossary terms have been acquired through a review of many sources, to include: Dearborn® study manuals, Merrill Lynch® glossary, on-line website sources (see list), mutual fund and insurance company brochures (John Hancock®, Hartford®, Franklin Templeton®, etc.), https://www.citigroupbank.com *Financial Education Program, Webster's Dictionary®, etc.*

The above definitions are offered for education purposes only. All definitions should be verified prior to executing any contract/sale/purchase/etc. Check with your Tax, Legal, and Financial Advisors. Not to be mistaken for advice.

Biographies of Our Quoted Sources

John D. Rockefeller – An American industrialist. Rockefeller revolutionized the petroleum industry and defined the structure of modern philanthropy.

Warren Buffett – U.S. investor, businessman, and philanthropist. Mr. Buffett is one of the most successful investors in American history.

Mark Twain – Samuel Langhorne Clemens is better known by the pen name Mark Twain. He was an American author and humorist.

George Soros – An American currency speculator, stock investor, businessman, philanthropist, and political activist.

George Burns – An American comedian, actor, and writer.

George Foreman – An American two-time former World Heavyweight Boxing Champion, Olympic gold medalist, and famously successful entrepreneur.

Vincent Lombardi – A famous inspirational football coach – named 'Coach of the Century' by ESPN in 1959.

Charles Dickens – 19th century English author, one of the most popular English novelists of the Victorian era.

William Feather – An American publisher and author in the 1900s.

Carl Levin – A Democratic United States Senator from Michigan and was the Chairman of the Senate Committee on Armed Services.

Walter Updegrave – A CNN®/Money® contributing columnist; Money Magazine; "Ask the Expert."

Gary Ryan Blair – "The GoalsGuy®", one of the top strategic thinkers in the world. As an author, speaker, coach and consultant, he is dedicated to helping his clients win by creating focused, goal-directed lives.

Thornton T. Munger – An American Scientist.

Albert Einstein – Best remembered for his theories of special relativity and general relativity. Einstein received the 1921 Nobel Prize in Physics for his services to Theoretical Physics. Einstein also discovered of the law of the photoelectric effect.

Benjamin Franklin – American scientist, inventor, statesman, printer, and philosopher.

Bob Hope – Comedian, actor and "first and only honorary veteran of the U.S. armed forces."

Henry Ford –American founder of the Ford Motor Company® and father of modern assembly lines used in mass production. Mr. Ford's introduction of the Model T automobile revolutionized transportation and American industry. Mr. Ford was a prolific inventor.

Tennessee Williams – An American playwright who received many of the top theatrical awards for his works of drama.

Elvis Presley – American pop singer and actor. Elvis was a cultural icon.

William A. Ward – An American author; one of America's most quoted writers of inspirational proverbs/ sayings.

Elizabeth Weintraub – Author and nominated by the CA Association of Realtors(r) as a founding member of the its Real Estate Institute(r) (RECI).

Sam Ewing – American writer and humorist.

Alan Greenspan – An American economist who served as the Chair of the Federal Reserve of the U.S. from 1987- 2006.

Thomas Jefferson – An American statesman, diplomat, lawyer, architect, philosopher, Founding Father, and the 3rd President of the United States.

John Maxwell – An American author, speaker and pastor.

Peter Lynch – An American investor, mutual fund manager, and philanthropist.

Ronald Reagan – American politician and the 40th president of the United States.

Abraham Lincoln – American statesman, lawyer and the 16th President of the United States.

Financial Prep **101:**

Simple Tips for the Next Generation

Teacher Lesson Guide/Activities/

Answers: janisrdickey.com

Janis R. Dickey, PhD

NOTES:

Web Sources:

Organization	Website
Markets.com	www.markets.com/investing
Money Math: Lessons for Life®	Copyright 2001 by The Curators of the University of Missouri ISBN 0-9709279-0-8
My Money®	www.mymoney.gov
National Association of Consumer Advocates®	www.naca.net
National Association of Investors Corp®	www.better-investing.org
National Council on Economic Education®	www.ncee.net
National Credit Union Administration®	www.ncua.gov
National Endowment for Financial Education - Education Programs®	www.nefe.org
National Foundation for Credit Counseling®	www.nfcc.org
National Urban League®	www.nul.org
NEFE High School Financial Planning®	https://hsfpp.nefe.org
Neighborworks America®	www.ng.org
Personal Financial Education®	www.federalreserveeducation.org/pfed
Personal Financial Education Group®	www.pfeg.org
Public Debt	www.publicdebt.treas.gov
Smith Barney's Young Investor's Network®	www.younginvestorsnetwork.com
Springerlink®	www.springerlink.com
The Certified Financial Planner Board®	www.cfp.net
The Federal Reserve	www.federalreserve.gov
TransUnion®	www.transunion.com
U.S. Treasury-Office of Financial Education	www.treas.gov/offices/domestic-finance
United States Department of Agriculture	www.csrees.usda.gov/nea
United States Senate Special Committee on Aging	https://aging.senate.gov
US Securities and Exchange Commission	www.sec.gov
US Treasury - Office of Financial Education	www.treas.gov/offices
Use Credit Wisely	www.usecreditwisely.com
Wells Fargo Home Mortgage®	www.wellsfargo.com/mortgage
Owners Library	www.owners.com/tools.library
Personal Fund	www.personalfund.com
FICO®	www.myfico.com

Organization	Website
2008 Tax Rate Schedules	https://taxes.about.com
360 Degrees of Financial Literacy®	www.forefieldkt.com
Acorn®	www.acorn.org
American Bankers Association Consumer Connection®	www.aba.com/consumer
American Financial Solutions®	www.myfinancialgoals.com
AMSA®	www.moving.org
Bank Branch Online®	www.bankbranchonline.com
Bankrate.com	www.bankrate.com
Citibank's Credit-ED®	www.credit-edadministrator.com
Citigroup® Financial Education Program	https://www.citigroup.com/citi/citizen/community/curriculum/adults.htm
College Cost Finder®	www.cnn.com
Credit Cards - Compare Credit Card Offers	www.creditcards.com
Credit Education Bureau®	www.crediteducationbureau.com
Credit Union® Online Library	www.cybercu.org
Department of Transportation	www.protectyourmove.org
Equifax®	www.equifax.com
Experian®	www.experian.com
Federal Deposit Insurance Corporation	www.fdic.gov
Federal Loan Program	www.students.gov
Federal Reserve Bank of New York®	www.newyorkfed.org/education
Financial Education Curriculum	www.citi.com/citigroup/financialeducation
Financial Finesse	www.financialfinesse.com
Financial Literacy and Consumer Education	www.scholar.google.com
Free Credit Report®	www.freecreditreport.com
Free Credit Reports Instantly®	wwww.freecreditreportsinstantly.com
HSBC Privacy and Security Policy®	www.hsbccreditcard.com
HUD	www.hud.gov
Institute of Consumer Financial Education®	www.financial-education-icfe.org
Internal Revenue Service	www.irs.gov
Jump$tart Coalition®	www.jumpstart.org